Repave is an offering. A full exhale. It is altar, fruit, and moonrise. The rush of release. It is screaming underwater. Picking blackberries through the chain-link fence. A song that you sing for yourself.

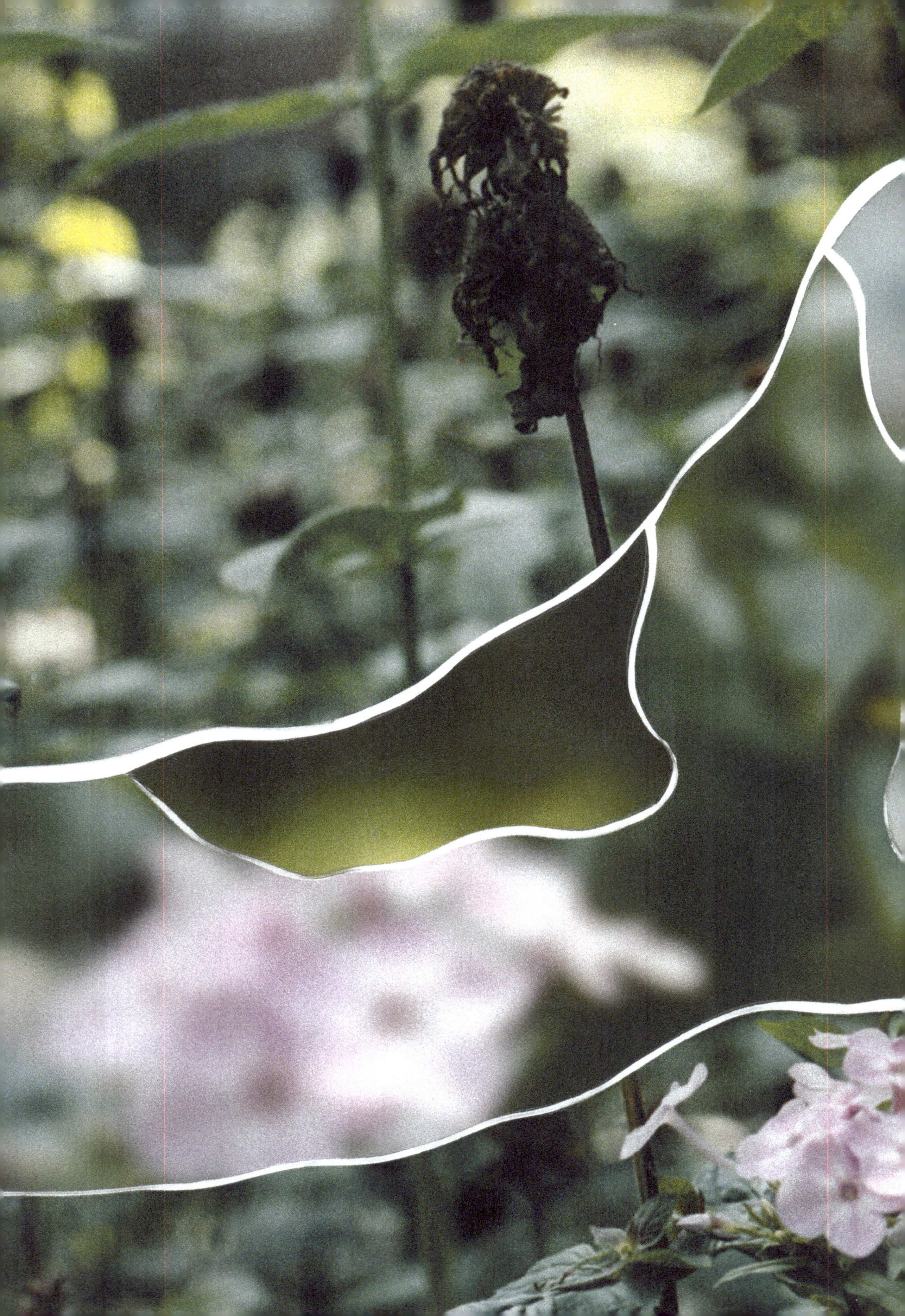

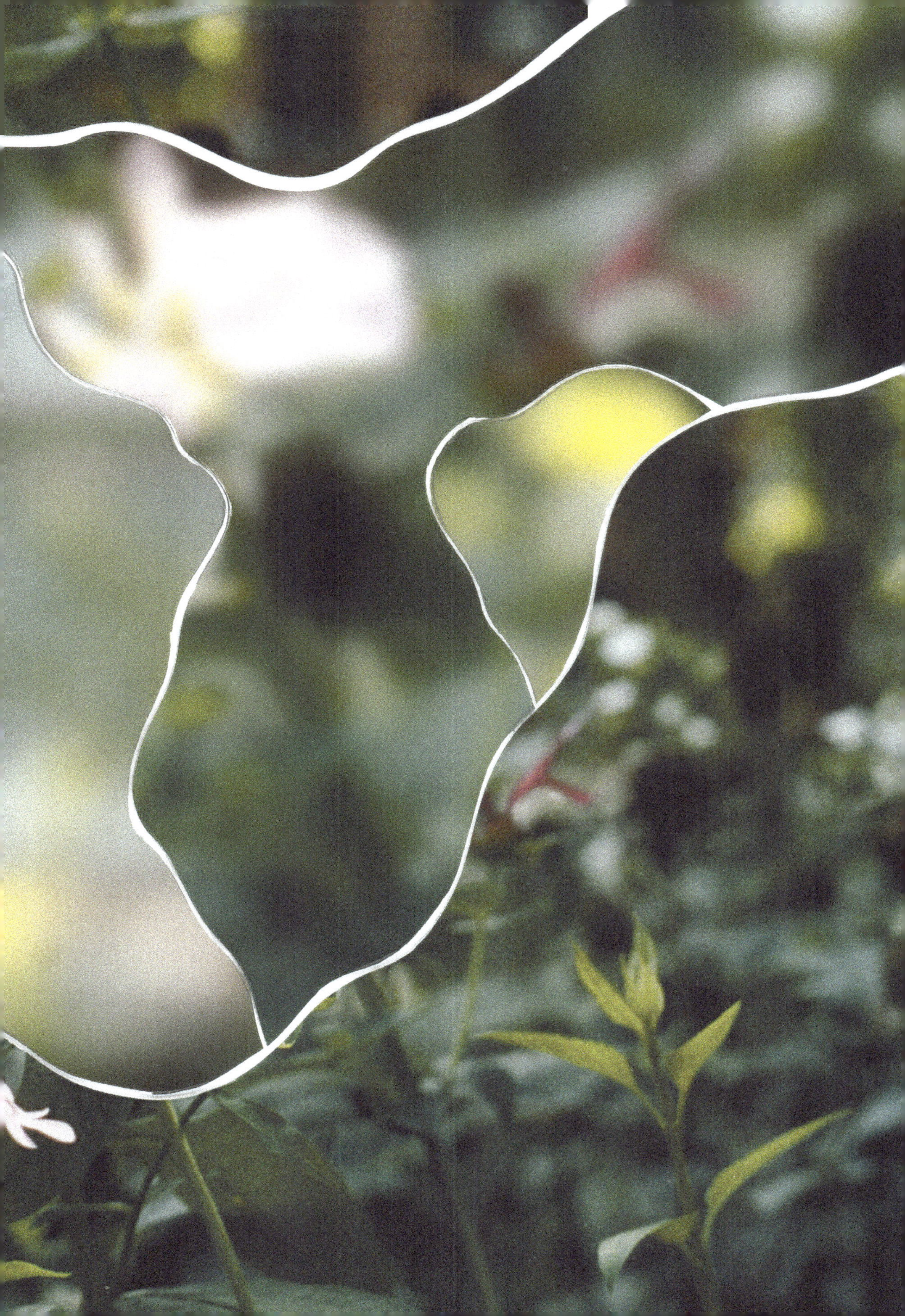

repave is an arts & literature anthology conceptually united around the axis of mental health and healing.

—

repave team:

Emmi Greer
Ryan Edmund Thiel
Rachel Zetah Becker

special thanks to:

Jude, Jan Osborn, Rich Perin, Andrew Shon, Joni Renee Whitworth, Tahra Wilkins, Megan Zetter, all our therapists, teachers, & healers, everyone who has helped us feel seen, accepted, and loved — and the Earth for holding it all.

The creation of this issue was made possible by funding from The Regional Arts & Culture Council. Thank you, RACC for enabling us to create and share this work.

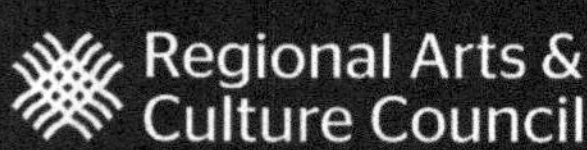

—

www.repave.org
@repavemag

contents

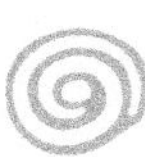

visual artwork

additional artwork provided throughout by e. e. greer, Rachel Zetah Becker, and Ryan Edmund Thiel

interactive interludes

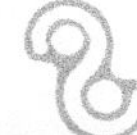

fiction

non-fiction

poetry

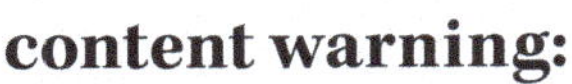

content warning:

This issue includes works that address self-harm, suicidality, violence, sexuality, abuse, and disordered eating. Lived experience with mental illness may often be uncomfortable, so we invite you to witness with openness and compassion. We also offer this warning so that you can proceed as is appropriate for you. Please take care of yourself as needed. Thank you for being here.

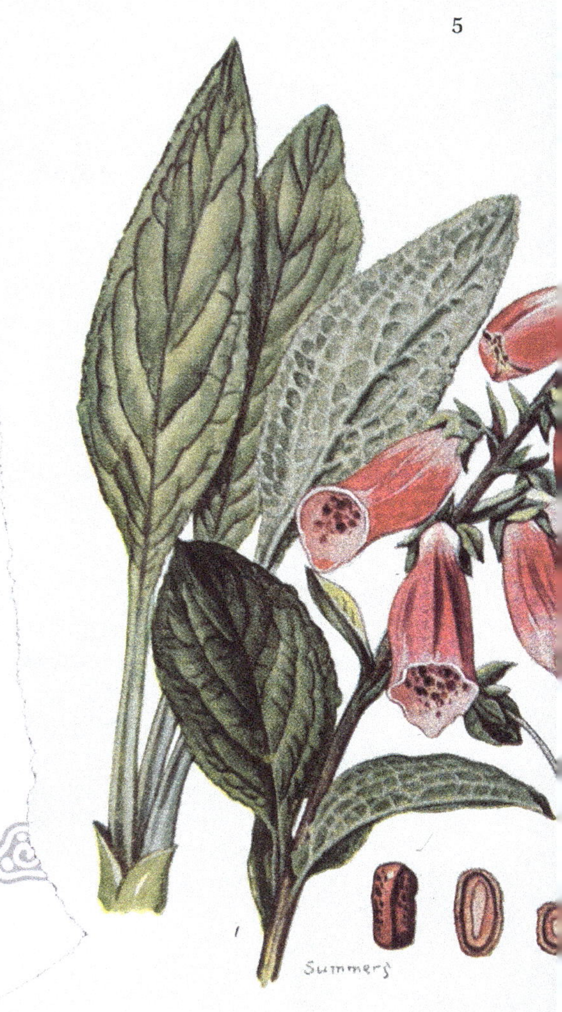

PLATE VI.—*Digitalis purpurea* (Foxglove).
mental Pharmacology and Materi

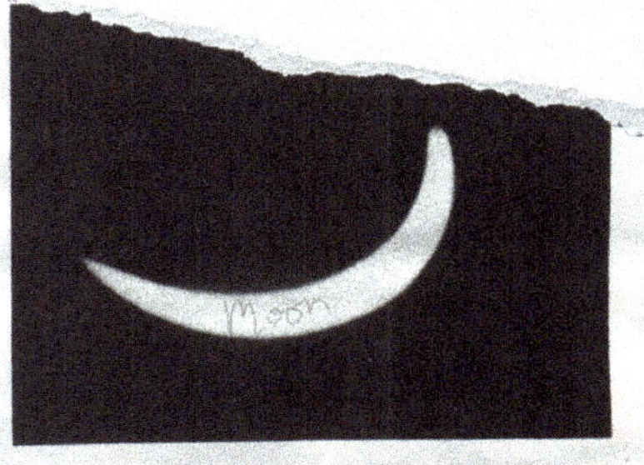

SOLAR ECLIPSE - FEBRUARY 26, 1979

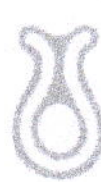

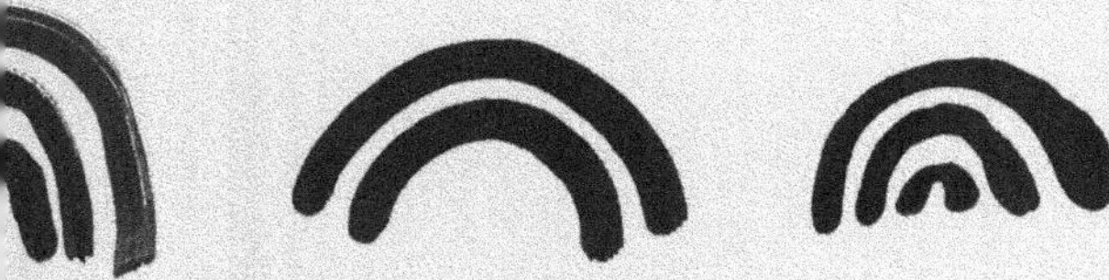

Aaron Clefton (he/him/his) is a white, heterosexual, cis man living with bipolar disorder. He is a civil rights attorney and managing partner of Rein & Clefton, a law firm focusing on enforcement of the Americans with Disabilities Act. He lives in Oakland, California, with his spouse and twin sons. He is dedicated to advancing the civil and economic rights of disabled, working and poor people. This is his first published work. (reincleftonlaw.com)

Anthony Ferguson can be found online at proxycult.com

Bailey Cheney (she/her) is a nice and fun and sensitive and sometimes cool girl trying to live beyond survival in her tiny corner of the planet (and internet). her art stuff is a means for coping with the excruciating pain and joy of having a brain and body 24/7, all the time. you can find bailey's work in her friends' bookshelves and recycling bins, as well as libraries, magazines, and museums of minimal notoriety. give her a follow on instagram @bailey_irl for pictures of cool dogs, cool skies, and cool art.

Bri Beck (she/her) obtained her Master of Arts in Art Therapy and Counseling from the School of the Art Institute of Chicago in 2019. Bri considers herself to have a social art practice and combines her fine art, design, and work as a helping professional to change individual and societal insight. She plays with color, pattern, shape, and scale to show emotional states and create alternative environments. In her art therapy and activist work, Bri is particularly passionate about working within the disability community. As a self-identified disabled artist and art therapist, Bri is committed to utilizing the arts to show the varied, beautiful, and complex story of disability, as well as creating an avenue for other disabled folks to do the same. Bri currently works as a team leader at the Dincin Center for Recovery with Thresholds. (www.briannabeck.com • @bri.beck)

Carissa Buganan (she/her) is a chef, houseplant addict, and music video aficionado from Portland, Oregon. When not cooking, she can be found listening to records or watering her begonias.

Cervanté Pope (she/her/they/them) is a music journalist and culture critic based on the West Coast. Her work has been published locally and nationally, particularly with *Revolver Mag* and *Kerrang*. Much of her personal work is informed by growing up Black and American Indian, fairly sheltered and just trying to figure it all out. (@ghettocross)

Dianne Wright (she/her) is a disabled poet who lives in the High Desert in Southern California. She has an MA in Rhetoric and Composition, and considers herself a Freelance Subversive. Her poem "An Accounting" about the shooting of Ahmaud Arbery is forthcoming in the journal *Writers Resist*.

e. e. greer (she/her) is a writer, educator, and hybrid-genre artist. she is forever obsessed with the polyamorous relationships between language, art, and consciousness. (emmigreer.com)

Emily Kendal Frey (she or they) is the author of the poetry collections *The Grief Performance* and *Sorrow Arrow.* Another full-length collection is forthcoming in 2021 from Fonograf Editions. (@emilykendalfreypoetry)

Emme Williamson (they/them) is an interdisciplinary artist, writer, and tarot reader who loves moss and post-it notes. Emme was born and raised in the Pacific Northwest and received their MFA from the University of Illinois at Chicago in 2018. Emme's work explores identity, rituals, and personal narrative, with a focus on gender, spirituality, and the body. Their short film *I think it's Wednesday*, made during and in response to the COVID-19 pandemic and quarantine, was shown in Northwest Film Forum's 2020 Local Sightings Film Festival. Emme features tarot readings and teachings online through their YouTube channel and Instagram (@emmetarot).

Goddess (they/them/theirs) is the Proud MoMo of Sun Seed Community; a platform for the practice of collective healing. Creating Goddess' tools of liberation took a whole community of support and they hope their village's stories can resonate with others. They graduated from the Healing Arts Institute of Massage in October of 2018 and continue to explore therapeutic and spiritual practices. You can usually find them in the "pagan" section of the bookstore, sitting in the back of a concert, caressing crystals at your local metaphysical shop, or binge-watching old sci-fi movies while cooking. (sunseedcommunity.com. • FB/IG: @sunseedcommunity)

Jenny Vu can be found online at jennyvutoday.com

Josephine Chien (she/her/ta) is a published poet/writer, and has received an honorable mention from the American Academy of Poets. She is working on a novel, *Paris-Taipei*, in which the heroine escapes her oppressive life in Taipei by dreaming of Paris.

Born and raised in Brooklyn, NY, **Kaleem Jones** (he/him) is an audio + visual artist. His work focuses on his experience as a black man living in American capitalism. His favorite things to do are drawing, writing poetry, and making beats. (@highlycoloured)

Kate Weimer (they/them/theirs) | amateur print-maker and sewing enthusiast. "wholesome and edgy at the same time." (@crunchwrath_supreme)

Kathryn Louise Herron (she/her) is a writer, photographer, and filmmaker living in Olympia, WA. Kathryn holds an MFA in Creative Writing from Pacific University and a Bachelor's degree from The Evergreen State College emphasizing creative writing and media studies. Kathryn is the author of "The Stranger Face" (Afterword Books, 2020), "The Blacklist" (Clash Media, 2018), "The United States of Rape Culture" (King Shot Press, 2017), and "Death and the Blue Blood Blues" (Great Jones Street, 2016). She is currently working on her debut novel and a collection of short stories. (@kathrynlouiseh • kathrynlouiseh.com)

L. Sparks (she/her) is an intersectional feminist, writer, poet, and creative. She is a brown, multi-racial, pansexual, woman living and writing in Colorado and is currently an editor with the online artist-centric news and media platform, Dirt Media. She has been published with *Spit Poet Zine*, *South Broadway Ghost Society*, *Tiny Spoon*, *Stain'd Arts*, *Suspect Press*, and *Cosmonauts Avenue*. You can find more of her work and connect with her on Instagram @sparksliza534, on Twitter @lizathepoet, or lizasparks.com.

contributors

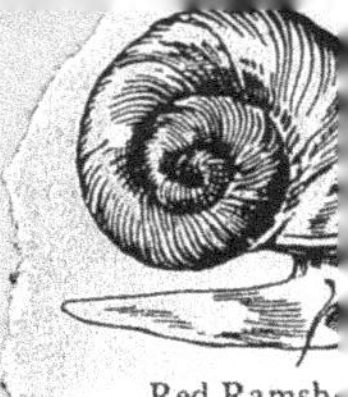
Red Ramsh

Maureen Boyd (she/her) is a Thai-Scottish American writer, born and raised in Los Angeles, California. She has published in *Joyland Magazine* and has work forthcoming in *Buckmxn Journal*. She is a former union organizer and is currently pursuing an MFA in Fiction at Pacific University. She resides in Oakland, California with her family. (maureenboyd.net • twitter: @Militant_Asian)

Miguel Ontiveros (he/him) (b.1994) raised on the Southwest side of Chicago is an artist who works between the media of photography and mixed media. Ontiveros' photo collages explore visual-spatial investigations from his personal surroundings. He deconstructs and layers reconfiguring fragments using collage scraps of ephemera in relation to self and site, exploring the materiality in connection with memory, place, and identity. (montiveros.com)

Rachel Zetah Becker (she/her) is an artist, graphic designer, and earthling based in western Colorado. She is fascinated by nature, trash, religion, and the times we are living in. Rachel created Church of Earth in 2016, an art project and spiritual practice devoted to healing our human relationships with the Earth. She loves a good dance party and wandering in wild places. (rachelzbecker.com • churchofearth.us • @church.of.earth)

Ryan Edmund Thiel (they/he) is an interdisciplinary artist interested in the liberation and manifestation of the self and its relationship to the environment and other lifeforms. They currently reside in Chicago, Illinois. (@talldarkandryan)

Ryley Schlachter (she/her) | Born and raised in Dallas, TX, although I have lived in California for the past 10 years. I mostly work with photography, but when I allow myself the time, writing is my other main art form. Most of the inspiration of my work stems from my experience with my eating disorder, as well as my daily work with the earth as a farmer. (@letsryot)

Sharon E. Crowley (she/they) | I currently live, write, and work as a union organizer in Seattle, WA. I am also a recovering academic. I moved here to study English at the University of Washington (terminally ABD). I also have a BS in Biology from the Lyman Briggs School at Michigan State University, and an MA in English from the University of Vermont. I grew up in Grand Rapids, MI. (@arguchik • arguchik.com)

Takeo Hiromitsu (he/him) | I am creator creature and find flow in creative processes. These take the form of painting, printmaking and music. I have a BFA in Printmaking from Colorado State University and have been working in the contemporary art museum world. For me, the act of making art is fundamental and the force is of creation and destruction. I am merely a resonant chamber that tunes into the frequencies and the byproduct of tuning in sometimes is an art object. (@ztkao)

Willow Brook (she/her) is an earth loving artist who weaves together art and the environment along with her deep devotion to spiritual study and practice. As an art educator who loves to play with all mediums, she uses available materials with a special affinity for vibrant colors. (@soul.invocation • soulinvocation.weebly.com)

Zohara Night (she/her) writes weird, dark, queer fiction and fantasy. She has an MFA and three cats. (zoharanight.com)

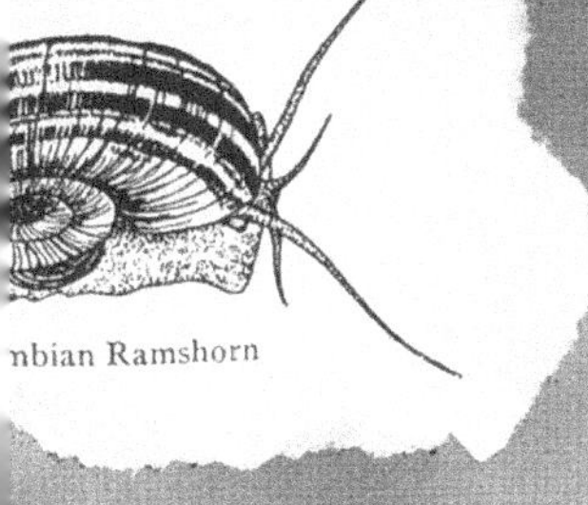

*art is the giving by each [person]
of their evidence to the world.
those who wish to give, love to give,
discover the pleasure of giving. those
who give are incredibly strong.*

— Robert Henri

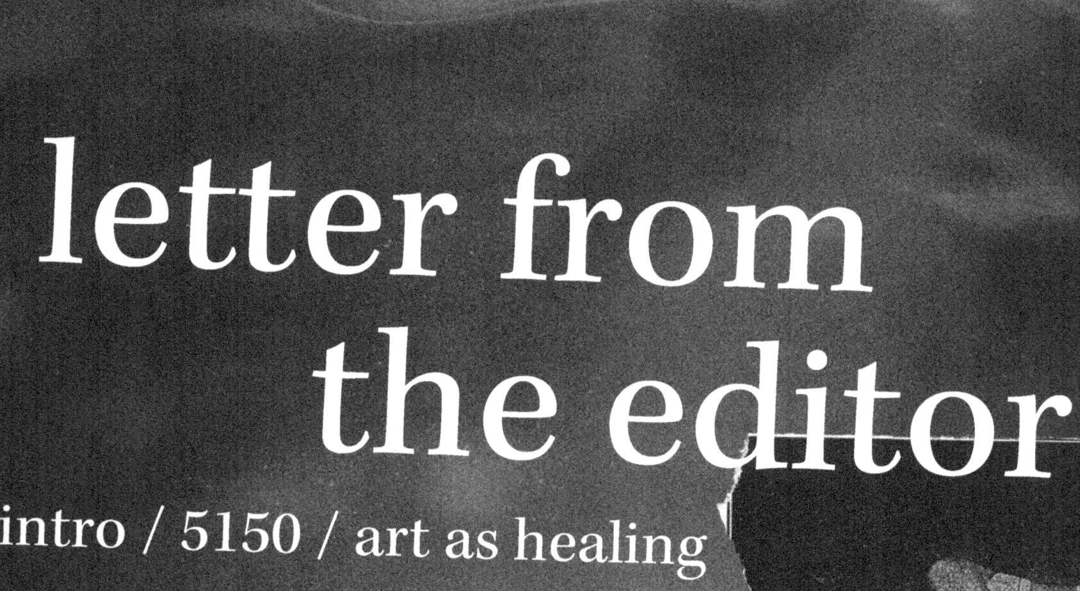

letter from the editor

intro / 5150 / art as healing

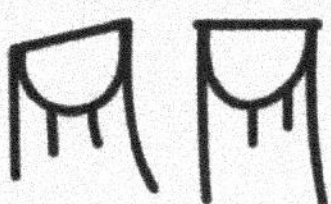

I'll be honest, it's named after an album. but only because, back then, the title revealed itself to me as a needed term, a way I could, for the first time, name my state. repave was that phase for me. such reclamation. the vast and immediate healing my simultaneous privilege and willingness allowed me.

as I'm writing this, it was exactly seven years ago to the day, my curling at the bottom of the spiral. didn't expressly try anything, mind you, but at that time, I believed it would be easier to die and in the panic throes, I thought I might act on it. people who didn't quite grasp but loved me got wind of that and all of a sudden, my stoop was stormed, and I was taken in handcuffs.

I denied and flailed and begged him to stay. but once in the hospital bed, I resigned to the situation. had to stay three nights. they call it a 72-hour hold, like you're a library book. but it was mostly blur. held my crisis close.

who knows how much further down my arc goes and for not finding out, for that most unpleasant rescue, I thank them.

I resent the methods, though. such awful stakes. how they drug us numb. only go outside for minutes per day, and even then, concrete on five sides. but—what it woke in me, I am so grateful. I say this because it's ok. to be visible. admit the waver. the breakdown. the haven.

before I had to go, I pleaded with the cops to let me change or at least grab a handful of clothes but they wouldn't. I hated that outfit. so, I went with no comfort. but someone getting released that day, a new mother, who had brought herself there gifted me her soft fleece.

after that, recovery, for me, became a living state. made it a noun. a constant shape of being.

Repave by the band Volcano Choir was released just a month before I faltered. when I was most frantic. I'm sure I listened before, but it didn't sink in like after. it's an album set in winter, an ode to the annual darker half. and so when I was emergent in that season, it became consumptive. a soundtrack to a future I hadn't previously realized and was now showing. this is not to say that it will be antidote for everyone, but those eight songs surely saved me.

the freezing sea on the album cover was how I felt. thrashed but vast and moving always. I fell into it, saw myself there. the raw byegones and my tiderays glowing. chanting *I am an anchor*. became an almanac.

got full on its spangly affirmations and throaty lamentations. *Repave* gave me some strain of understanding I hadn't been offered before. told me to:

shed skin / for kin / shed skin / like a master

wanted just to be what it said:

shameless and humming.

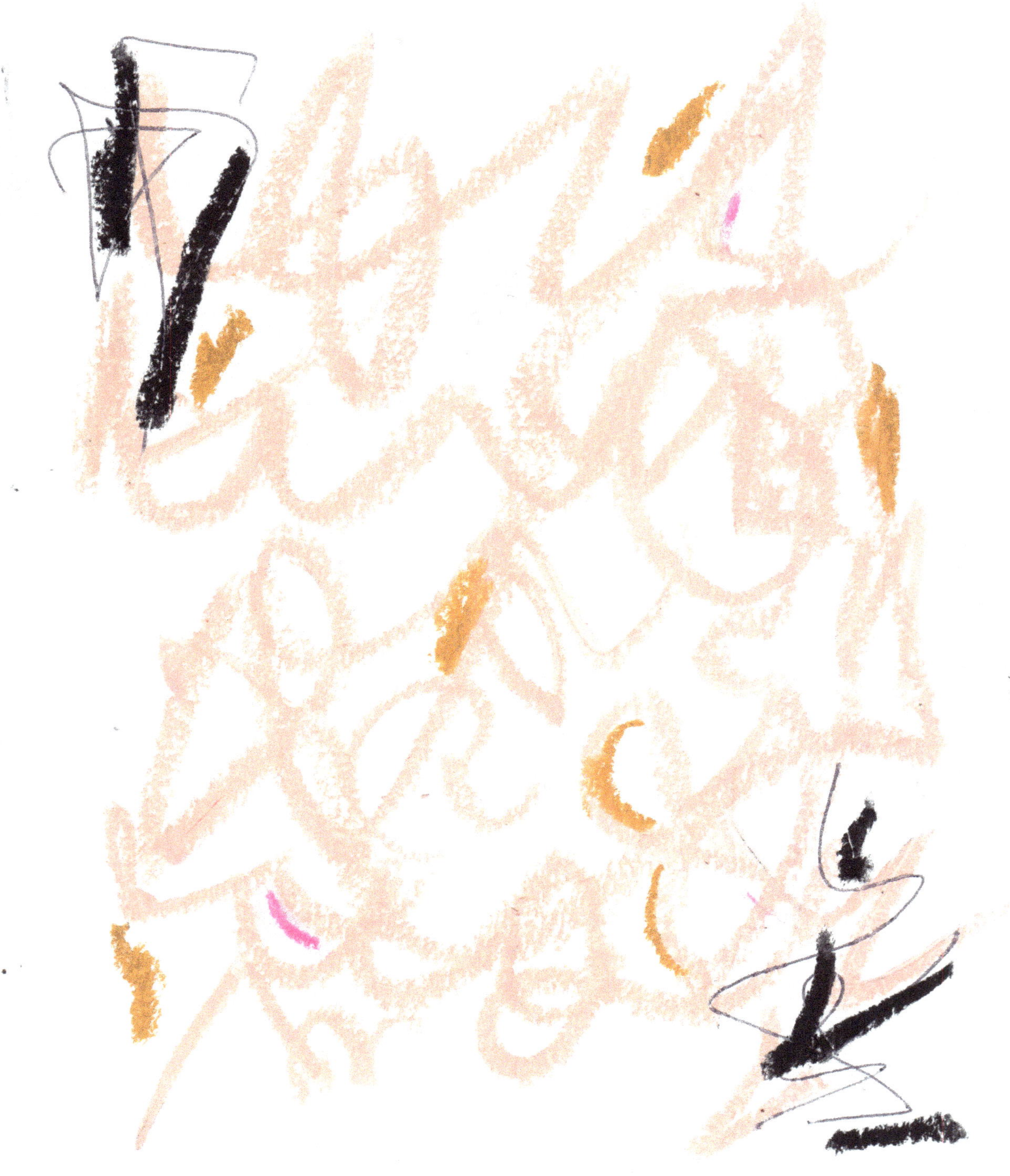

back then, I was a precipice, and certainly, I still struggle, but from that steepest chasm, I came back. and just like that music, I did it parts gentle and brave and smashing and cagey. part art and meditation. and now I constantly imagine what care could really be. one thing I know: no handcuffs.

we are not wrong or criminal. but able to feel things deeply, and we need that capacity in this world. because we suffer the fever sometimes, it seems we have opened a channel. a spectrum stretched and we know the edges. so we must discuss benevolence. how to put it into remade systems. to have it feel not like trouble, but actual help. nonjudgement.

My recreation is cyclic and constant, but I don't think it would have initially been made possible without art. art as a generative and healing practice. what a potent vehicle it can be. a pure realm. proof of transformation. and doesn't it already have something to do with death. we are the only species to know we are temporal. and have to live with that. so, we desire this tactility, to create. make. render our own image. and in doing so, transcend our lifetimes.

that's why it's easy for me to believe that some of the utmost acts you can perform are art and healing. both individual and collective, two wings that lift together.

and that's what I hope this to be. step in somewhere where you are seen, invited, respected. a portal you can hold in your hand. and the letters themselves, in the word, look to me, a lot like us—burdened, rising, dignified.

back to the term. It was a container for remaining myself. a holy claiming. because I wanted so badly to look and say: *that was before, and this, here, is a new me.* but that would be superfluous and untrue. at a time, it may have felt like asphalt tearing, like the totality of self-destruction, but it was, instead, a fortification.

to repave is not to exile any existing material, but to allow it to rest, condense, and be used. renewed. all the selves we've sent. all the times

I have resurfaced, gone over and over. doubled down, got smoother, stronger. owned my own rubble.

of course, I have no cure. of course not. but it's not nothing because I came through. was young as clover. sobbing on the sidewalk. doomed myself. harm rows. went from that— to transcendence. often inside its shimmering brackets. so the least I can do is talk about it.

thank you for braving this tender age with me. I know our emotional thrones have not been cleared yet. hardly space even enough for our passage. so let us create that for ourselves where and however we can. and then adorn it. adore it.

I am alongside you and there is some vase of the state in everyone's mind. and anyway, it's not linear, or easy. but most likely worth it. because to show some version of what our minds are like will open worthy eyes.

and as we heal, we do not need to seek perfection or hustle at it. whatever speed and whatever muscle. there are so many shards already. sharp measures to hurt ourselves with.

what a difference it makes to just be permeable, open.

and as the song says:

it's softening to be softening.

if you are lonely or swollen or bruised through

or in the thick of headgrip, this is for you.

let's make mental health mainstream.

I'm saying now, we've spent the shallows.

I swear,

you look good

in that depth.

— *emmi*

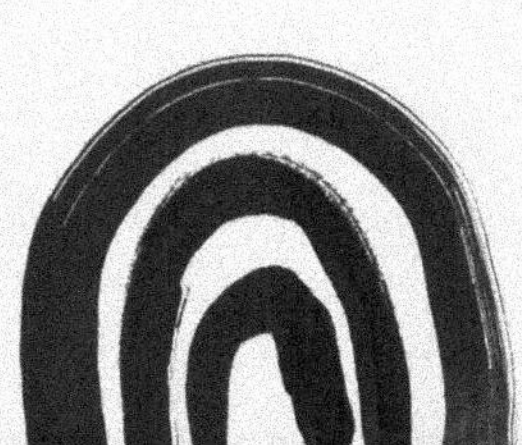

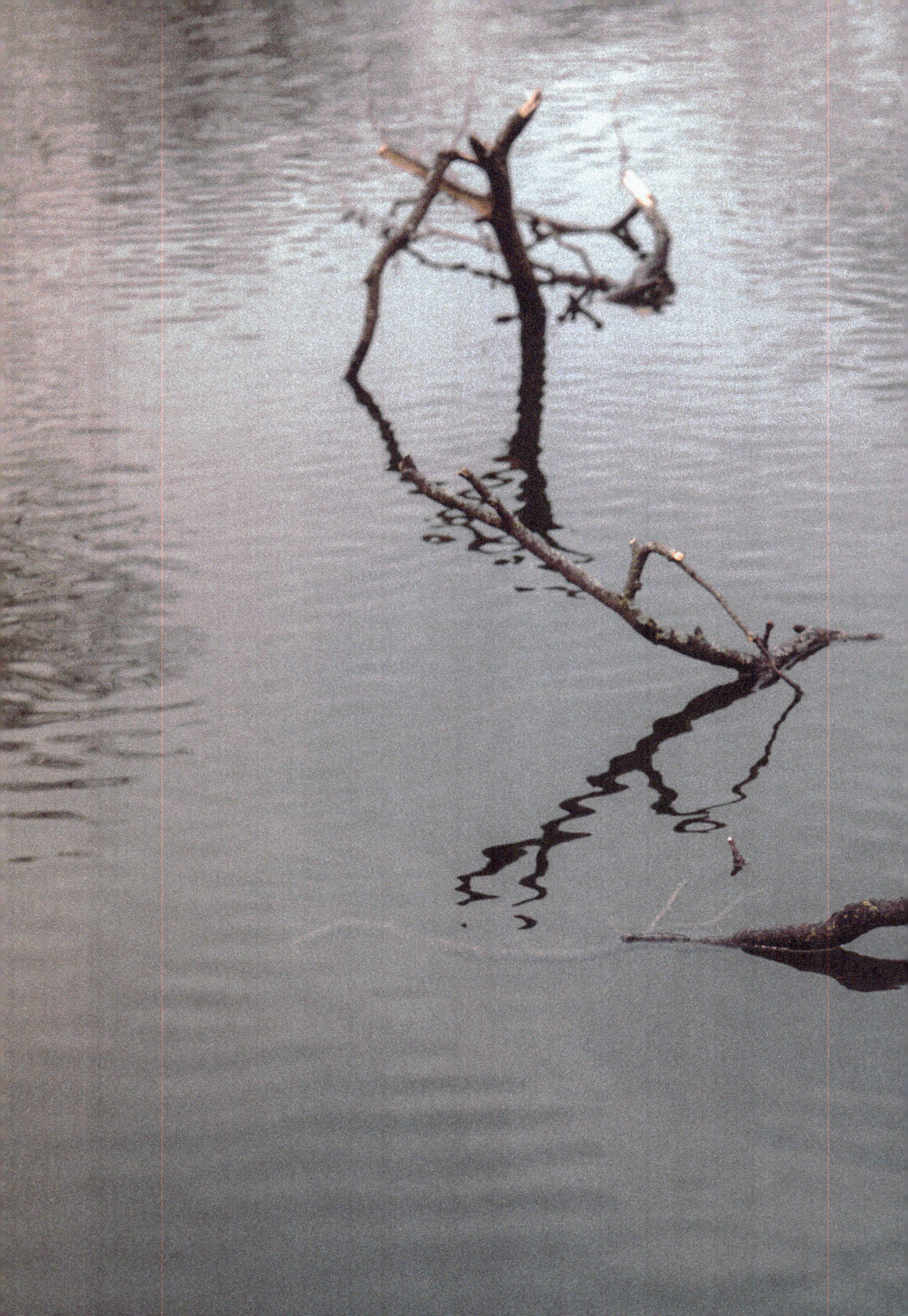

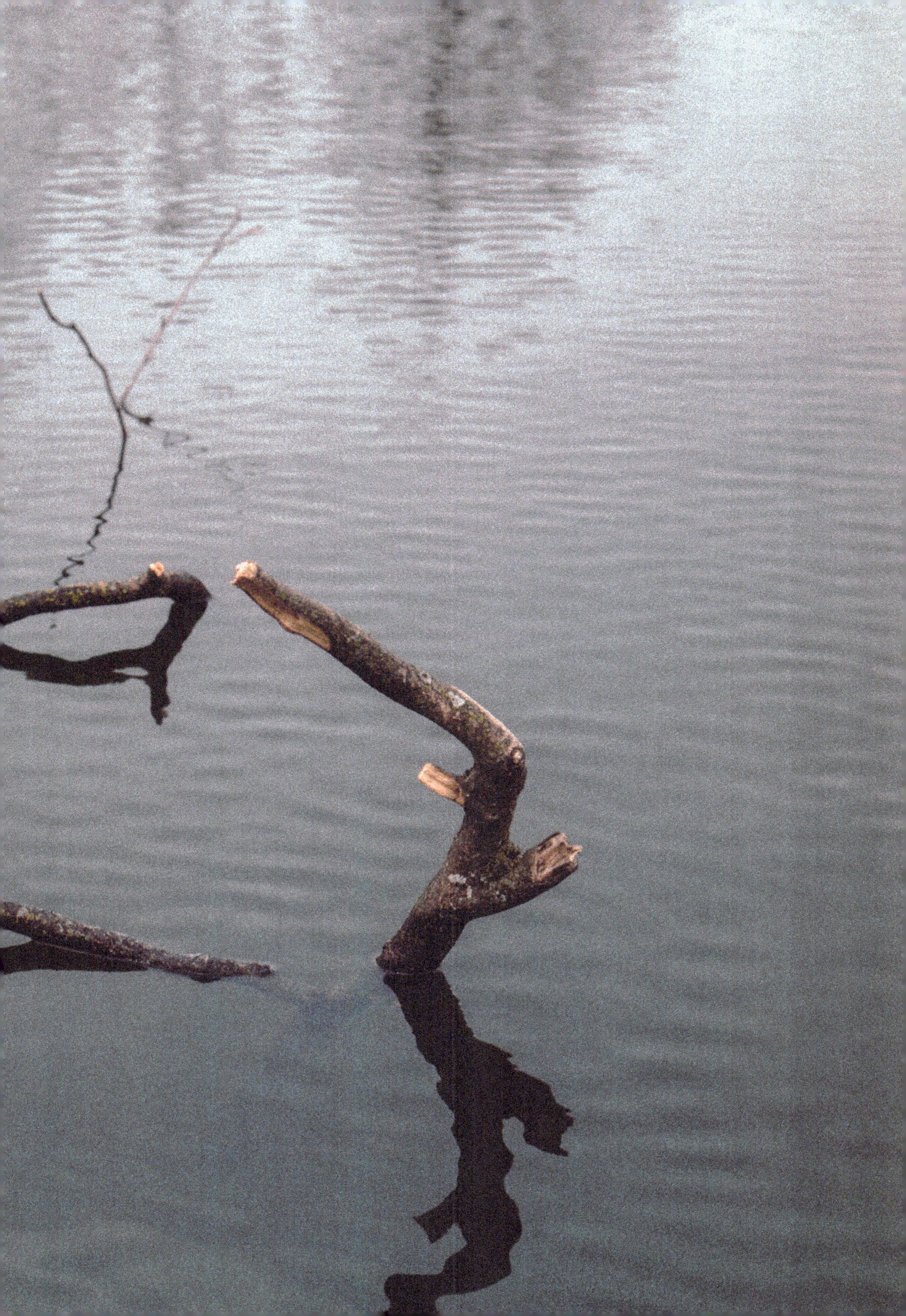

MESSENGERS

BY ZOHARA NIGHT

The first time Poppy saw her ghost, she was standing outside the bakery wishing she could have a goddamn cigarette. She'd quit four years ago, during the Summer When Everything Changed, almost a year before she met Meera and only a few months after she cut for the last time.

She and Meera started coming here the past few months to buy challah. Over the years, baking challah together on Fridays had become one their favorite activities—it was intimate, holy, and very, very gay. But there'd been a shortage of yeast for a while now, and when they couldn't get a hold of any, they'd come here to buy the bread instead. She missed baking, but she hadn't really felt up to it lately, anyway.

Poppy always waited outside, both because of social distancing measures and because the baker's son Jacob was a total fucking creep. He always hit on Meera. But never Poppy—probably because you couldn't clock Meera with a magnifying glass, whereas Poppy was just shy of six feet, broader-shouldered, and didn't bother to hide the fact that even after five years of hormones she still couldn't grow decent tits. Still, Meera insisted on being the one to go in. Poppy knew she could take care of herself.

Poppy's phone dinged. Meera—a lone emoji, eyes rolling. Poppy turned around and looked into the bakery window. Jacob was leaning on the counter, yakking away, despite Meera pretending to be busy on her phone. Poppy laughed.

Just then, a delivery truck laid on the horn as it passed, and Poppy nearly jumped out of her skin. "Fuck," she shouted, giving the long-gone driver the finger. It was at this very moment that Poppy saw her for the first time.

It was the hair that caught Poppy's eye first, because you don't see hair like that these days. Down the block, across the street, stood a lanky teen boy with long, jagged black hair, over-straightened bangs pushed dramatically to one side. Poppy half-winced, half-smiled, but the expression quickly melted away because she realized she was looking at her younger self.

It was Poppy. It had to be. She was even cloaked in her old favorite shirt—the knitted gray one she wore almost every day of freshman year. It was baggy enough to conceal her boy chest and emaciated frame, with sleeves so long that she could hide her balled fists in them.

Poppy felt a gasp escape her throat, so quiet she couldn't herself hear it. But before she could do anything at all, another truck drove by, and in that horror-movie way, once it passed, the ghost standing there had disappeared.

"It's about time," Meera said, appearing beside her carrying a brown paper bag. "God, that guy is such a blowhard."

Poppy blinked, trying to collect herself. "Yeah. Too bad his mom makes the best vegan challah in walking distance." She forced a grin.

"You okay?"

Poppy considered telling her what she had just seen. But she didn't, because she would sound utterly out of her mind. Never mind that she *felt* utterly out of her mind. "Yeah, I'm good. Let's go home?"

Meera hummed, and broke into a smile. "Coffee first." She took Poppy's hand, and they took off down the block, trailing the scent of fresh bread behind them.

* * *

Saturnalia didn't have the best coffee, but it was on the way home. Poppy and Meera decided to sit outside a while, basking in what was surely one of the last truly warm summer afternoons. Meera was working on her novel again, after months of writer's block, grazing the pen across her lower lip as she thought. Poppy watched the crowds go by, still noticeably thinner than they had been before the pandemic hit. But each time she looked up, she felt a pang of panic in her gut, terrified that at any second she would find herself once again staring up at the face of her teenage self.

"Do you think the restroom's open?" Poppy asked.

Meera nodded. "I saw someone go in a minute ago."

It was a tiny cafe restroom, single occupancy, and dimly lit. A fake wood sign hung over the toilet that read *Coffee is my love language* in gaudy cursive. Poppy peed and flipped on the faucet. She was checking her teeth when she saw, standing behind her, the face of her teenage self.

"Jesus," she gasped, hearing the blood pounding in her ears. "What the fuck?"

The ghost said nothing, just gazed at her from behind that mop of black hair. She was leaning against the wall, looking as numb and boyish and helpless as Poppy felt at that age.

"What do you want?" she pleaded.

The way the kid looked at Poppy betrayed her palpable confusion, and at last, she said slowly,
"I died."

Poppy shook her head. "That's...impossible."

The younger Poppy raised her arms. The long sleeves were stained red with wet blood, from the cuff almost up to the elbow. Yes, this was how Poppy had looked that night—the first time she had tried to end her life.

Poppy couldn't take this. Not now, and probably not ever. "I'm sorry. I can't help you."

She unlatched the door and thrust it open. Light streaming through the cafe windows blinded her. She stumbled out and found her way to the patio, back to where her girlfriend still sat jotting lines in her notebook.

Meera took a sip of her americano and gave Poppy a smile as she sat. If Poppy looked as shaken as she felt, it seemed that Meera hadn't noticed.

It couldn't have been real. She didn't die. She was sitting right here. Why now? Why *that* version of Poppy—that teenaged, effeminate, emo boy version of her? Am I supposed to help her somehow? she wondered. What can I possibly do?

"Meera," Poppy said. "If you could say anything to your teenage self, what would it be?"

Meera sucked her teeth. "Easy. Go to the doctor and get yourself some estrogen shots."

"No, no. I mean—yes, of course, but I mean more like, in a sagely, older-queer-to-baby-queer sort of way?"

"Hmm. I guess I'd have to think about it." Meera put down her pen. "Where's this coming from, anyway?"

Poppy shook her head. "I don't know. Never mind."

At the next table over, an elderly couple sat nursing their coffees. Poppy eyed the woman, who could have been anywhere from 60 to 90. Rivers of wrinkles flowed down her face. Her husband was talking and gesturing wildly. Between sips, she smiled at him and nodded her head quietly. Poppy wondered if they, too, were living on borrowed time.

* * *

The candles were lit. "L'cha Dodi" crackled through the speakers, and the room swelled with the sounds of accordions and fiddles. Poppy lit a joint and cracked open her book,

popping small bites of challah in her mouth. The thick, herby smoke curled and danced with the music.

Meera polished off her wine and set the glass on the coffee table in front of her. She stood, rounded the table, and plopped down in Poppy's lap. Poppy smiled and set her book down on the armrest. Meera planted her lips on Poppy's. Her fingers grazed Poppy's neck. Kissing her harder, Meera started to unbutton her shirt. Poppy put her hand on Meera's arm.

"What's wrong?" Meera asked.

"I don't know. I'm just not feeling like myself lately. All this anxiety, and…" She shook her head. "Just kinda fucked up. As always. You know…"

"Hey, it's okay." She kissed Poppy's forehead. "Me too. Everything's fucked right now. Want to just watch something instead?"

Just then Meera's phone dinged. She groaned and reached for it on the end table. Her face lit up with white light. She frowned as she read.

"What's up?"

"Sydney. She asked if I could pick up her paycheck and drop it off at the shop."

"Go on," Poppy said. She took her hand and kissed it. "I'll clean up."

"You don't want to come with?"

"Hell no. I'm exhausted." Always am these days, aren't I? she thought.

Meera attacked Poppy's face with kisses and walked to the front door. Her keys jangled as she strapped the bike helmet under her chin. "Love ya," she said.

"Love you, too."

"Be back soon." The door closed behind Meera, the sound of her footfalls diminishing down the hallway. With each one, the silence in the apartment swelled. Poppy took another hit of the joint, then put it out. She looked at the empty armchair and sighed.

As if the very thought of it had called her forth, Poppy's ghost appeared. Sitting there in her bloodstained shirt, looking every bit like the boy Poppy had so desperately tried to be.

"So, this is how it's going to be from now on? You're going to just... show up sometimes?"

The kid looked down at the floor and shrugged. "I don't know." She stood shakily, wincing with pain, and circled round the armchair. "I'm sorry. I didn't ask for this. I was just supposed to die."

"No, it's... it's okay. I didn't mean that. I'm just confused."

She imagined how confused the kid must feel. Either way, the ghost seemed not to hear. She was examining the framed photos scattered about the bookshelf. She picked up the photo of Poppy and Meera taken in Toronto last year and stared at it for a while. "You look so happy. You're beautiful, you know."

Poppy sighed, and let out a small laugh. "Thanks."

"I can't believe you actually did it. I kind of suspected, but I thought it might be like, a sex thing or something. I mean, honestly... I've been really hoping it was."

"Ha. That certainly would be easier. But no, we're a girl."

The younger Poppy nodded, a wave of relief washing over her face, where a single tear appeared. She wiped it away, smudging her guyliner. "Mom and dad... we probably lose them, huh?"

"Hmm. In some ways. But no, they're still around. We do lose a lot of people. But we gain so many more than we could have imagined."

"Like..."
The kid gestured at the photo.

Poppy smiled. "Meera, yeah."

Young Poppy gritted her teeth then, seeming to steel herself. "Who is Sydney?"

"Sydney?" Poppy frowned. "Oh. No, it's not like that. Meera's nothing like...him." She meant Poppy's first boyfriend, freshman year. "Or any of the rest. It took a long time to find someone like her."

The younger Poppy broke into a grin. "Soulmates, huh?"

Poppy couldn't help but mirror her grin. "I guess so. I think... I think I might ask her to marry me." She saw the confusion on her younger self. "Oh, yeah—that's legal now. But I don't know. Maybe it's not the right time."

The kid stepped toward her. "What do you mean?"

"Things are...complicated right now. In the world, I mean."

"Who the fuck cares? If you want it, do it. I've dreamed about my wedding day since I was like, five. Except I could never imagine myself—"

"—in a tux," they both said, and laughed.

The young girl's face grew solemn. "But I guess I'll never see that, now."

"Wait. I don't understand. I tried that night, but I didn't *die*. I'm sitting right here. I remember all of it."

"Maybe *you* didn't. But I watched mom find my body. The aspirin, the razors...it had been hours."

"No." Poppy shook her head. "No, she came home early that day. Her last client canceled. I remember. I barely even blacked out."

"That's not how it happened for me."

Poppy must have been tearing up, because the kid put her hands up reassuringly. "It's okay. I wanted this. Remember?"

"We didn't know any better," Poppy snapped. "You don't know what I know."

The kid just watched her, detached, unmoved. Then she shook her head angrily. "Don't you dare cry for me. You know we never wanted that. Not from anyone."

"Well, maybe it was what we needed."

"Just forget it, okay? You lived. Look at your life. You were right—I could never have dreamed of this." She paused. Her lip quivered. "If you want to know whether I regret it, fine. Seeing you, seeing all of this, I guess I do."

"We did regret it." Poppy wiped her eyes. "Girl, we regret it every time."

"You mean...I try again."

Poppy nodded, lips tight. The kid seemed to brace herself, her jaw clenching, eyes distant.

"More than once."

"Yes. Things got a lot worse, for a long time."

The younger Poppy's voice cracked.

"Why do we keep fighting, then?"

"That's the fucking question, isn't it."

Silence swelled between them, benevolent, before Poppy opened her mouth again. "Things are so good, finally. I know. That's the problem. It looks perfect from the outside, but when I'm in it, all I can think is how terrified I am to lose it. I never expected to make it here. To have this life. And now I feel like I don't know how to."

The younger her scoffed. "What, do you think God or something is gonna realize their mistake and snatch it away from you?"

Poppy laughed a little through her tears.

"If you should have died at fifteen, every day after that is a fucking *gift*."

"Yeah, you're right. But you don't understand what I mean."

The kid shook her head, scowling.

"What?" Poppy asked.

"You're going to sit there and tell me I don't understand?"

Poppy cracked a smile. "Yeah, I guess you're right. It's just that now I'm so close to finally getting it together, all I can think about is, what if it all goes to shit? What will I do then? Death was like an old friend, you know? Always there, waiting to take me in. And now that's gone. I finally don't want to die. I'm *scared* of it."

"Well, yeah. Speaking from experience, choosing to live is way fucking scarier than choosing to die."

Poppy nodded. "You're brave, too, you know. Way braver than you know."

For a lingering moment, the kid watched her quietly, then went back to exploring the studio. She looked so young to Poppy, her eyes ever-searching and full of wonder. "God, this place is fucking adorable. It's like a dream." She reached Poppy's dresser and began looking over her jewelry. She picked up one of Poppy's silver necklaces, the one with a small, strange pendant of a sapphire hanging in the shadow of a crescent moon. "Beautiful."

Poppy stood and walked over to her fifteen-year-old self. "That's one of my favorites. I've had it for years." She took the dainty chain and held it up to the light. "God, I don't even remember where I got it." She unlatched it and draped it around the kid's tiny neck. "You know, it looks better on you. Take it."

"Really?" The young Poppy beamed in the mirror, then smiled at her older self. "Thanks." She frowned, then, as if listening to a voice Poppy couldn't hear. Her eyes lowered. "I want to stay longer, but I think I have to go now."

"It's time?"

"Yeah."

"Will I see you again?"

The young girl shook her head. "I don't think so."

Poppy sighed. She swallowed back another wave of tears, the strongest one yet. "Thank you. I wish I could do something more for you."

The younger Poppy shook her head. "Do more for yourself."

Poppy blinked, and the ghost was

"THANK YOU. I WISH I COULD DO SOMETHING MORE FOR YOU."

THE YOUNGER POPPY SHOOK HER HEAD. "DO MORE FOR YOURSELF."

gone. She walked slowly to the sofa and lay down. Tears welled in her eyes. "I'm sorry," she said to herself. "You deserved better. You deserved better." She cried for a while, in the silence, just existing, just allowing herself to exist, feeling the warmth of the throw, the softness of the pillow beneath her head.

* * *

"He's awake. Nurse!"

She recognized her mom's voice. She opened her eyes, but the world was fuzzy and oversaturated. It made her want to vomit. She saw an IV needle sticking out of her arm. Her wrists were wrapped tightly with gauze. Her mouth was heavy with charcoal and ash.

She tried to remember how she got here. Her brain felt filmy and dark—there was only the tub full of warm, red water, and this. She watched her mom stand and rush to the doorway, calling for the nurse again and again. On the table next to the chair where her mom had been sitting, she saw her black jeans, her stained grey shirt, and a silver, moon-shaped necklace she didn't quite recognize.

Her whole body was ablaze. She closed her eyes, tried to speak, but no sound came out. She drew a deep, deep breath, smelling the faintest hint of weed and sweet bread. She squinted at the clock on the table. A mess of green lines came together. She saw it was a few minutes past midnight.

The door opened and Meera stepped through with a small, crumpled white bag. She unclipped her helmet and crossed the kitchen to where Poppy was drying the dishes and kissed her deeply. "Sorry that took so long."

"Fuck. Do I smell churros?" she asked Meera, who wagged the bag in her face. "Oh, you do love me." She gave Meera another quick peck on the lips and snatched one from the bag.

"Girl, you are not going to believe the drama with Sydney. Wait, let's open a window. It's fucking gorgeous out right now."

Poppy crossed the studio to the window, the churro dangling from her mouth, and pushed it open. Outside, she saw sapphire. She tried to remember the name of that trans dyke with the jewelry shop on 10th, drafting a mental note to make an appointment for this week. She slumped into the couch next to Meera, who had already started her story. A light breeze came in through the window. For the first time in months, the city sounded alive.

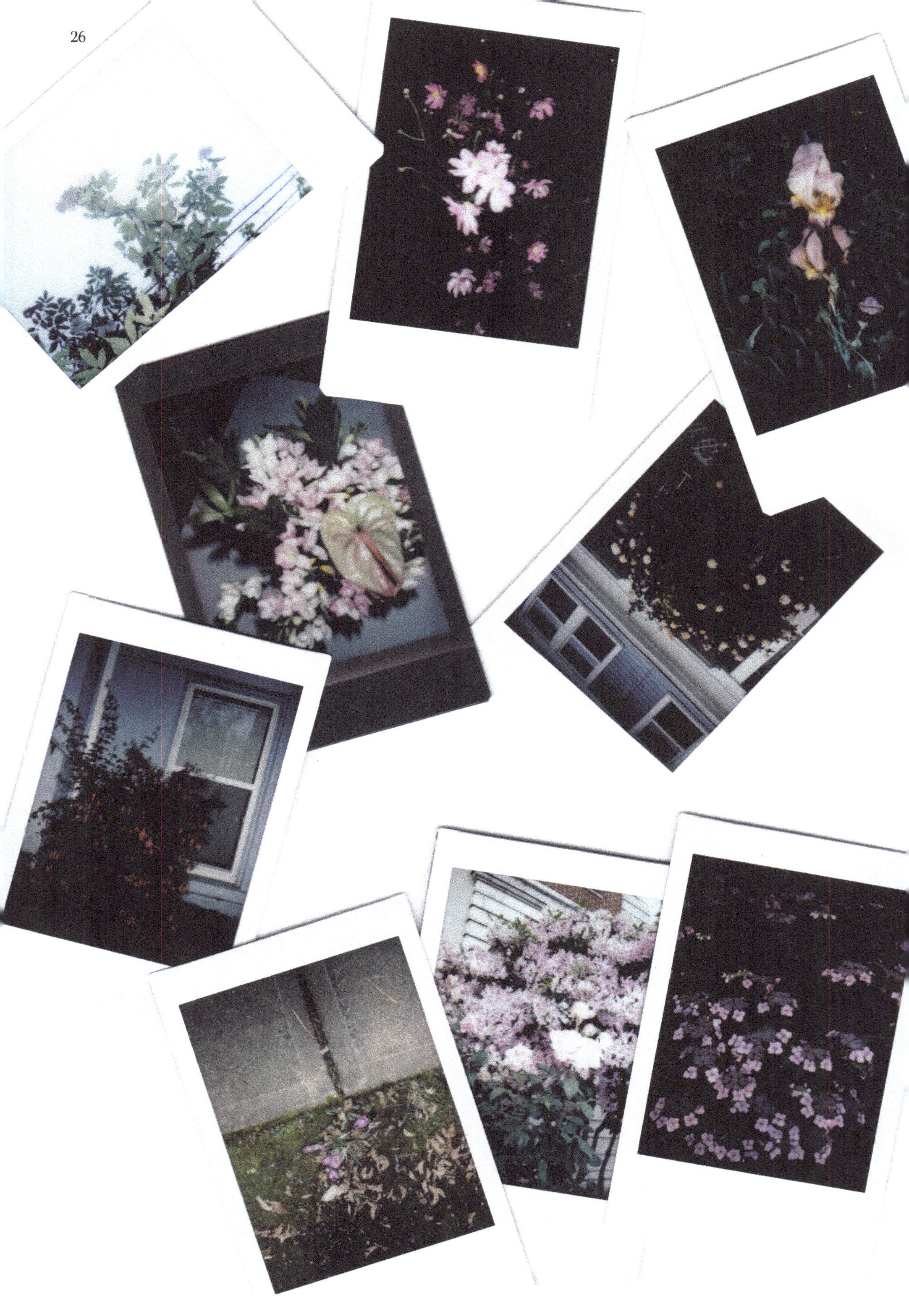

come on, there is
volume now, let's
cull the fullest light.

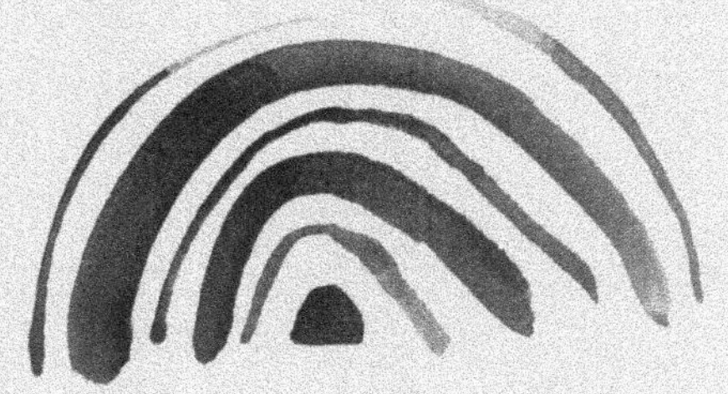

Past Lives

BY L. SPARKS

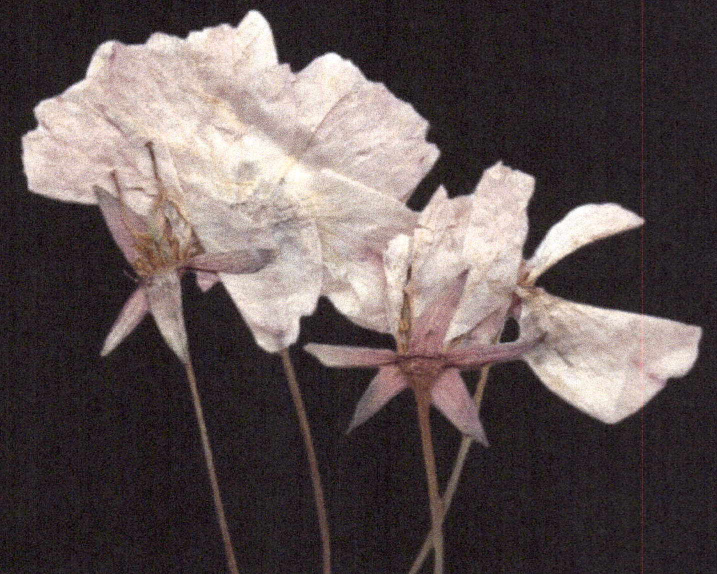

maybe I have already lived many lives   died many deaths
a spider falling into a sleeping human's mouth
a gazelle in the jaw of a lioness
a tree growing one hundred years before being struck by lightning

today I got out of the shower
and said *I love my brown skin*

someday I will be a decomposing body
or a body burnt to ash

I will not be thinking about all of the times I hated myself
does the spider   the gazelle   the tree
hate themselves?

I watch an ant scurry across the boulder I am sitting on
they are working so hard to stay alive

maybe I have already lived many lives   died many deaths
a mosquito
a housefly
a gnat
under a human palm

when will I finally be done suffering?

maybe I can love myself
maybe I can rub my own skin like a prayer
maybe I can find all of the beautiful places
expel the teeth and the lightning
before I get swallowed again
into a mouth that isn't mine

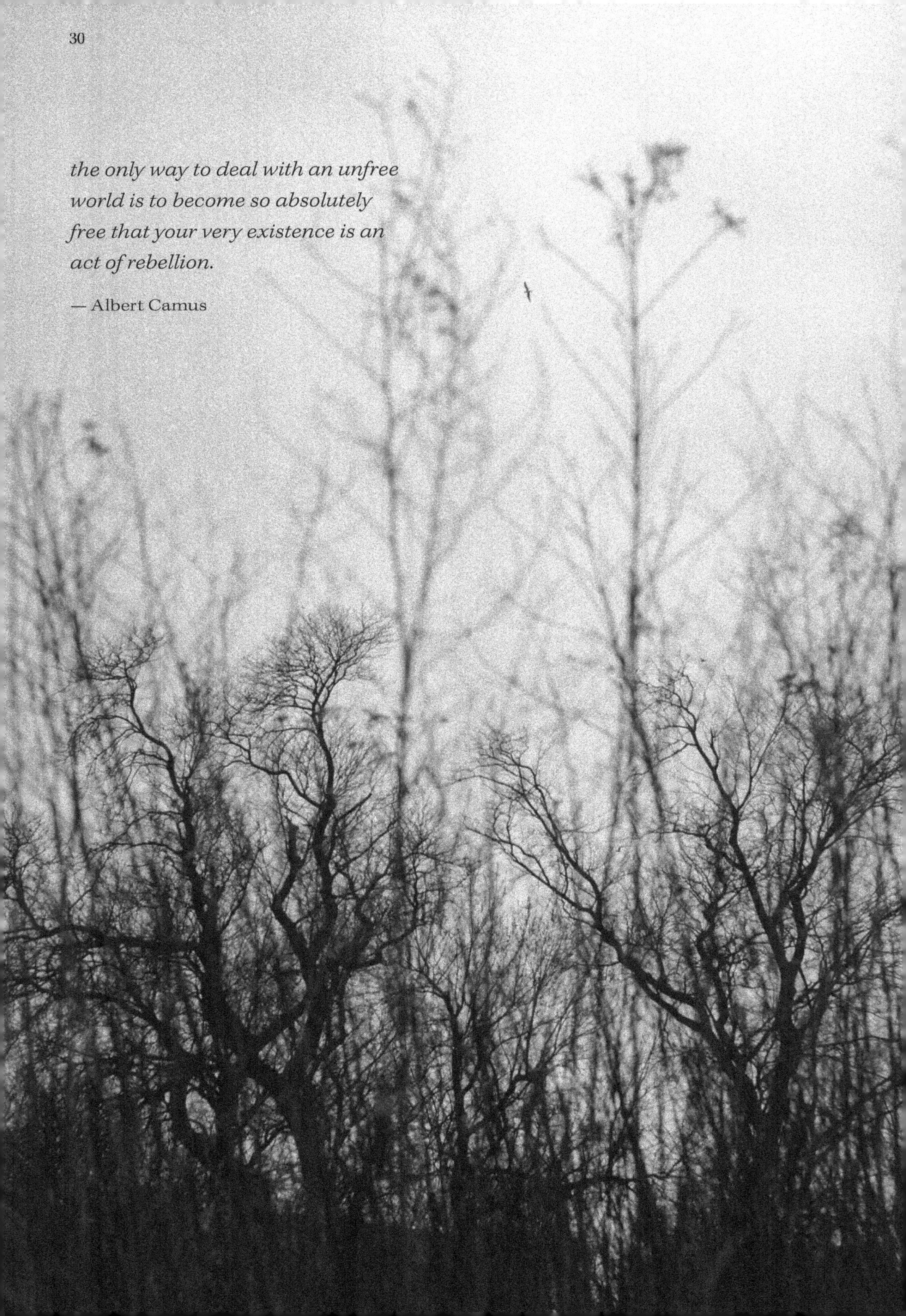

the only way to deal with an unfree world is to become so absolutely free that your very existence is an act of rebellion.

— Albert Camus

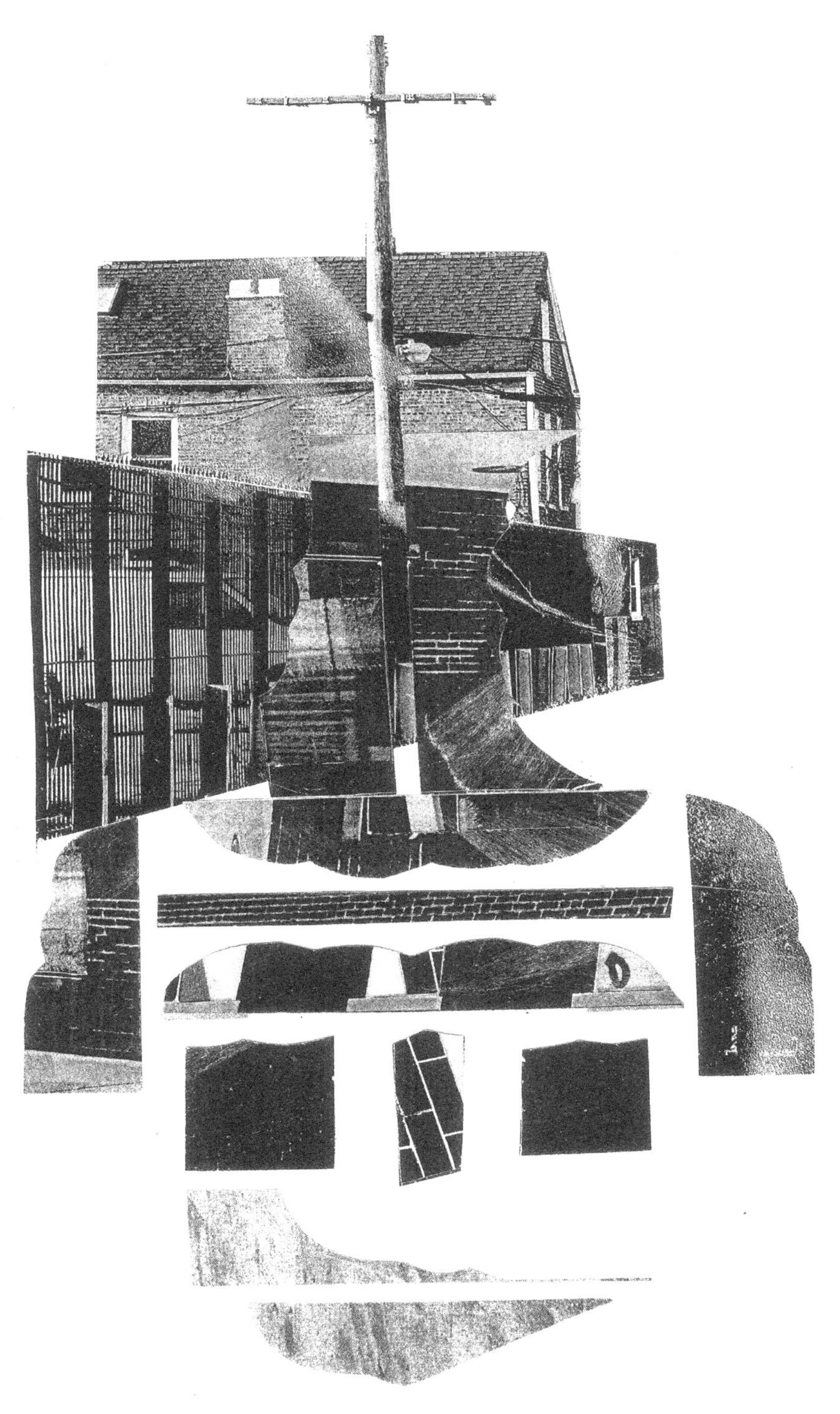

TOWER | Miguel Ontiveros

OUR LOGO, A BLACK RAINBOW,

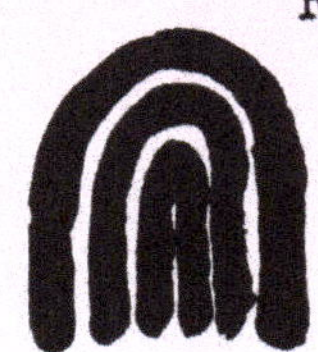

REPRESENTS THE LAYERS OF LIVED
EXPERIENCE. WE LIKE TO THINK
OF THIS SYMBOL AS A PORTAL,

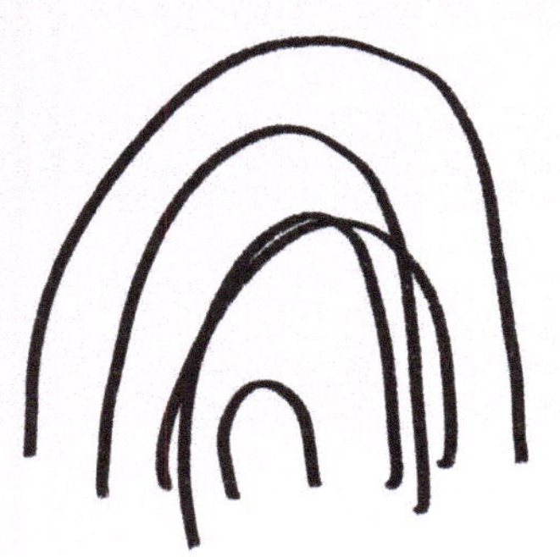

A CAVE, AN ARC, A SHELTER.

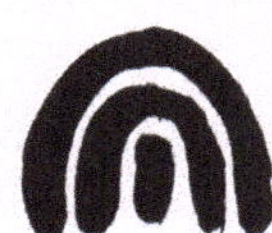

A GATEWAY FOR WONDER, RELEASE,
REST AND REPAIR.

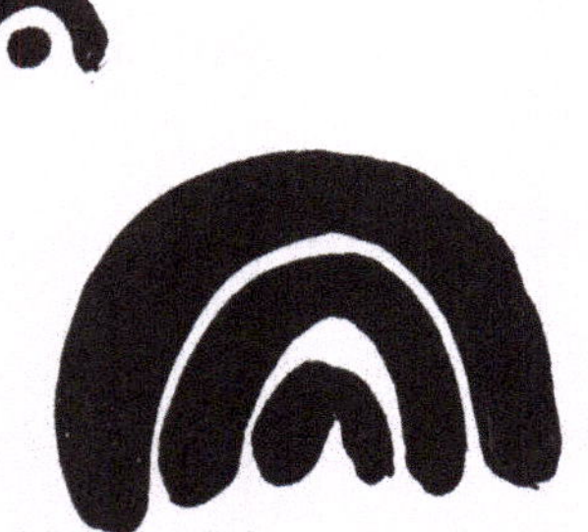

AN AFFIRMATION THAT THERE IS
BEAUTY IN DARKNESS

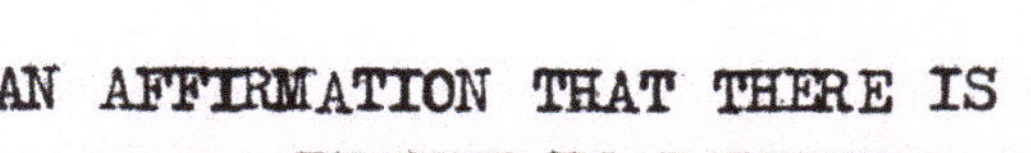

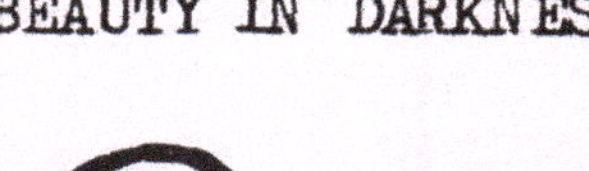

A REMINDER THAT EVEN THE DENSEST
STORM WILL DISSIPATE.

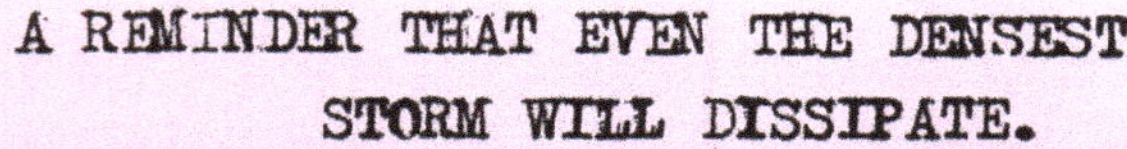

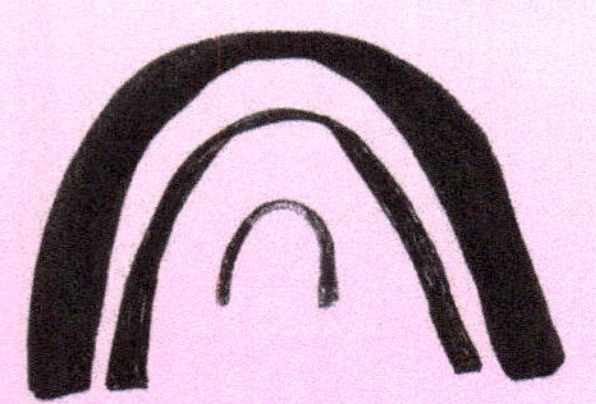

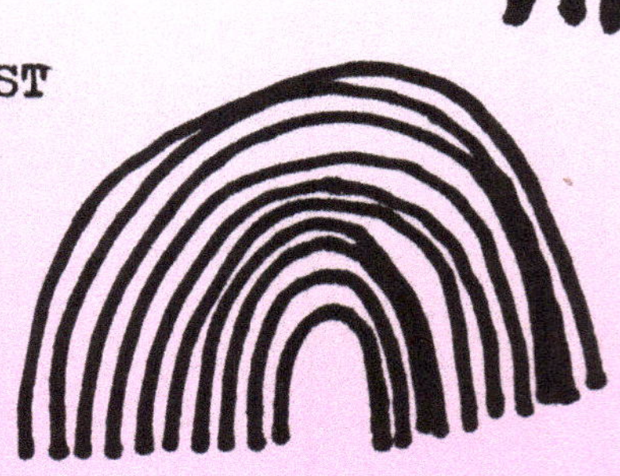

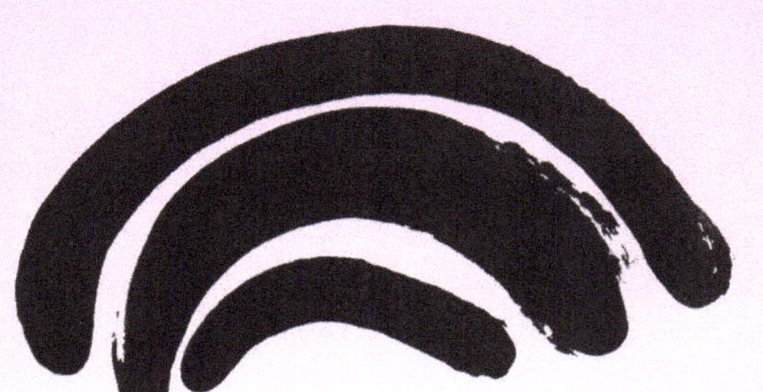

THE RAINBOWS HERE WERE
DRAWN BY OUR CONTRIBUTORS,

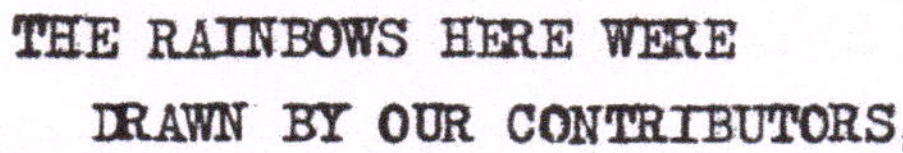

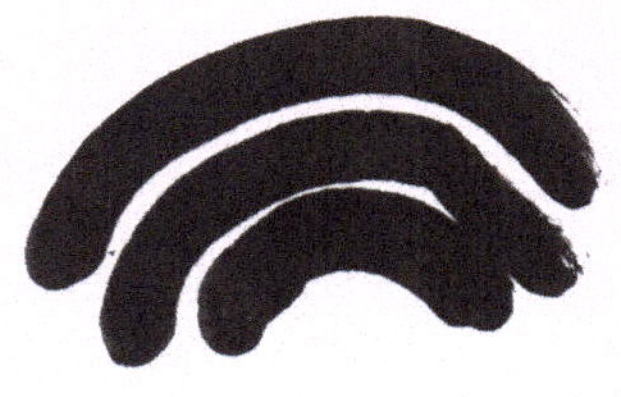

A VISUAL EXPRESSION THAT
HEALING LOOKS DIFFERENT
FOR EVERYONE.

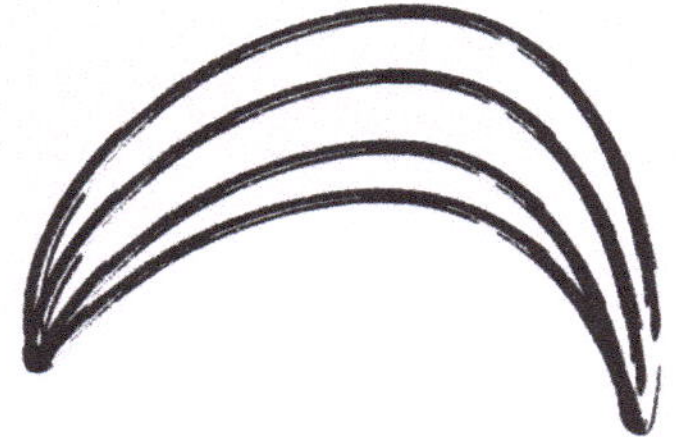

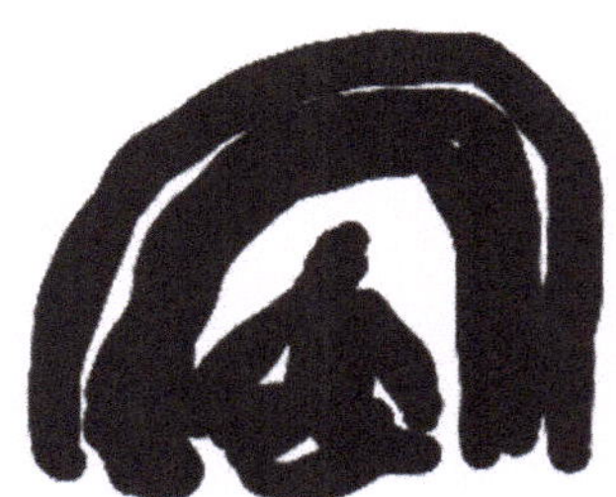

THERE IS SPACE AND INVITATION
FOR YOUR VERSION AS WELL.

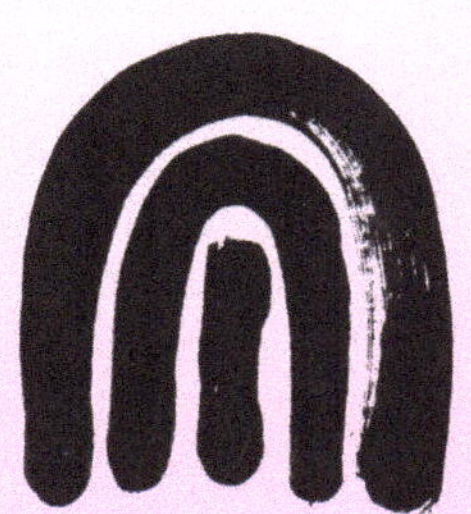

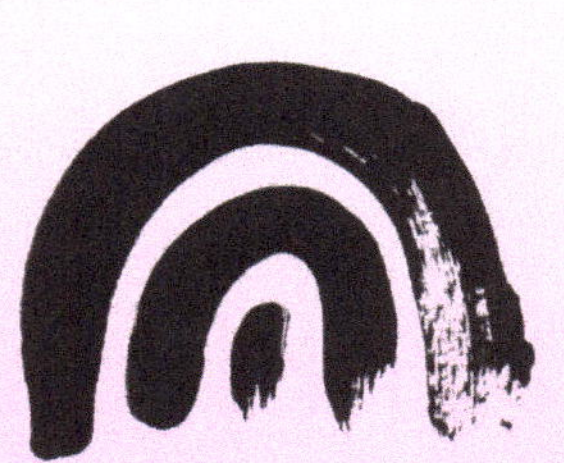

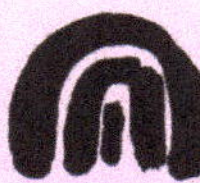

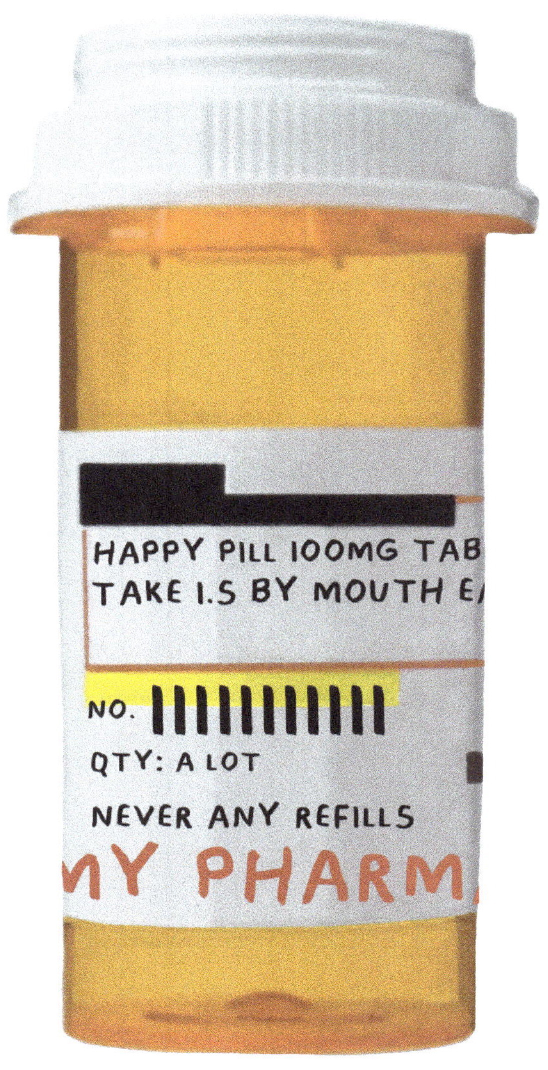

Tiny Capsules of Chemicals that Help Me Exist

ILLUSTRATIONS BY BAILEY CHENEY

*for those who could have been
saved by life-changing medication*

Letter to Myself

BY AARON CLEFTON

Dear You:

If you are reading this it means that you have survived the worst of bipolar disorder, and your struggle is about to begin. As you know, mental illness brought me within nine millimeters of my life. You would think when I dropped the gun, a weight would be lifted. It wasn't. The steel landed on the carpet with a muffled thud. It remained there. I picked myself up, and I walked out of the room.

What I want to tell you, younger me, first and foremost is: *Take Medication.*

Like sunscreen, the long-term benefits of taking psychiatric medication have been proven by scientists, whereas any other opinions on good mental health are based only on my own meandering experience.

What I need to say next is: It doesn't get better. It doesn't get easier. At least not in the way you hope right now. Your denial looks a lot like hope minus acceptance. You'd know I was lying if I said otherwise. You are living with bipolar disorder. Let that sink in. You are *living with* bipolar disorder. Let *that* be your hope. Let that be a light in the long dark of recovery ahead.

I think that you will come to understand in time. You cannot imagine it now, but bipolar disorder is different than what you or anyone would suppose, and luckier. If you shift your perspective, begin again to trust what you see, you may leap to something like acceptance. Something like peace.

You'll begin to see bipolar for what it really is. Not a mystical curse, or cage, discursive regime, or an end to life as you knew it. No. It is much more funda-mental. It is a permanent disability. Like other disabilities, it is one that requires you to learn and adapt, to use technologies that at first you don't understand, like medication, until using them becomes second nature.

The first casualty for us was truth, truth about yourself, and truth about relationships with others. The second loss is trust, trust in your ability to perceive those truths at all. Beginning to survive mental illness is like trying to figure out where a pattern starts. You imagine it like one of Escher's ouroboros-like staircases, rising and falling at the same time, one leading toward another in an impossible circle. Bipolar wants to return the weapon to you, put those crooked dice in your hand and invite you to play, again and again. No matter how many times you want to make progress, there are always more steps to take that return to the beginning. Mental illness is exhausting.

Mental illness plays you. In the beginning, especially, you need to stall to get your bearings. You play a fake death to prevent a final one from coming. You stall. You kill time. You play the hand you are dealt after you checked into the hospital. The hospital is alright. Mostly everyone is losing except the hospital's bottom line. However, the doctors mean well, and it can be safer than the outside on your own in those early days.

The hospital is like a tutorial for the rest of your bipolar life, practice for the real world. Knight takes apathy. Counselor takes Pawn. Depression takes Rook. Medication castles King. Manic Queen Checkmates. The King falls. The weight returns. The nurse suggests playing again. You look at the board, silently missing your father, wondering how it came to this.

Aaron, it turns out that mental illness is not all about you. But you won't know it for a while. Life changes when you decide to live, choose to live with bipolar disorder. Relationships change. Some fall. Some need to fall. Others rise and support you.

A lot changes when you receive a bipolar diagnosis, but some things don't change at all. One feature of my person that stayed the same was my pale skin color, what Paul Mooney called the "complexion for the protection." After my first hospitalization, I lived at my cousin's house in a mostly white, middle-class area of North Seattle. During my worst clash with bipolar disorder I recall believing I was receiving special secret messages from the TV telling me to hurt myself. Lying on the floor in my own piss, I wanted to die. My then best friend, a gifted Black musician and artist, stayed with me during the worst of this. It was far more than what a friend should have to do, and a testament to who he is. Imagining it now, I am humbled by the sheer bravery and care it took to stay with me through the entire episode. He called my cousin, who called the police. And the police did come, hands on hips, fingers 9mm from their weapons. I can't recall what they asked me. They must not have considered me a threat because I am still alive. I had the correct complexion for their protection. The same was not true for Daniel Prude

the struggle for your sanity is linked with the

or Charleena Lyles or so many other people of color doing their best with their mental illness. The medics came after. They strapped me to the gurney, and took me to the hospital. My friend had wagered his life to stay with me. I didn't really understand what his act meant back then. The decade delay in understanding is the measure of my privilege as a white man. I'm alive today because of kindnesses from those who didn't owe me anything.

If you ever read this, Omari, thank you for risking your life to save mine.

Now, I am writing back in time to say: There is life after mental illness. But you will struggle, and you *need* to struggle. Mental illness is very real, but the madness of our age rules us all — racism, and capitalism, and oppression. The struggle for your sanity is linked with the struggle to heal the collective madness of our age.

Let me remind you much of your struggle connects to that of the collective. Your recovery, in large part, will come from learning about our place in this world in relation to other people's struggles. For one, mentally ill people are more likely to die at the hands of police. This is especially true if the person is also Black or brown. We should be defunding the police and redirecting those resources to suicide prevention and emergency mental health response services. Ending police funding isn't political if you are mentally ill—it is survival and a necessary path to healing.

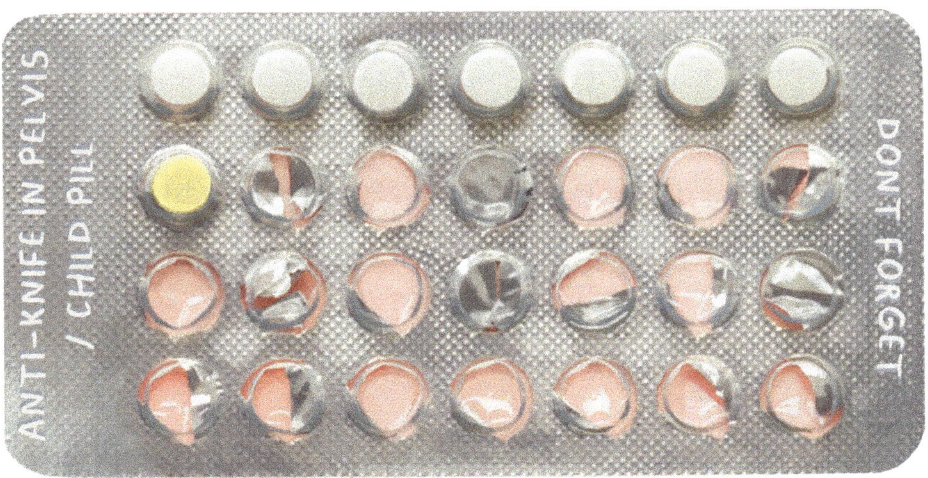

struggle to heal the collective madness of our age.

you need to know in your bones that you are not alone.

For another, drug companies and hospitals make millions on the chemicals that we need to survive. If you or someone you know has a mental illness, you should be demanding universal health care. Period. We who are mentally ill will never get the mental health care and services we need until we demand it openly. We can't do that when we hide our disabilities.

To demand better we must be out about our conditions. How can we ever feel safe when there are so few resources to support us? The relationship of working people to their employers must radically change to accommodate mental illness and stop exploitation. As Marx says, "From each according to ability, to each according to need." I can think of no more apt phrase to describe the relationship of mental illness as a disability to the rest of society. Until workers have control over their own labor, we, as people with mental illness will be easily overlooked and left to poverty and struggle.

And lastly, when will we all learn the truth about war from the millions of mentally ill veterans who have not found peace? How much mental illness could the military budget heal? How many unhoused people could be given homes?

Finally, you need to know in your bones that you are not alone. The best way to do that is in a community of others struggling for justice. No justice, no peace. No peace, then madness. We're done with that. You need to learn your recovery is with others and become the sanity you want to see.

Remember, that when bipolar tries to take away, you must hold tight. Years ago, you decided not to relinquish the last inch of me. I am so grateful and proud that you did. I know someday you will be too.

And trust me on the medication.

With love for the future,

Aaron Clefton

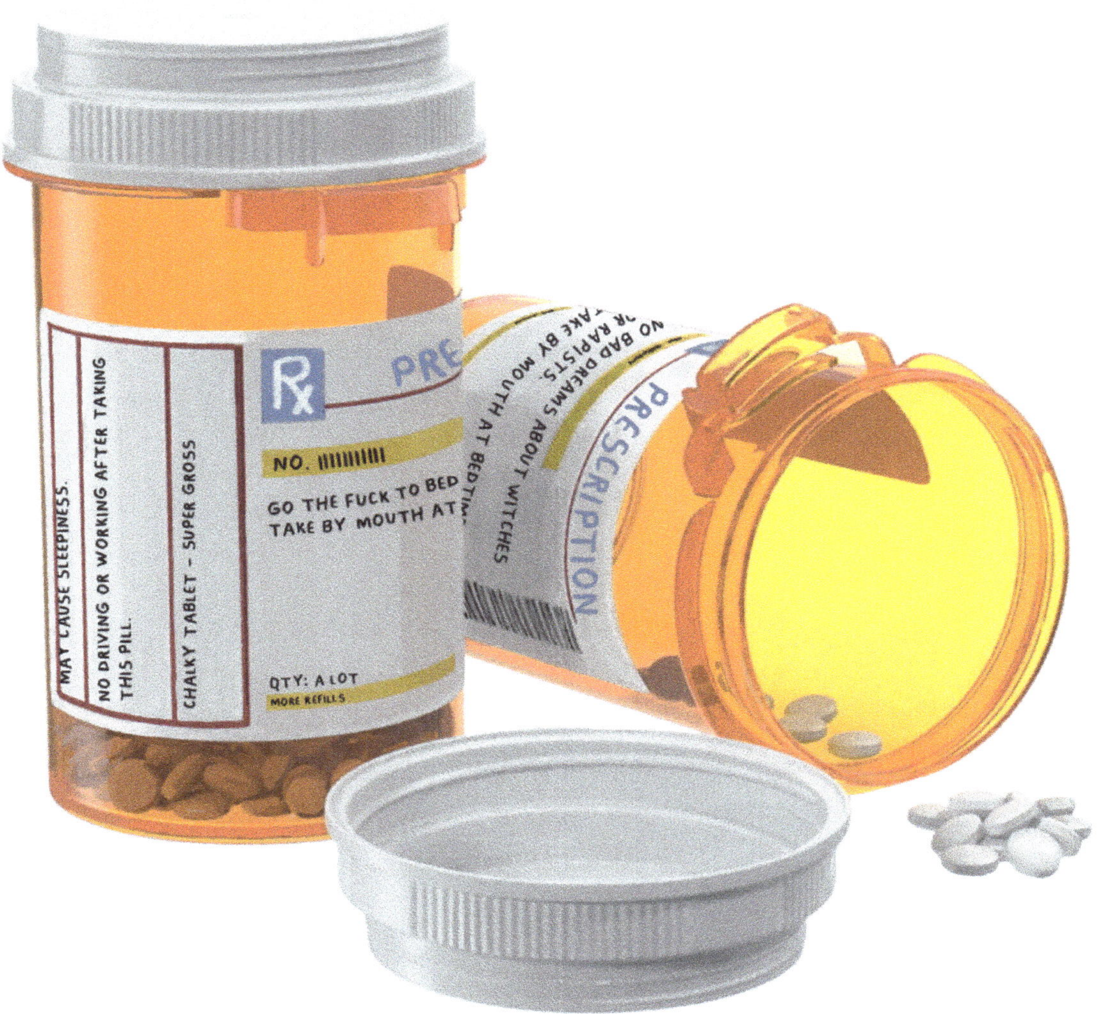
MAY CAUSE SLEEPINESS.
NO DRIVING OR WORKING AFTER TAKING THIS PILL.
CHALKY TABLET - SUPER GROSS
Rx
PRE
NO. IIIIIIIIII
GO THE FUCK TO BED
TAKE BY MOUTH AT
QTY: A LOT
MORE REFILLS
PRESCRIPTION
NO BAD DREAMS
OR RAPISTS.
ABOUT WITCHES
TAKE BY MOUTH
AT BEDTIME

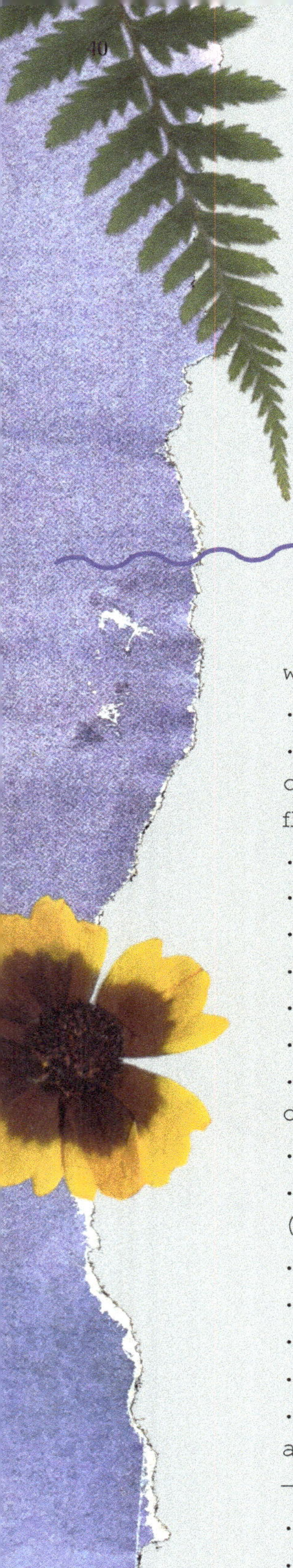

dear reader:

as part of creating this issue, we asked our contributors to share their thoughts on questions relating to personal healing and well-being. as you see these prompts throughout, know that you are also invited to add your own answers, questions, sketches — bring yourself to these pages.

when I feel truly seen by a loved one. —G ....
....
.... when in doubt, dance it out. playing
one of my favorite songs is a guarantee to get my energy
flowing and moving my body feels GOOD! —WB ....
....
.... saying the truth. —EKF ....
....
....
.... writing. —LS ....
....
.... to be in the presence
of smart, caring, and progressive people. —DW ....
....
.... oat milk hot chocolate, touching moss
(especially in the rain) —EW ....
....
.... moving my body. —RZB ....
....
....
.... being warmed by the sun
and feeling the warmth of the sun radiating from a surface.
—TH ....
....
.... waking up early in the morning, before
the city starts to move, and just enjoying the silence. —CP
....

.... reading. swimming in natural bodies of water. extravagant meals. genuine laughter. flowers. —EEG .... puppies, painting my nails, street corn tacos, blaring music in the car, snuggling with my partner, reality tv, card games, Lays Baked BBQ chips. —BB .... being seen. —MB .... arguing in Federal Court on behalf of my clients with disabilities for the protection of their civil rights. —AC .... compassion. —JC .... expressing my creativity through writing and photography. -KH .... drawing, sex, weed, therapy, being honest -KJ .... dancing. —KW .... walking in the mountains —RS .... running, hiking, and knitting. —SC .... laying in warm direct sunlight, wearing my rainbow sweater, putting my face in my cat's belly fur, drinking a warm cup of chai —BC

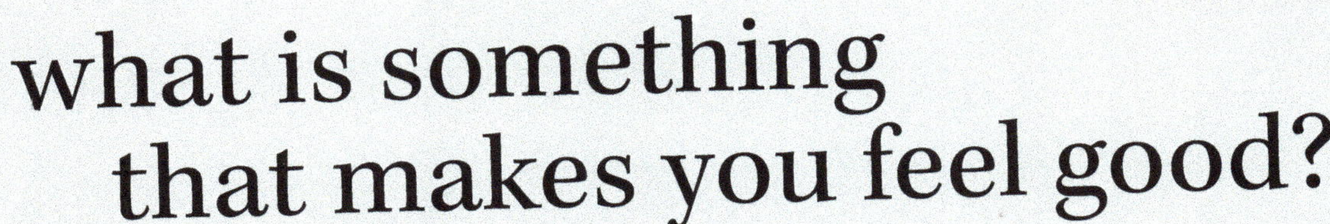

what is something that makes you feel good?

visits with my vagina

by Goddess

The chaotic yet hilarious ongoings of my brain at my first trip back to the OB-GYN after a traumatic experience with my previous doctor.

author's note:

This article was written as I was in the beginning stages of healing from a toxic relationship. If you find yourself deeply entwined with someone who causes you to doubt your worth, or you find you are doubting others, please know that it is okay to say you need time apart. It is okay to say you want no contact. Trust your instinct. Know that community repair and self-healing is possible if we can all show up with our full selves, brave love, and boundaries rooted in self-love.

"Hello, can I please have a to-go container for my pho."

"Sure, how was everything?"

Goddess, you are about to have someone look at your vagina.

"So good, thanks."

Racing to my car juggling two books I did not even touch while stuffing delicious bits of spicy noodles, shrimp, and vegetables down my throat, I kick myself for stopping for lunch. I can not be late to this appointment. I need this referral for medicaid to cover my pelvic PT.

"Play with my pussy but don't play with my emotions..."

Doja Cat gets cut off by the ring of my phone.

For the love of all that is holy, please be about a job.

"Hey (deadname) it looks like you didn't sign your lease. Do you remember doing it?"

"Ummm, I don't know. I apologize for the GPS in the background. I'm on the way to the doctor's office right now *(to get my vagina looked at)*. Can I check and call you back in a few hours?"

"Okay, thanks!"

I have got to pee as soon as I get into that office. Pat yo self on the back, boo, for pre-checking in online.

. . .

"Mam, *(Fuck, seriously?)* do you need help?"

Des Moines, IA has only one LGBTQIA+ clinic, and it's open Tuesday evenings (a day and time in which I have to work).

The next closest clinic with a staff fully trained in gender affirming services is 131 miles away.

A very kind and very oblivious hospital volunteer leads me down the hall while explaining there's a closer place to park for my next visit, and that they've gotten over 10,000 steps in for the week already.

"Thank you."

Follow the mechanical lift thingy the humans call an elevator to get your vagina looked at.

I walk in and there are families.

Some children with two parents.

Some children with no parents.

And some adults with no children.

When will my little ones be peering at strangers as I sit in a waiting room?

"Hello, what's your name?"

"Goddess."

The receptionist click, click, clicks and says, "Okay, we have you down."

Thank god I'm in the system with the correct name! Thank you, receptionist, for the hookup days before.

"persistent and intentional refusal to use a transgender individual's preferred name and pronoun and insistence on using those corresponding to the individual's sex assigned at birth constitutes illegal sex discrimination if such conduct is sufficiently serious to create a hostile environment."
— ACA Section 1557

"Can I go pee real quick?"

"Sure, then we'll get you set up for the sonogram."

Oh, shit! They are really going to be looking at MY VAGINA. I thought that was just a saying like, "it's raining cats and dogs." Nope, you knew Goddess. You just didn't want to think about it....except you did. All the time.

First they weighed me.

Good god, I need to stop eating so much B-Bop's and crab rangoons.

As I get undressed I regret everything. Like not taking a shower, and deciding to feed my craving for spicy Vietnamese soup right after laborious work instead of going home and changing my underwear.

Thank goodness the sonographer turned off the lights.

We talk about the difficulties of finding work after college as they probe and press into my innards. The tender spots I let no one go these days.

Oof, yep. That's my vaginal wall crying. Remember your exercises and relax.

vaginismus / vag·i·nis·mus / vajə'nizməs
—
noun: painful spasmodic contraction of the vagina in response to physical contact or pressure (especially in sexual intercourse).

Google it (no seriously, Google it).

Next, the doctor's room.

Pictures cover the walls of happy families with their babies. As I enviously look at smiling, mostly White families, I get my blood pressure checked. And then I see you.

Your name.

A unique name, everyone I've ever introduced you to stumbles to pronounce, under a newborn's peaceful face.

Weren't we supposed to be doing this together? I flashback to the image of my mother sobbing in bed, the covers pulled so tightly to her chest. "Why isn't he here? He was supposed to protect me!" I have no answer. I'm 15.

We were planning on asking my uncle to be a donor, or maybe your brother. Green Bean was going to have your eyes and my whatever...just as long as they had your eyes.

No, fuck that. I got this. THIS is for me. I'm doing this for Green Bean. I am not alone and can be a single parent. So I turn away from that beautiful smiling baby with your name printed under its sleepy eyes, and look elsewhere.

Oh my god! Did these people name their child after a gun!?

The doctor introduces themselves with their pronouns and asks mine.

I've been asked this maybe three times since moving back to Iowa. As a state, we need to do better in expanding our language and behaviors around race, gender, sex, and pretty much everything. But please, let's never stop saying things like "ope," or "cool beans," and "okie dokie."

"Are you sexually active?"

"No."

"Do you want to get tested today?"

"Yes."

"Well, you are due for a pap..."

Congrats, dude! Another person is going to go inside of your vagina!

"ummm."

"Do you have pain with them?"

"Yes... but I'll do it. I need the referral to go see a PT my sex therapist recommended."

"Mind if I ask why you are in sex therapy?"

"I have some... past trauma....," I say as I look everywhere but her face.

Fuck all these pictures of happy families!

"That's good to know. I'll make it quick and painless."

And it was.

"Do you have any questions for me?"

"Well...um...I want to have children..."

"Okay, I'll get you some prenatal vitamin samples and test your (this, that, and the other) levels."

"Well...no...not right away I just want to make sure...I'm healthy enough..."

Do not cry right now, dude!

"Your womb looks great, and your cysts are gone. There is one very, very small one left."

You did it! I did it! I released those unfertilized little dudes that were clinging on so hard to me. I released pain, people, and behaviors that I was clinging so hard to.

As I wait in the lab room, the older person who kindly made space for me in line so I could talk to the receptionist says to their partner, "There they go talking about Trump again." Everyone looks at the TV.

Their partner says nothing. Just breathes through the tubes attached to their nose. The parent across from us holding on to their child in a wheelchair says nothing.

I hold on to my goodie bag.

I released a lot last year.

Self-Healing Remedies for Anxiety (A FLOW CHART)

by: Rachel Zetah Becker

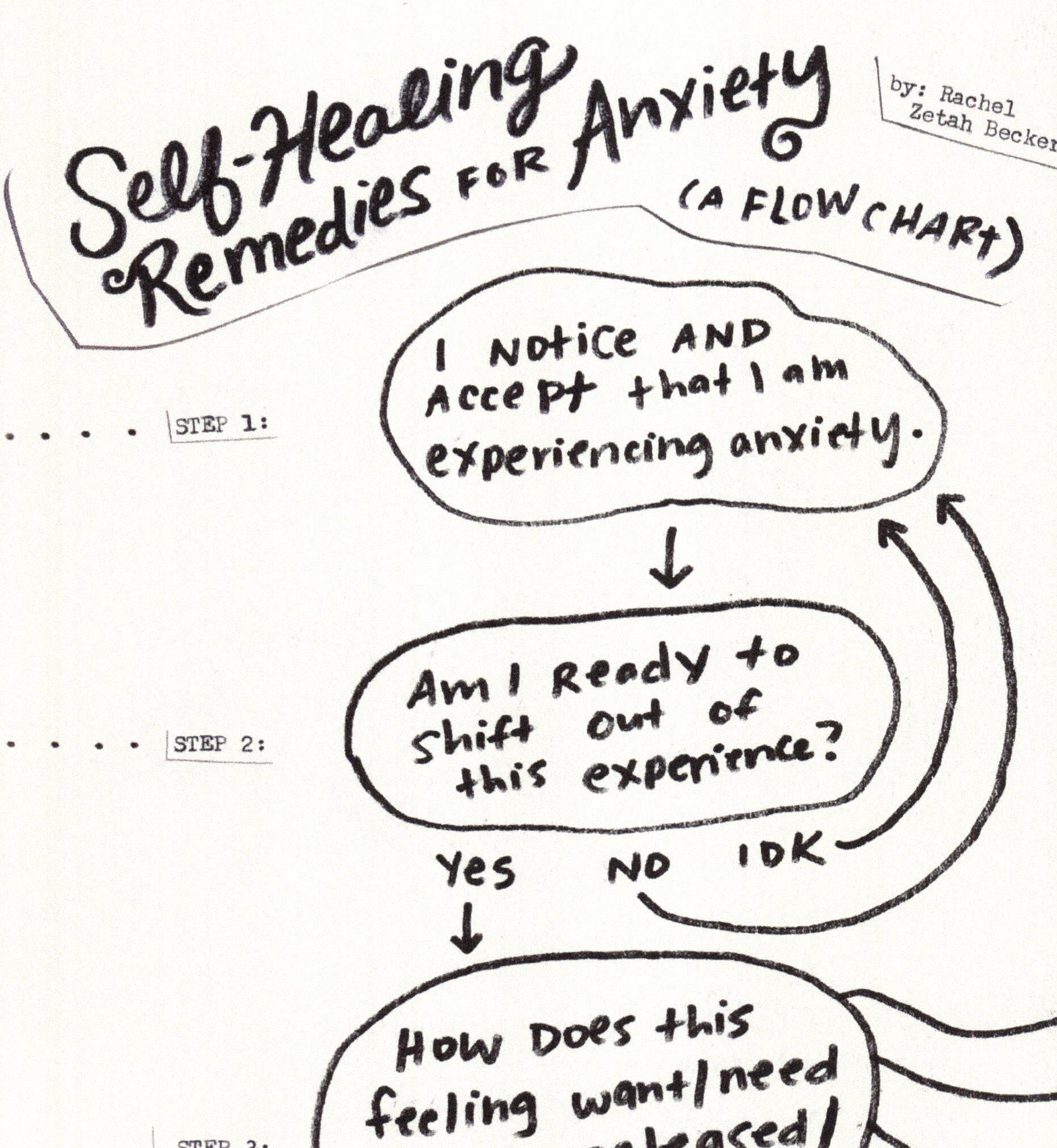

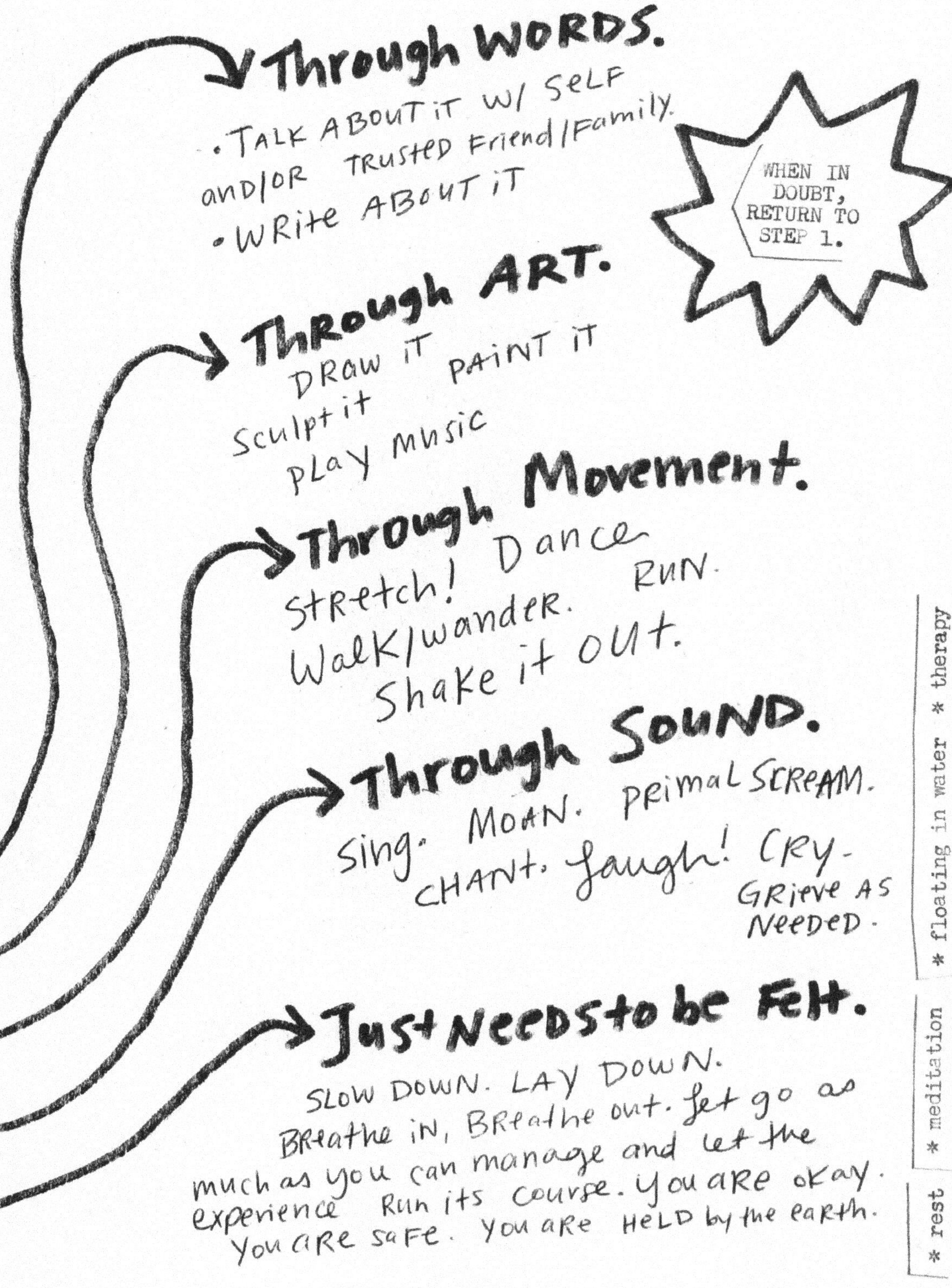
Through WORDS.
• TALK ABOUT iT W/ SeLF
and/OR TRUSTeD Friend/Family.
• WRiTe ABOUT iT

WHEN IN DOUBT, RETURN TO STEP 1.

Through ART.
DRaw iT   PAiNT iT
Sculpt it
PLAy MUSiC

Through Movement.
STRetch! Dance
WaLK/waNDeR.   RUN.
Shake it OUt.

Through SOUND.
SiNg. MOAN. PRiMaL SCReAM.
CHANt, Laugh! CRY.
GRieve AS NeeDeD.

Just NeeDs to be FeH.
SLOW DOWN. LAY DOWN.
BReathe iN, BReathe out. Let go as
much as you can manage and let the
experience Run its course. you aRe okay.
you aRe saFe. you aRe HeLD by the eaRth.

* therapy
* floating in water
* meditation
* rest

pictures of outer space | * hugs | * being with animals | * time away from internet / phone !

Treading Water

This collage really alludes to growing up disabled and embodying a "heroic" identity that is often placed upon you by others and then internalized. In my personal experience, internalizing that my existence was a source of strength for others pushed me to be an overachiever that pushed all trauma/emotions down and caused me to intellectualize everything. For much of my life, I existed from the neck up, while my body was somewhere else (depicted in the collage with my head above water and my body below.) To face the existence of my body as disabled or as the product of so much surgery, scars, and medical trauma, was a terrifying prospect. In the same vein, my head above water in the collage depicts barely hanging on while showing up for everyone else with a smile. Long story short, living this way for much of my life eventually led me to find myself in a mental health crisis when I was about 21, and I have struggled with anxiety/depression since.

Ironically, I did become a therapist after this crisis because my own journey with therapy/mental health was so profound. Sometimes, I laugh and even cry thinking about how I probably, on some level, did so because I have always felt it was my duty to remain steady and hold the pain and discomfort of others while interacting with me. And though that truth is something I am still working through, I more so feel I went into this profession because I feel disabled people, and those of all marginalized identities, have a specific psyche, trauma, and experience of the world that needs space to be processed, understood, and held by a mental health professional, but even more so by a loving community. My work as a therapist is more and more becoming redefined as I work within yet attempt to push back against an often oppressive and fraught clinical model of care.

by Bri Beck

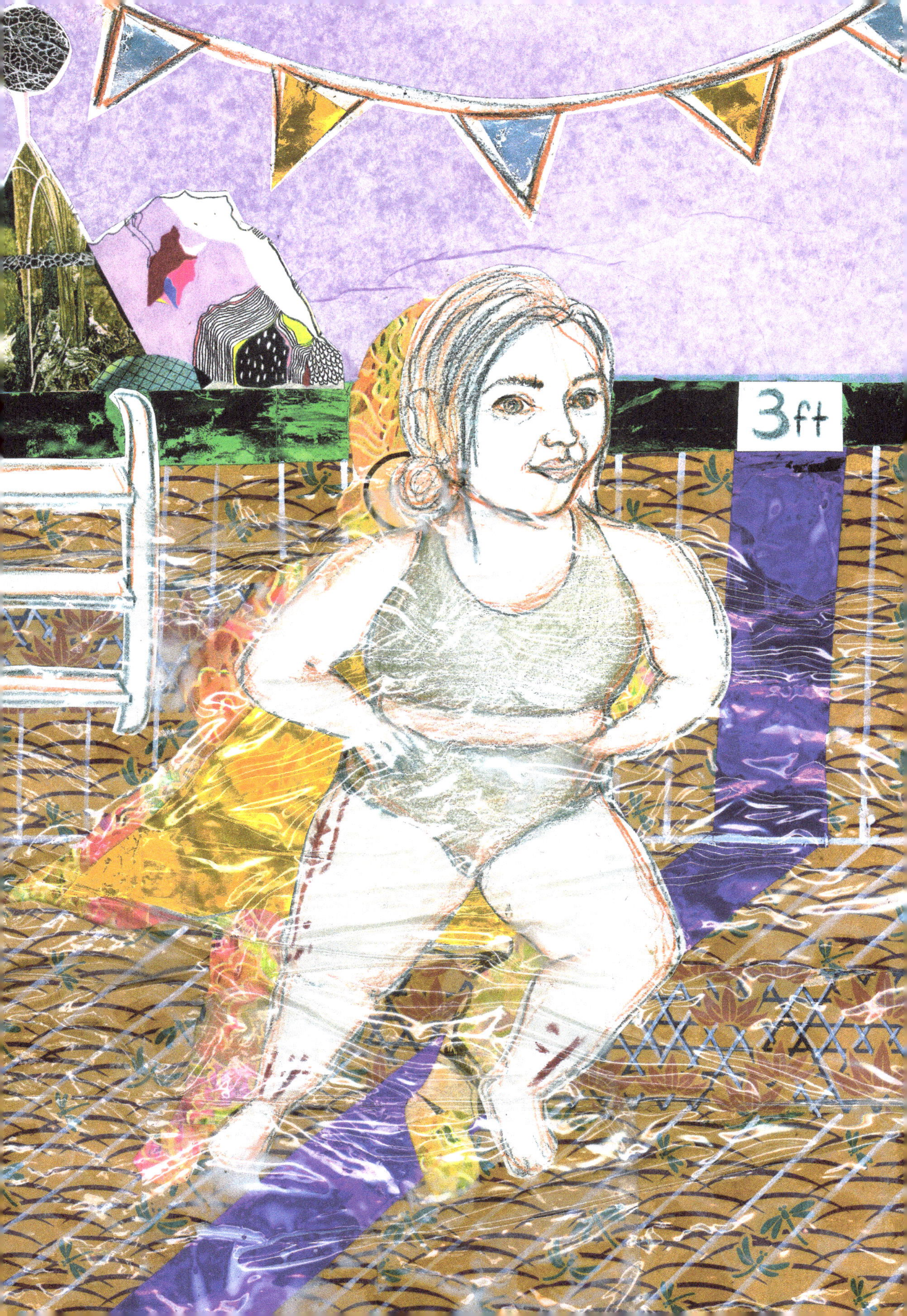

3ft

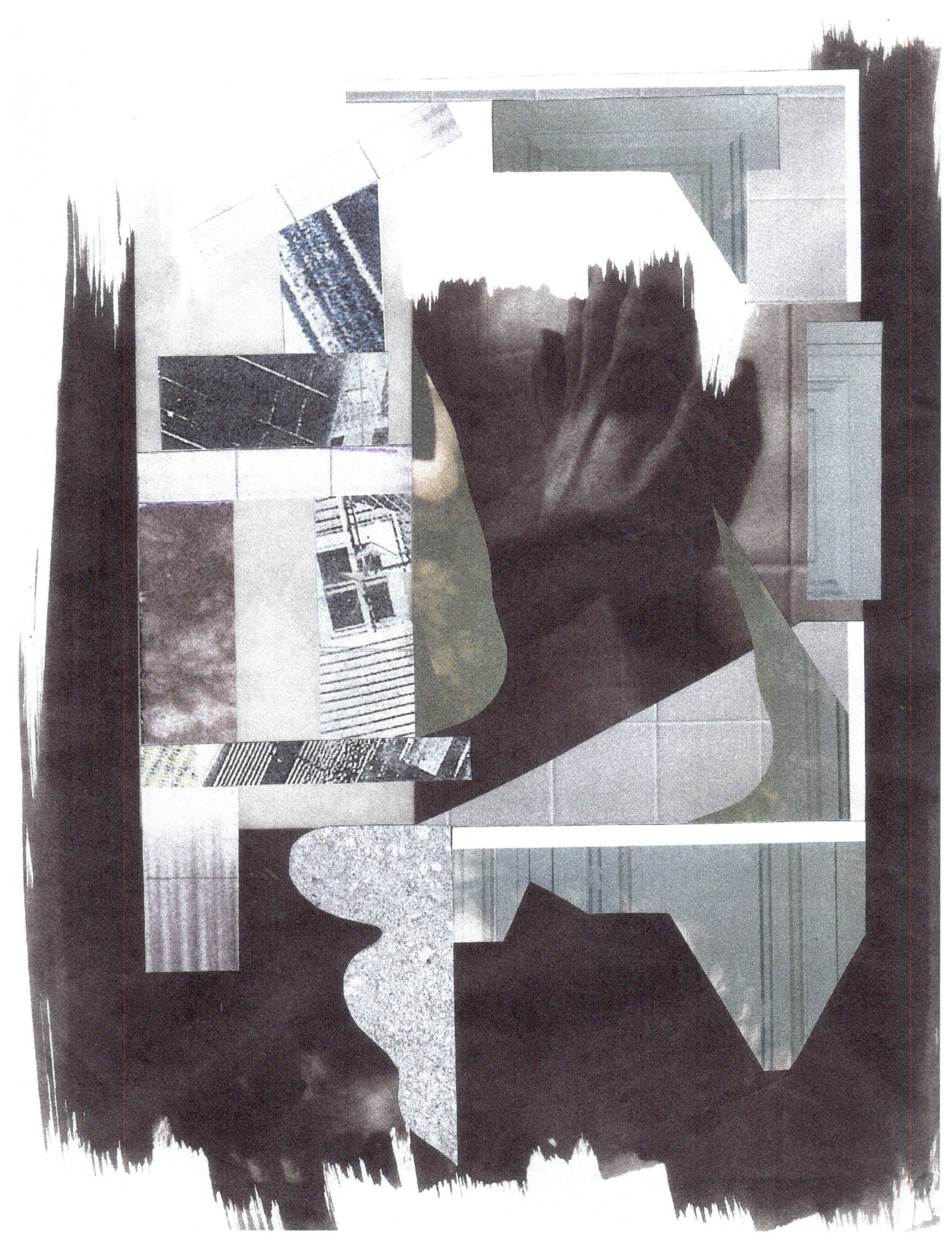

STILLNESS AND BROKEN THINGS | Miguel Ontiveros

Larch Ave

A Life A Story

by Dianne Wright

We've been hurt and need to say how.
Someone died before we got to say so.
Sand in your eyes just from opening
the front door. Windy again. Hand made
things forever lost. Ceiling pulled down
by professional tenants. Cameras stolen, too,
with pictures on their chips. Hours lost
to worry in a life hell-bent on outdoing all
records for paranoid fantasia. And the wind.

*I didn't go to your wedding because I knew
it was a mistake* as the friendship slowly
strangles itself. Being judged and found
severely wanting. Dying alone. Dining out alone.
Windowpanes above the desk shake loudly
from charging winds. Fear of falling. Staring
at my shoes when the ER doctor asked them,
How long ago did this happen? Not dropping
the new baby—Hold tight!

Feral cat refuses to be rescued, forcing me to
continue to feed him. Failure pays the price
and it backs up in my heart like an old toilet. Fear
of not writing. Of writing too much. 24/7 unwelcome
jukebox clamor-in-the-brain constantly claims my
attention. Again the winds. Noise, noise, and noise.
Sharks, crocodiles, yellow cryptopids threaten
from filthy broken file cabinets in the garage attic.
Voter suppression with a side order of racist cop violence.

Fraught close relationships. Self-indulgence leads to
manipulation and the refusal of moral support. The gaping
dearth of praise not just once but always. Losing face.
Strategic forgetting with forced horrid memories. Slapped
upside the head—knocked down in front of beloved cousins.
Ecocide in the Rainforest and everywhere else. The body
my body. But the wind! Pregnancy in the wrong place.
Official aftermath = getting dumped by the Department
Chair. Your BF. You failed but won the Booby Prize:

Academic Incompletes. Try to print a missive but the
WiFi is down. Nullibiety: you're it! Brakes go out on a wild
Dolores Boulevard ride. She wonders aloud if he did it.
Torn up photo taped to the forehead. Yes, she did that.
Pigmentocracy again and always. You failed to notice.
You noticed and overcompensated. And then waiting.
At the podium before 850 rich enemy donors. Concussion
from falling off the heights of kitchen cabinets searching
for love. I mean, candy. The winds rise to a screech.

Dog lying on the side of Amargosa Road, fur softly
blowing in the breeze. Pandemic TV repeats empty
Big Noise Patriot movies. Further chaotic interference
of any thought. Primarily from the clamorous jukebox.
Still and always random paranoid jaunts. You said that
already. But anyways and again come the winds. Mother
tells funny stories you can't recall, yet triggers of torments
remain active and in use. Waiting for the noise to stop
and wondering which fresh injuries will take its place.

Jukebox Duplex

We've been hurt and need to ask why.
Sunday afternoon fades into lamplight—

        Sunday down/lamplight up, darkness returns
        and your gut squeezes into a lump of coal.

Lump of coal gets hungry but you've nowhere
to turn for solace and relief from daily terrors.

        Solace and relief from daily terrors eludes
        while the 24/7 jukebox rages for attention.

Raging jukebox drowns calming thoughts,
raising fears that a gaping silence will take its place.

        Gaping silence inspires wretched scenes of past injuries.
        Then something happened but you wait too long to scream.

Waiting too long to scream opens a void for you to think,
we've been hurt and we need to ask why.

Jukebox Mashup

We've been hurt and need to tell someone.

Dark Sunday evening in the ER and all you can do
is watch your feet in your shoes after the doctor
asks them *how long ago did this happen?*
The look of shame on their 2 faces in apparent
response. We want to know more but the jukebox
psychosis drumming a wall of sound in my brain.
And the wind. Homeless kittens across the
busy street from their food. Again and still: voter
suppression, violent pigmentocracy. New meds for
$856 trip up your false hopes. Time to break into your
own house because she's forgotten the keys.

Again.

We've been breaking into our own house on a dark
Sunday evening and all we've got to show for it is a
24/7 psychotic wall of sound as a shameful response.
We want to know more but the wind. Scared kittens
across the street while we witness police violence and
suppression. Still and again pigmentocracy rules the day
or all you can see is $856 for one month of a drug you need.
Time to forget the keys!

Again.

Breaking into my own house in the ER where the doctor
seeks a shameful admission but the jukebox ejects my
thinking, interrupted by the barking dog scaring the cats
into the street. Racist police violence and still the wind
blows away the $856 you don't have for anti psychotic meds.
You won't say 'I' and we think we know why. Because we've
been hurt and need to tell someone.

Again...

the drench of moon
when it's ripe.
like the root.

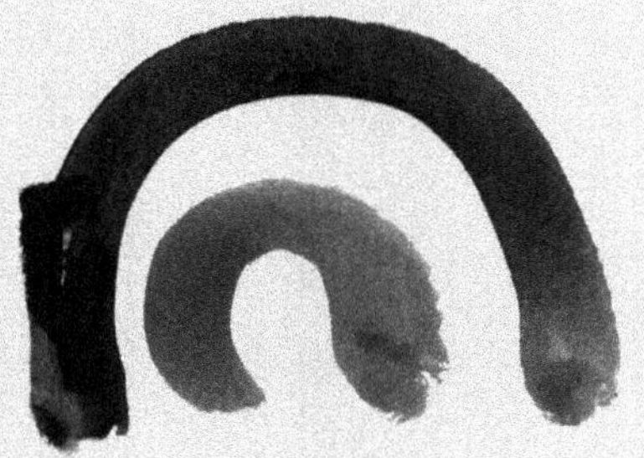

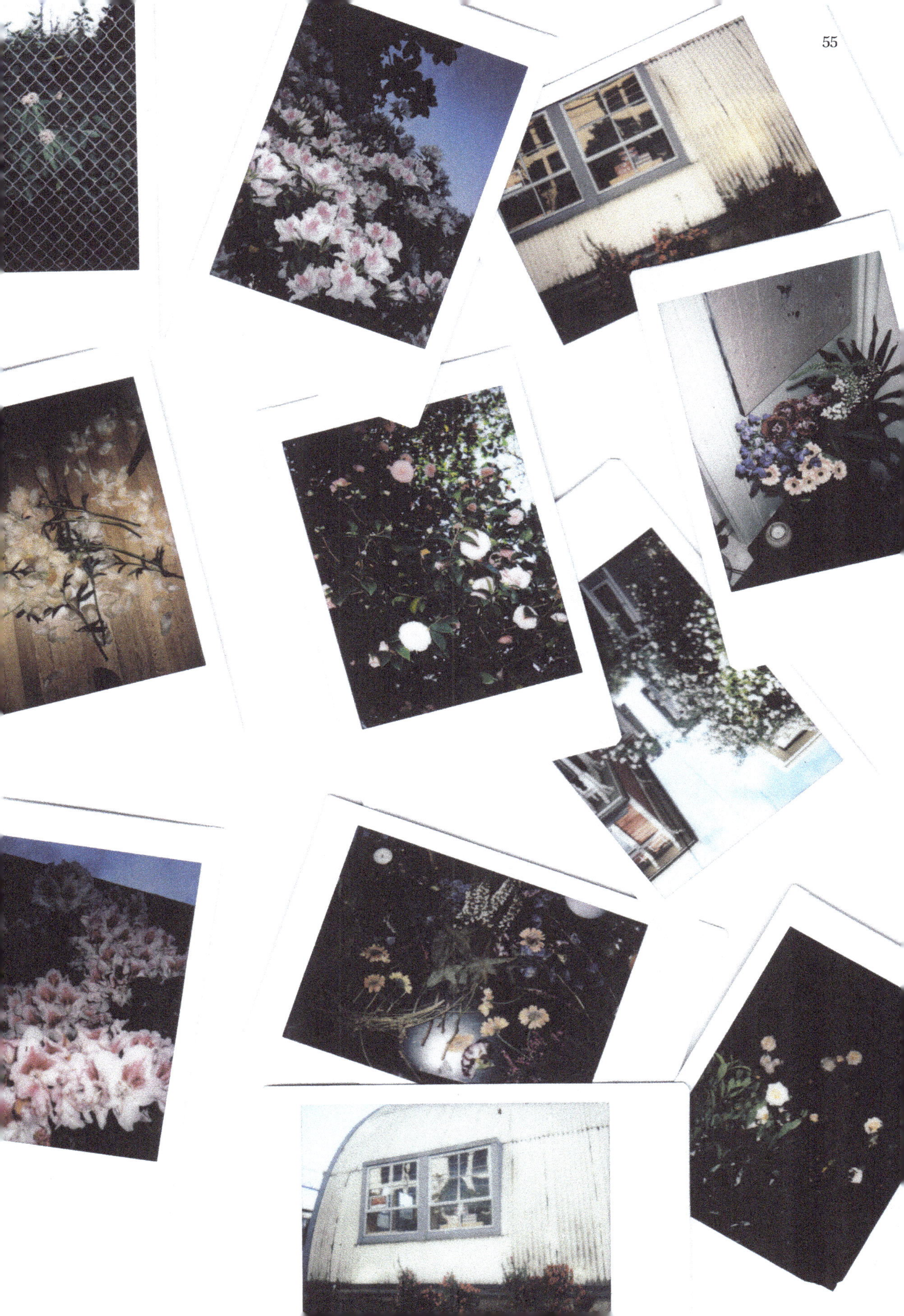

Insatiable

BY RYLEY SCHLACHTER

I remember the beginning so clearly.

He asked me to go to a Miniature Tigers concert with him. He packed vodka and chasers in a cooler in his car. We sat outside the venue in the parking lot, drinking. I didn't really like him at this point, but I liked the feeling of being liked openly; not being a secret or the girl that guys text late at night because they're too embarrassed to talk to you at school. He asked me out on a date, and he probably told his friends about it, which made me feel like I was good enough.

Jason is the first guy who truly made me feel wanted. The first person I explored myself with sexually without feeling utterly used. I didn't even like him that much…until he told me he was in love with me right when I moved away to college. I thought about him a lot after that.

He stopped responding to me, and probably stopped thinking about me, which only made me think about him more. This abrupt rejection sent me down a spiral of shame and self-doubt that I had to find a way to stop. I snapped my hairband on my wrist every time his name came up in my head. Maybe this is when food came in. I would think about him most while I ran, which only made me run harder and more often. I allowed my grief to flow freely as sweat would run down my face like tears. This release of my own self-restraint was the only liberation I would give myself the rest of the waking day.

I remember the first time we hooked up at his house. I laid down on his bed with my pants off. He was exploring my insides with such curiosity.

"Do you like this?" He would ask. "Or this?" He wanted to know what felt good to me and explored all the possible places until my fluids were literally dripping out from inside. I was a little embarrassed at first, but he loved it, and for the first time I felt unashamed of my body. Being wet was okay, feeling pleasure was okay, and it was okay to let myself go.

I closed my eyes and just felt him explore me, and it felt so fucking good.

When I came back home for winter break everything had changed; he had changed. I don't know what happened during his freshman year of college, but he wasn't sweet anymore. I tried my best to not contact him. I would ignore him at parties and pretend I wasn't thinking twice about him.

AUTHOR'S NOTE:

The process of recovering from my eating disorder took understanding what it was truly about. In this piece, I reflect on my resistance to feeling fullness, the last memory I have of feeling satiated, and when I began resisting it. Although it does not seem like a healing story, allowing myself to relive this trauma with compassion and understanding stripped away its hold on me. Recovery from any mental illness is difficult, ongoing, and open-ended, but awareness, compassion, and reconciliation with ourselves is what allows us to move forward.

Every couple of weeks he would text me with just a simple, "Hey." Most times, when I would respond, he wouldn't even text back – making me feel stupid, bathing in shame all over again.

Occasionally, he would ask me to come over. Of course, I would, hoping that those feelings of being seen and wanted would come rushing back into me.

We would have sex, but not the same kind of sex we had before. Not like I remembered it. It felt rushed, and he finished quickly, leaving me feeling unsatiated and used. He would have me leave soon after that, eluding that we would hang out soon.

This happened multiple times, and each time I felt more of myself get hollowed out and left on his bedsheets...I kept going, because those five or so minutes of being wanted felt worth it. I kept telling myself that things would be different; *maybe this time he will actually see me.*

We went over to his grandmother's house when she was out of town. We were crossfaded and this made hooking up feel even more intense. For the first time since the beginning, I was letting go, and just before I was about to release, he pulled out without warning and came all over me. As he began to wipe himself up, I asked if he would finish me off. He scoffed in my face like it was the most absurd thing I could ever ask. It was the most ashamed I had ever felt about my sexuality. How dare I even think to ask for what I want; how dare I even think I deserve to be satisfied? I felt my insides trickle down my leg. Just before he left the room he looked down at the wet spot on the bed and said, "Jesus, you made a fucking mess. Clean it up."

I sunk deeper into myself. For a long time after that, I had this inability to ask for what I wanted. Not just sexually, but in every aspect of my life. I felt overcome with shame, like I was undeserving of feeling satiated, complete. I stopped listening to my own needs, holding them so deep within myself that I forgot that they were even there. I made myself believe that the only way I would ever be loved is if I kept it all in.

This control of my voice and emotions manifested into a control of food and my body. For so long, I believed that this was the only way to survive. It took shrinking myself until my body was merely skin and bones to make me realize that this was not surviving, it was dying.

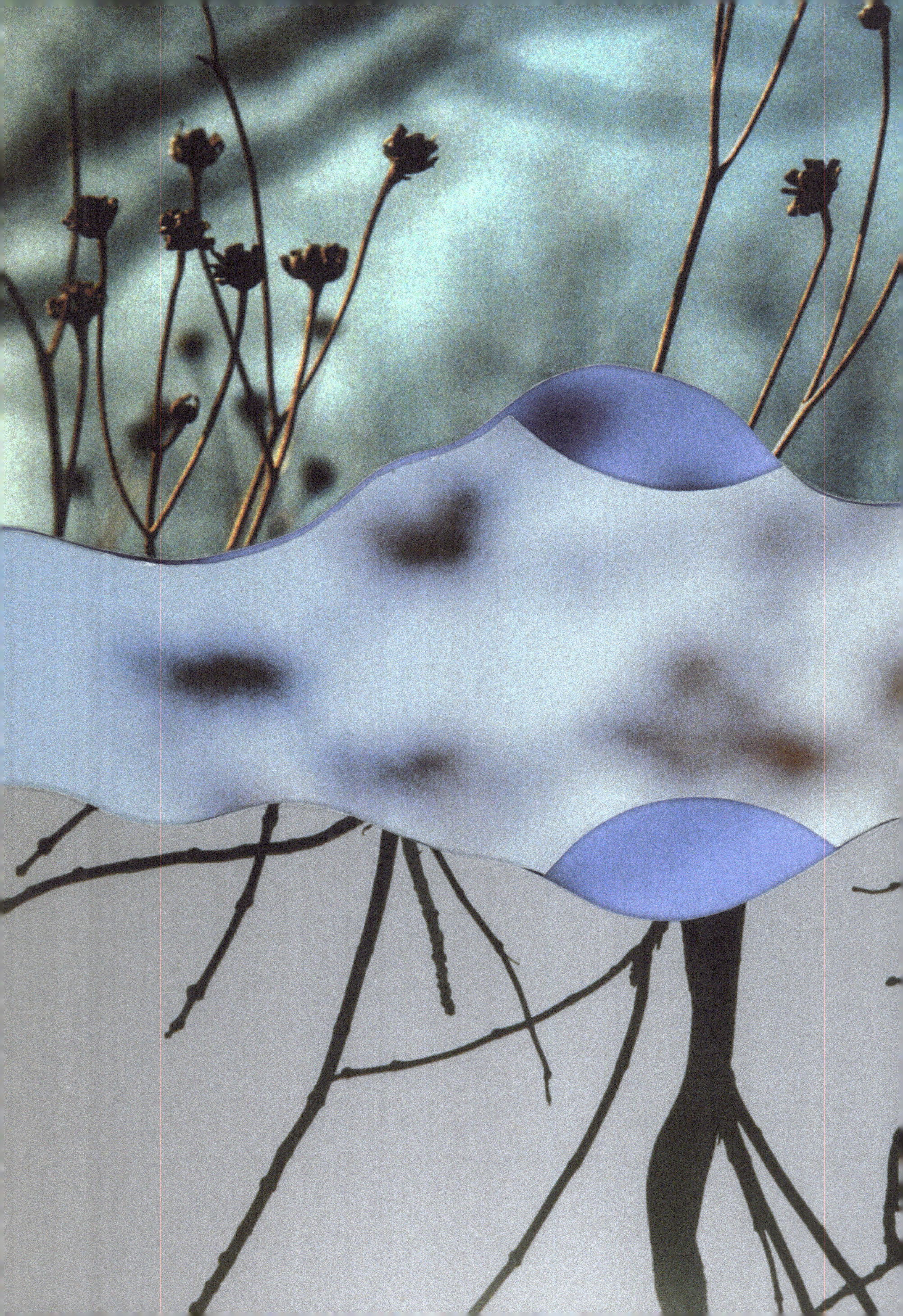

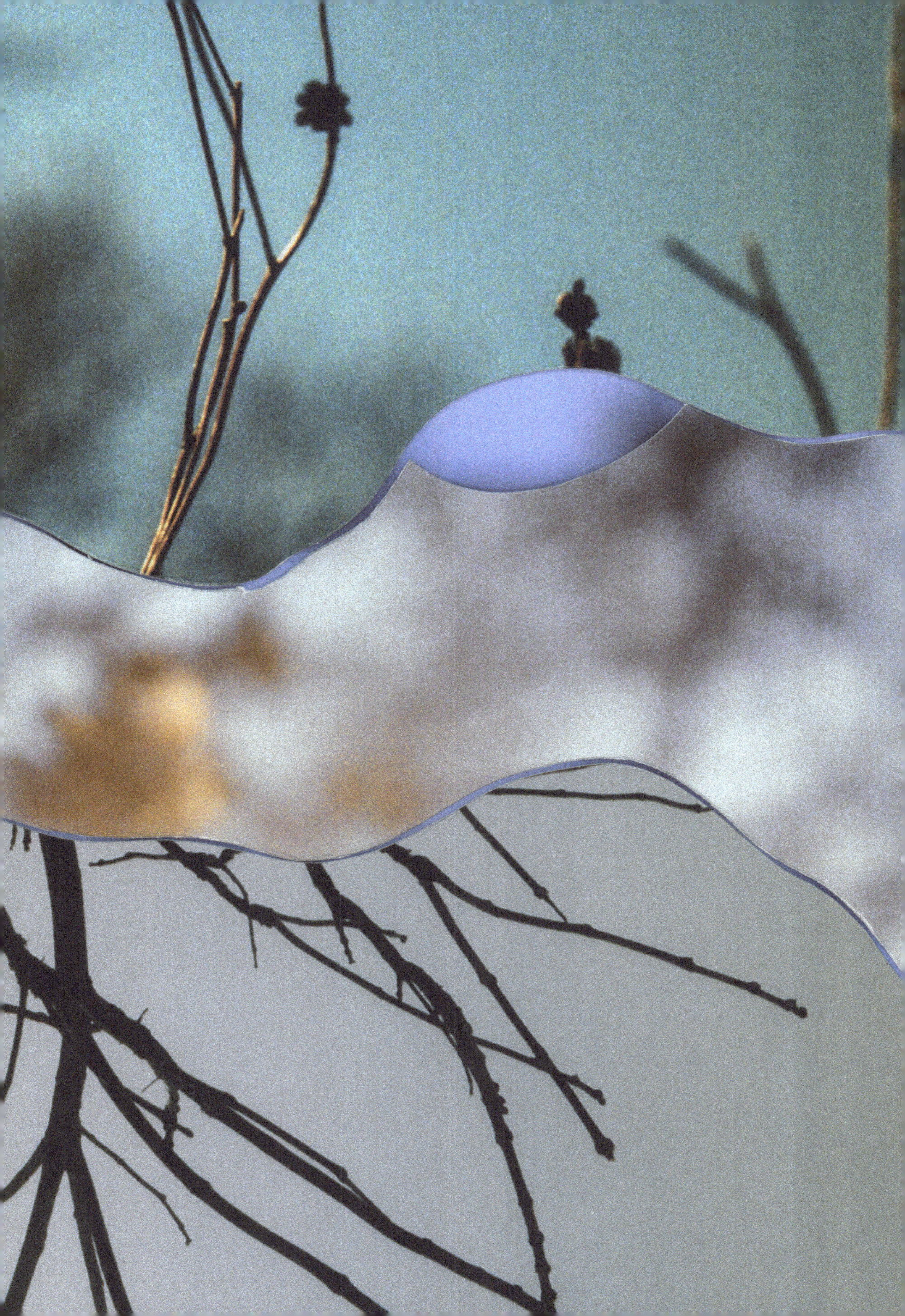

Crossing Lines

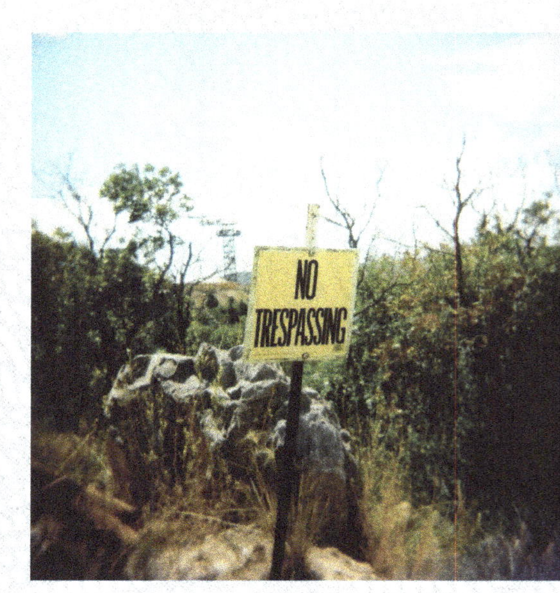

by Cervanté Pope

Lines aren't necessarily meant to be crossed. And this is a relatively new discovery for me. As someone who's dealt with fragile mental and emotional states my entire life, the foundation of my boundaries has been blurry, and often my own lines were transgressed without my knowledge.

My entire life, it was drilled into my head that there is a bridge between mental agitation and weakness. I've been told over and over that the real resilience comes in the way you handle adversity, in your ability to find calm in the strife put upon you by external forces—often other people. The idea of having to endure turmoil, to suffer perfectly, did not seem an authentic solution to me, but it took me the whole of my years so far to try to do something about it.

I resisted letting go of the stigma instilled in me, that Black people—and Black women especially—don't need to seek help mentally because we are stronger than that. Because we don't need that. While I appreciate the inherent strength that comes with this identity and my Native American identity that enriches it, swallowing strife for the sake of strength did not sit right with me. And I noticed this at a very early age, even though I didn't have the intellectual bandwidth to articulate it.

The first time I remember noticing this mental and emotional injustice was when I was around five or six years old. My cousin, who is a year younger than me, kept poking me and touching my stuff after I repeatedly asked him not to. I told my grandma, my mother, and my aunt, just to have them each explain that he's a boy who will just "do what boys do" and that I shouldn't be so uptight about my personal space and belongings. Even in my young eyes, I believed I had the right to feel however I wanted regarding myself and my stuff, and I still feel this way to this day. That was the first time in memory someone crossed by boundaries, and I was told to simply let it slide. That would soon become a theme within my life.

Not being believed and having to continually put up with that nonsense, though it seemed fairly trivial, was actually anything but because it became the first seeds planted, which would grow into the overwhelming notion that one's lines will always be crossed. That the support systems you think you have are not always what you think they are. And because I made it out of that and situations which followed seemingly unscathed, the stigma was reinforced. In a sense.

Whether it was conscious or not, I channeled the confusion and isolation that stemmed from my autonomy not being acknowledged into other avenues of my life. But soon, I watched those other avenues get backed up, muddied, and messy. A necessary light of realization began to shed.

The realization that I've spent years of my life with my boundaries constantly crossed. In itself, telling someone to ignore their mental health for the sake of what it would "look like for the culture" is crossing a boundary. I am so thankful that now, it feels more acceptable to look inward and focus on what's in your own head, but what it took to get there—collectively and for me, personally—has been a lot to trudge through. And we still have a far way to go.

For me, this consciousness began in the midst of a rough relationship—the only solace I found while enduring everything with that person were frequent conversations with myself, living in the fantasy of escaping. Once I finally did, years later, all the damage became apparent to me. If I'm honest with myself, that harm is revealing itself now more than ever. I made rules for myself that I continued to break—through my own actions or through letting the actions of others prey on me. Afterward, I told myself I wouldn't get into another relationship for a long while, that I needed time to figure out and reflect on the person I had become. Instead of listening to myself, I got into another relationship, and when that one failed, I got into another one after that. I crossed my own boundary. I had never really learned what it was like to abide by them anyway.

No one wants to be told they need help, yet at this phase in my life, it seemed like everywhere I turned, someone was speaking on that idea. The thought of it offended my character as someone so deeply entrenched in the stigmas against it. My pride attacked, I soldiered on with stubborn intent and a bull-headed confidence that I was just fine—that I had already been through such difficult things in my life so far and made it through that nothing could really be worse.

It's funny how wrong you can be sometimes.

What I am starting to figure out about boundaries is: that they're always in place, whether they've been spoken into establishment or not. I've lived my whole life within the confines of limitations—be them the religious ones (my family was Jehovah's Witness), the racial ones (oh, to be Black and Native American), or the socioeconomic ones (Section 8 for life)—my entire existence has been shaped by what I could and could not do, by lines I could and could not cross, by what I did and did not have access to because of who I am and what I have or haven't been afforded. While the mental health aspect of this is new to me in actualization, it's always been there conceptually. I've come to see that my avoidance of certain situations, topics, or people was because I had some underlying sense of what was within my capacity or not.

And though this may seem a simple concept to some, it's a difficult concept to many. Myself included.

When you're accustomed to a life in which things happen to you, it's difficult to see a life in which you make things happen. That's where, personally, I've discovered how imperative therapy and seeking help can be. I don't naturally envision a world in which I have any say or play in its workings, and that applies to the tangible world as well as the one that exists inside my head. Even though I have control over what happens in the latter, my grasp on reality is too strong to lie to myself, even when everything is of my own doing. In the outside world, it's easy to become coaxed into this general "understanding" of how the mind and mentality are supposed to be. And while there seems to be a universally accepted way of having mental outbursts and dealing with the fallout, the more you let your present state get blurred, crossed, or denied, the more you see the fallacy in so much of that rhetoric. Part of being an individual is figuring out all of the special nuances within yourself and within others and that's a journey that lasts a lifetime, stigma and societal acceptance aside.

In the last relationship I found myself in, post-abusive one, I began analyzing my thoughts and actions towards the person I was with, wondering how I ended up with them in the first place. There was something missing inside myself that I finally understood I couldn't find within a partnership, and though I didn't know exactly what that missing piece was, I knew I had to be on my own to find it. You can have a support system without giving up your autonomy, and when that finally hit me, I left that relationship to focus on my mental health. Instead of worrying about how it would make the other person feel, I made the conscious choice to stop worrying about all the ways I wasn't living up to being a good partner. You can't be good to anyone else without being good to yourself first. I hadn't taken the time I needed to do that before, but I'm taking the time to do that now.

What's been beaten into my head since I was a child was entirely wrong. I see instead that there is strength in vulnerability, in "weakness." It's dismissive to imply anything other than that, to perpetuate a notion that fragility is the only possible explanation for outwardly experiencing emotions. I'm done with the idea that my identity means I have to make up for other people's offenses or walk through life stomped on by their perceived power and privileges. That's a boundary I'm establishing right now, and I won't let it get crossed anymore. If anything, you're crossing your own boundary of nonbelief by choosing to acknowledge whatever is there. At least, that's what I'll keep telling myself, and it seems I am getting better at listening.

what would you say to your younger self?

Follow your love of literature, reading, and writing, rather than always prioritizing the need to make a living. — DW

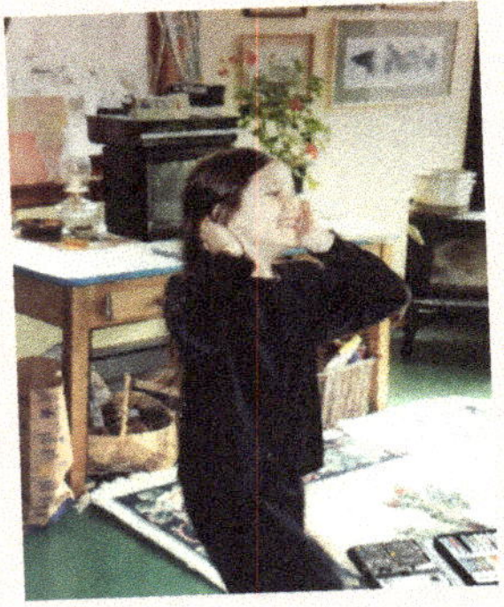

You are enough, in every way, just as you are. —RS

Fail forward! Yes! —JC

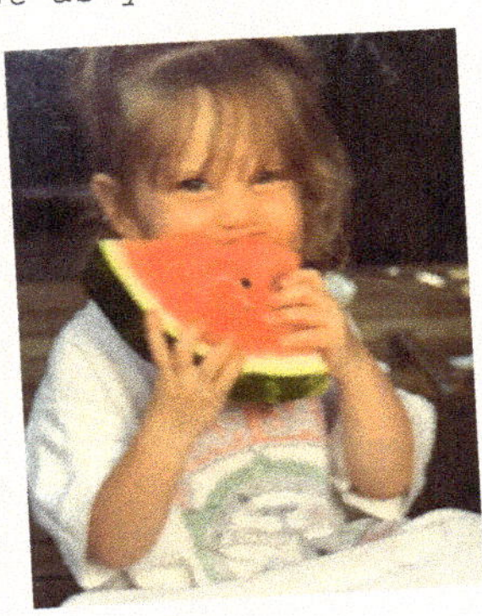

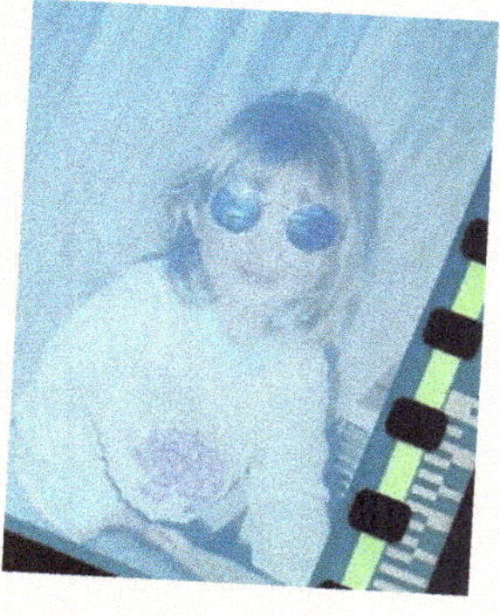

You are healthy and whole just the way you are. Do your best to question the beliefs the world gives you that don't affirm your inherent wholeness. Healing is possible. You weren't an accident. The challenges you experience can deepen your ability to engage with life in a loving way. —WB

You are exactly who you were meant to be. Also, dude, you are super queer. —G

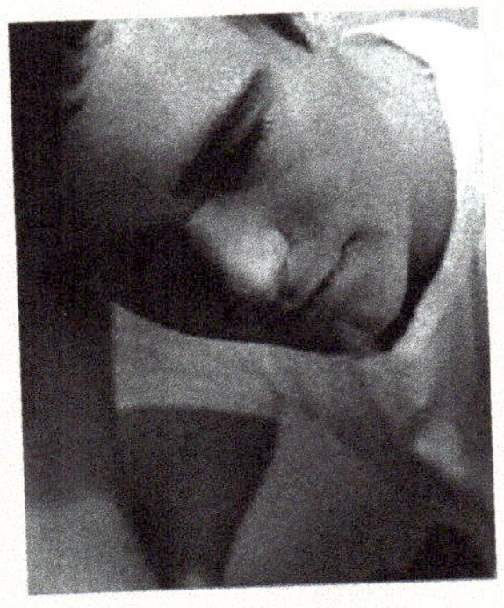

Take Medication. If I could offer only one tip for the future, Medication would be it. —AC

Don't Quit! —LS

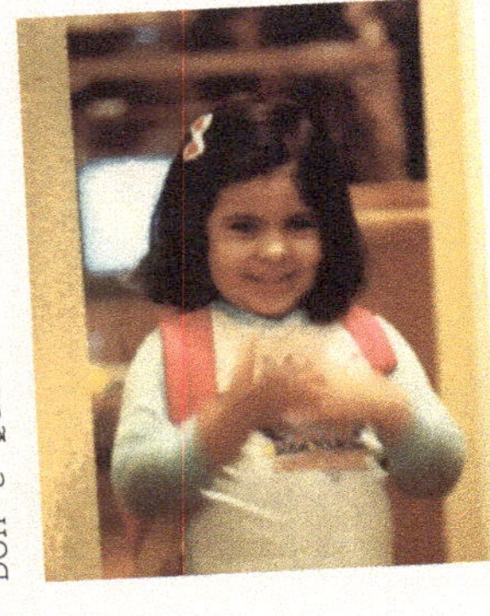

You don't have to carry everyone's pain. You are loved for who you are, not for what you can do. Learn to be with your emotions; let them show you what they need. —EW

Don't be scared to go hard for what you want, even if you end up failing. —KJ

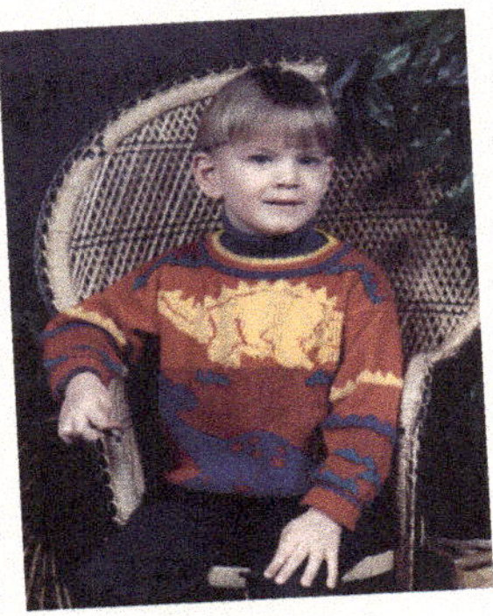

Be fearless, don't stop creating, and love your entire self. —RET

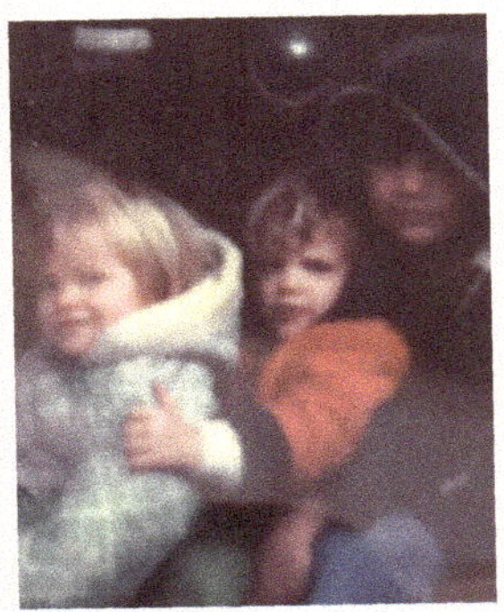

you know what's true.
—EKF

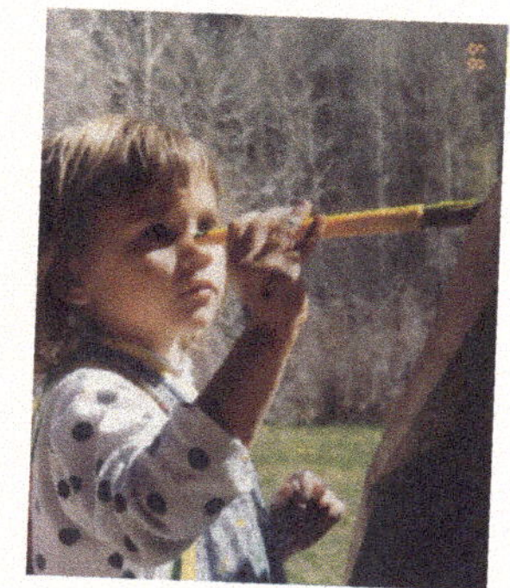

you will find everything
you need. —EEG

Do more for yourself.
—ZN

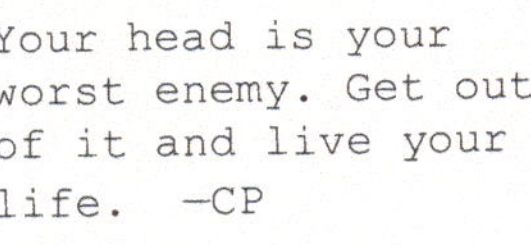

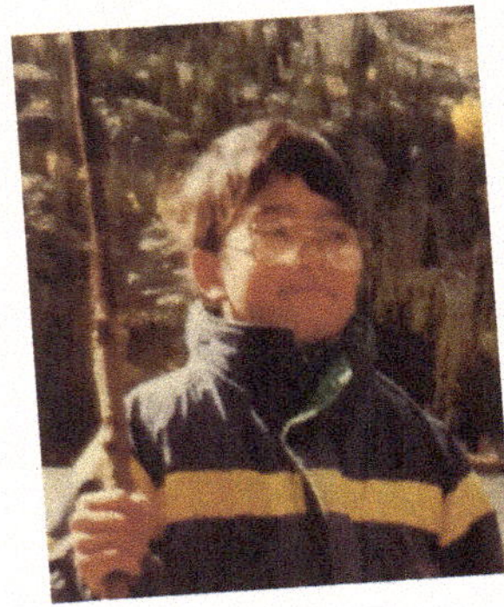

responsibility for
your whole life is
yours whether you
want it or not. —TH

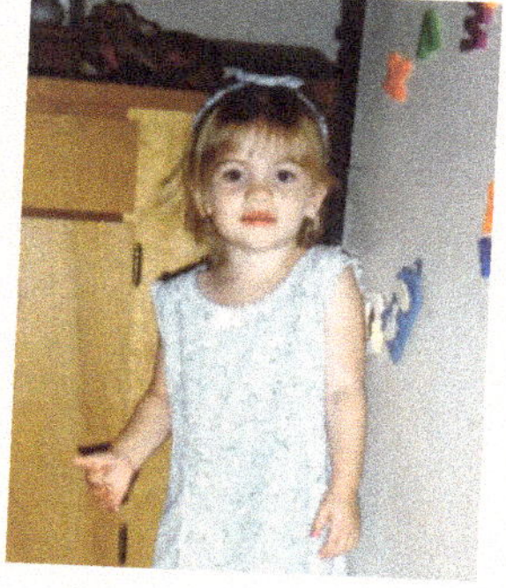

you are worth it and
you don't need to
shrink yourself for
anyone. —BC

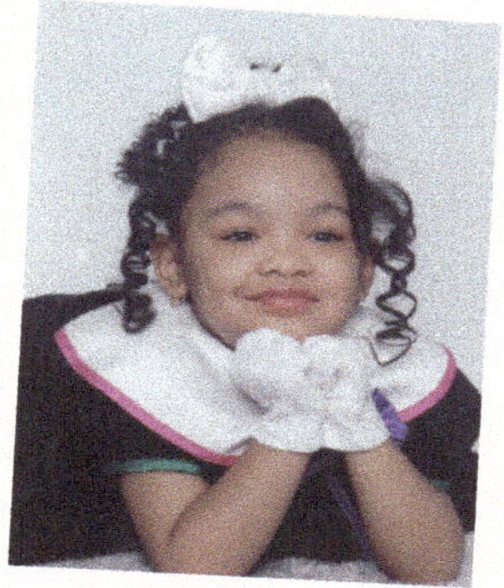

be kinder to
yourself. —CB

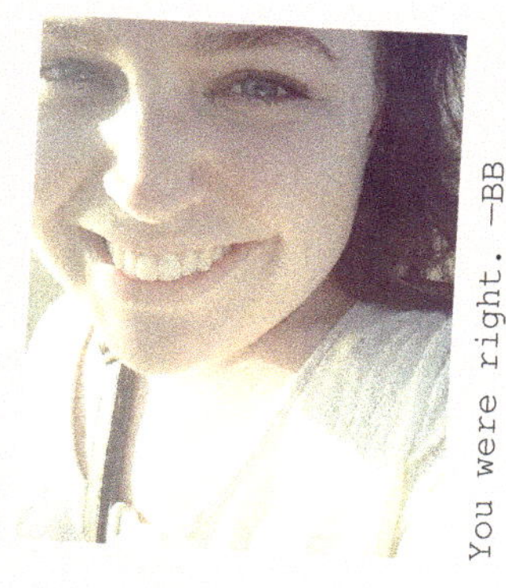

You were right. —BB

. . . .
. . . .
. . . .
. . . .

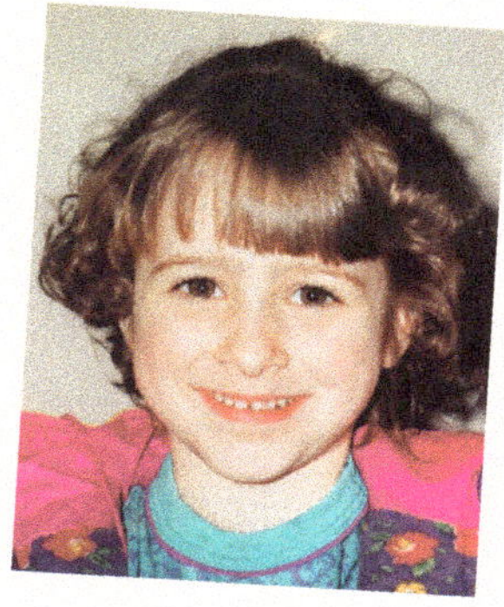

You are worthy
of love. You are
incredibly strong.
You're going to be
okay. —KH

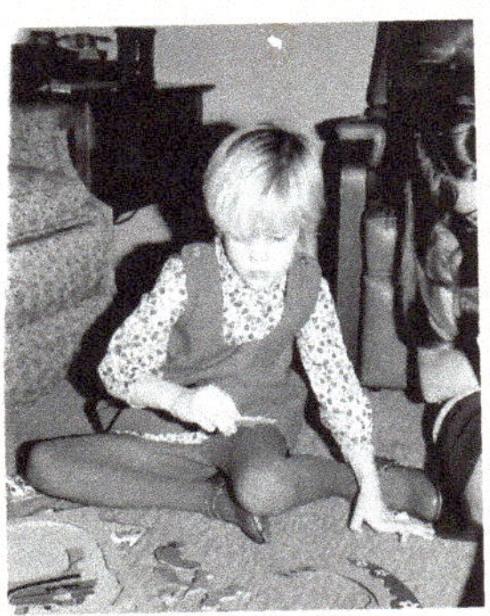

Keep working on
the puzzles. —SC

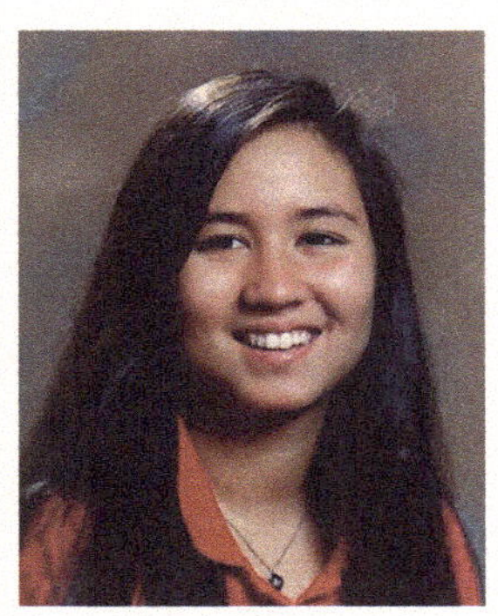

Find the people who
you love and who love
you and don't let go.
—MB

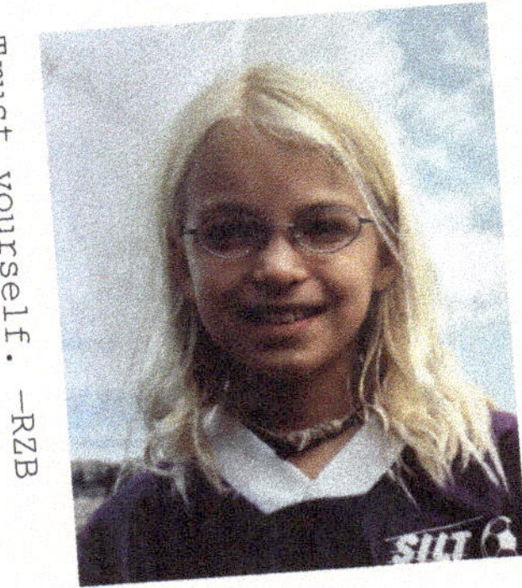

Trust yourself. —RZB

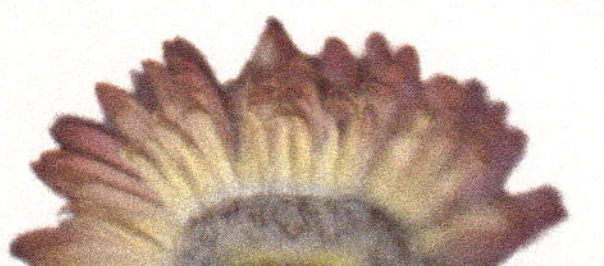

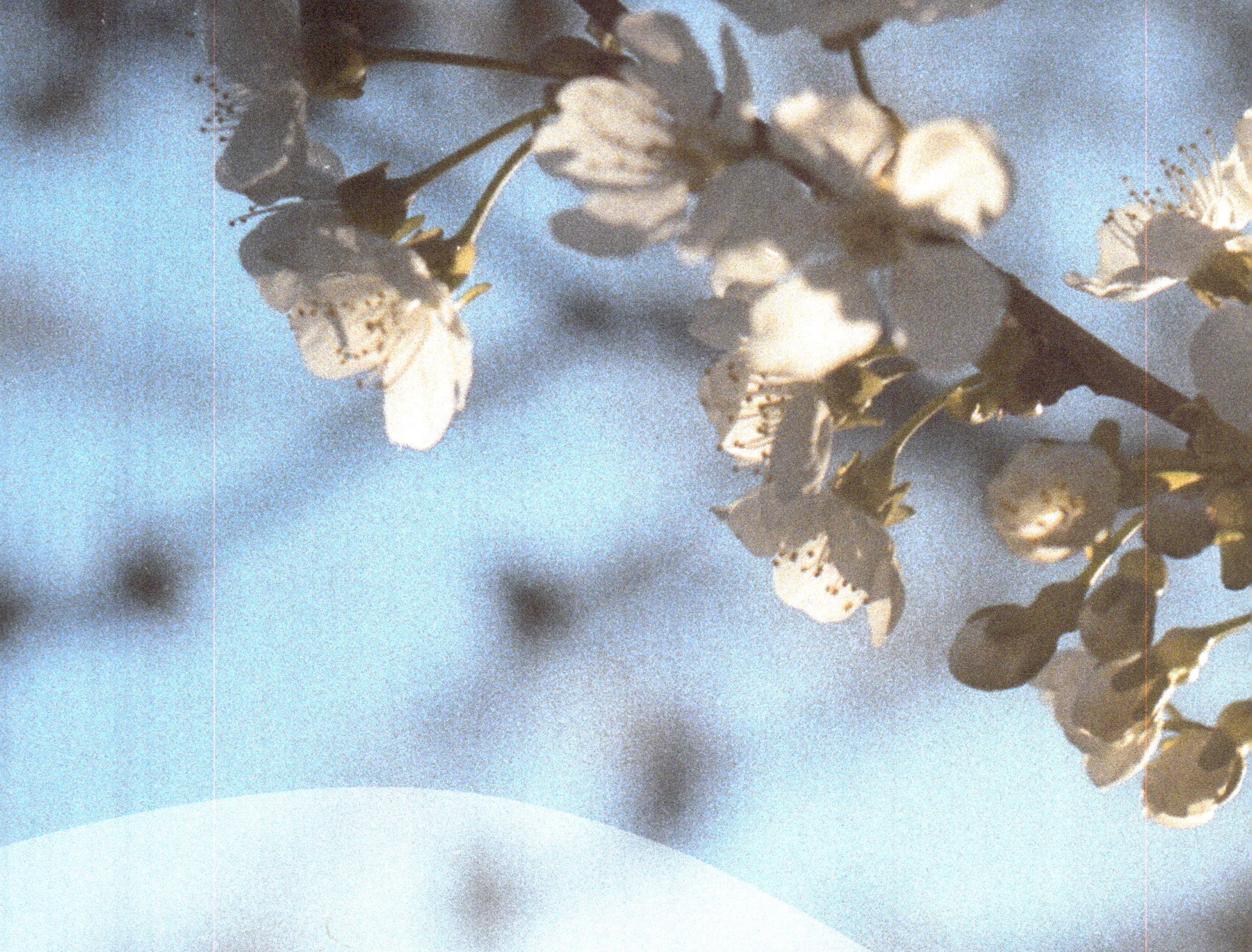

My love is a practice
It is a boundary
A safe haven upon a treetop
It is a nest made of precious sticks I have found on my life's journey
In between these lost-and-found branches are warm mementos
Ribbon and yarn, all the shades of my expressions, that once tied me to another
Fluffy tangles of fiber that resemble the confusion and inner turmoil I can now shape into
experiences that fill the cracks of my sanctuary

My fortress is not weatherproof
       And yet it is a soft place to rest my head as the rain comes
       May I take what I need from the moment and may the rest find its way out and
            back into Earth Mama
              To be reborn

My foundation is not sound
       And yet I am a diligent bird
       I shall pick up more memories
       More tools
       And more obtuse bits of my being and repair the parts of my abode that need
tending

MY LOVE IS A PRACTICE

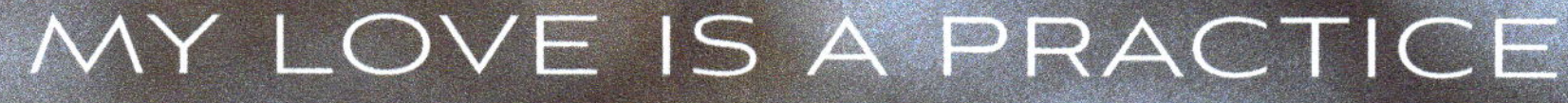

BY GODDESS

My love is a practice in healing
My love is a practice in accountability
My love is a practice in repair

My love is the continual choice to know myself
To care for myself
And to be myself

My love is a practice
It is a boundary
A safe haven upon a treetop

and the day came
when the risk to remain
tight in a bud
was more painful
than the risk it took
to blossom.

— Anaïs Nin

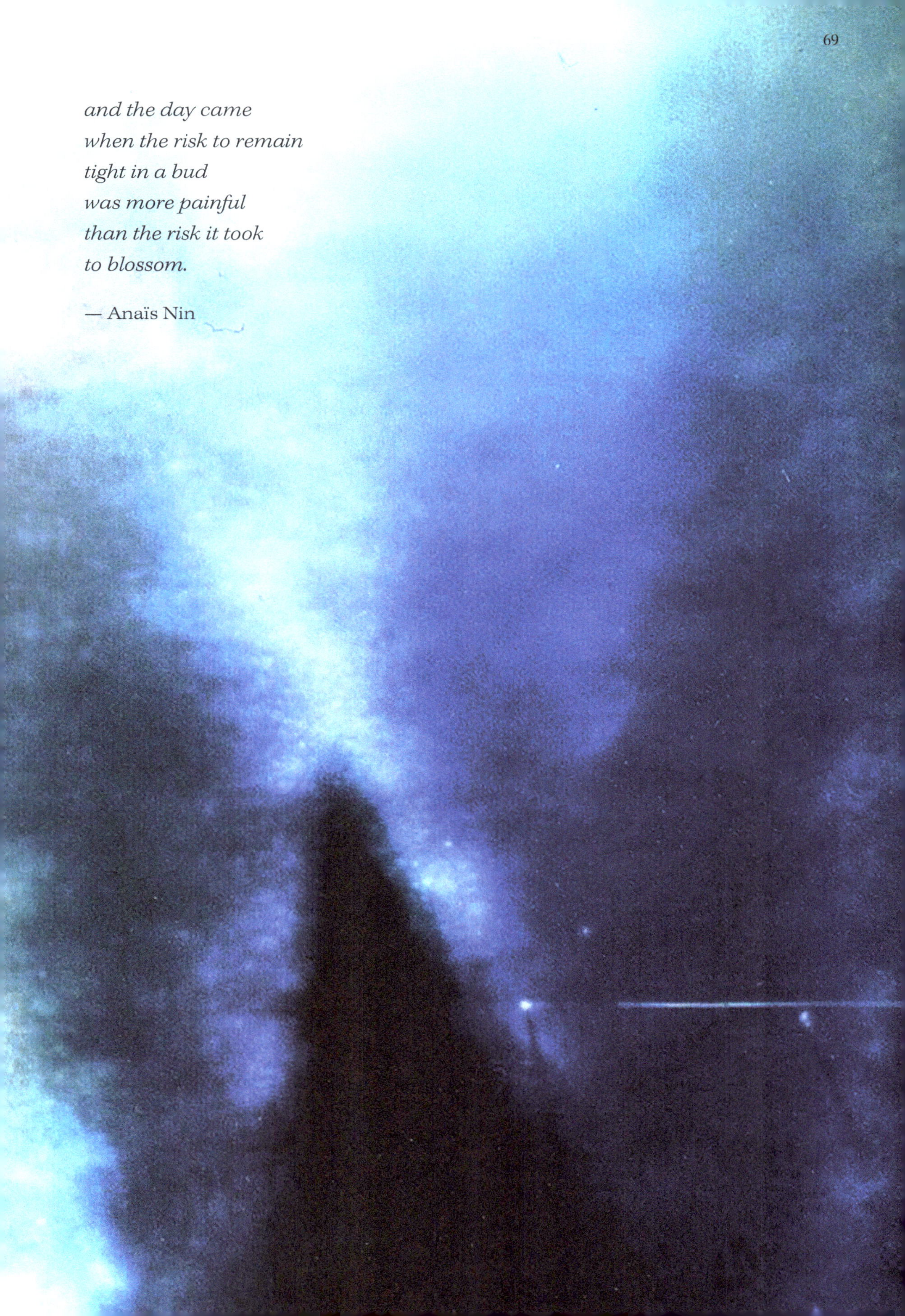

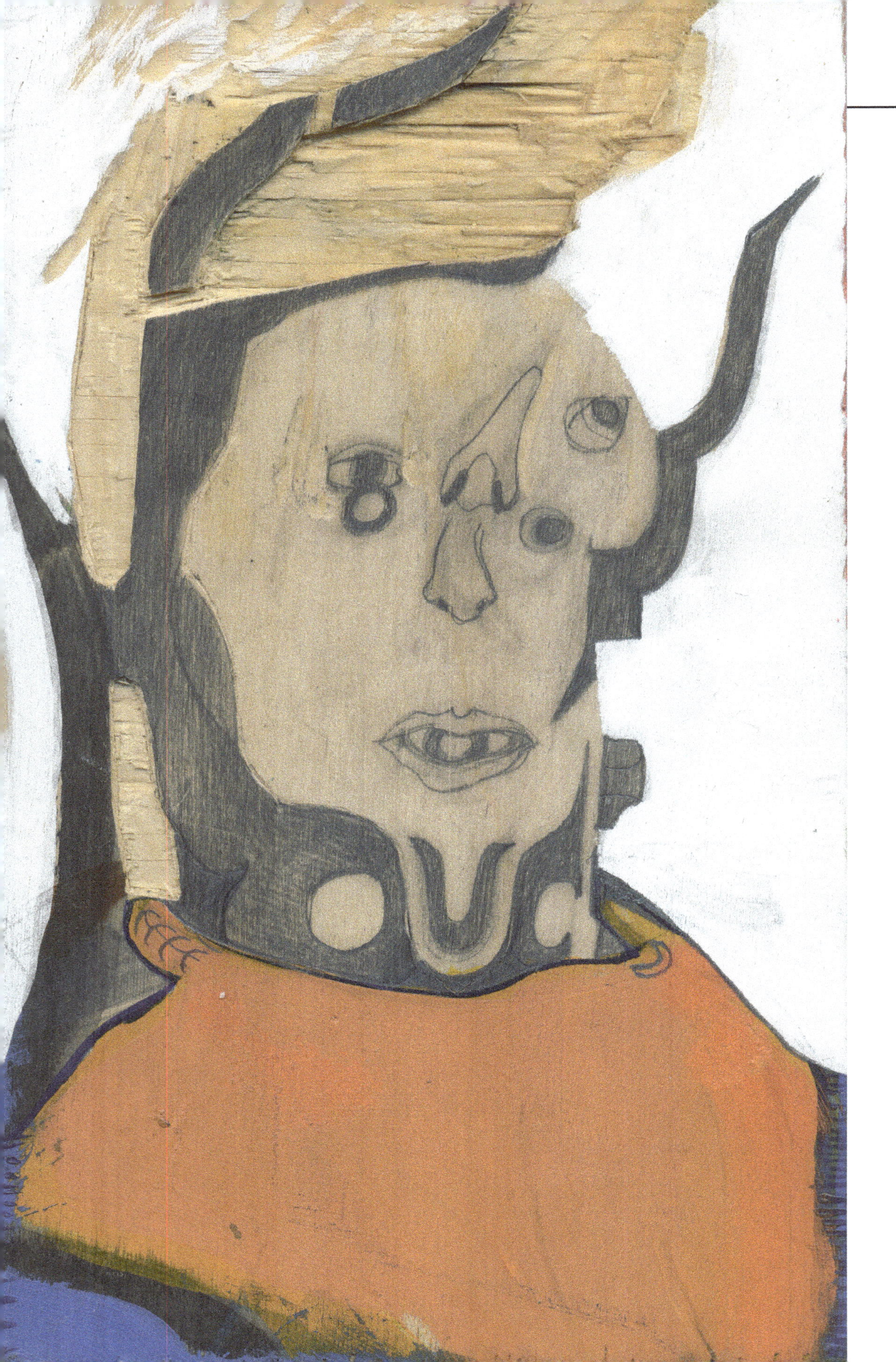

Mino II

Untenable Existential Conniption

A Day-Long Brain Fart by Takeo Hiromitsu

I heard recently in an interview, with a man I admire, a perspective on success and the pathways to it. He touches on the relationship between inner success and outer success. I take this to mean: how I personally perceive that I am successful and how it shows up to others. He mentions that his path to happiness was indirect due to the signifiers of success he was conditioned to focus on. He reflects and contrasts this winding way with the observations of the successful people he has met in the 'millennial' age group. He notes that this generation seems to have few qualms around happiness being the main heuristic framework for choice-making and guidance. Making decisions based on intuition and feelings of intrinsic joy.

I loved hearing this. It provides me with an anchor point for reflection. My many qualms around using happiness as my main filter for choice-making are heavy and full of fallacy. My parents, who I love and respect, wanted me to know of the pain and suffering of the world. Their hearts were in the right place, as this was intended to cultivate compassion and gratitude. At this time, the seeds of gratitude and compassion were planted, but my adolescent character focused on the flaws and I ended up cultivating a tangle of confusion and rage instead.

This is in the 1980's and I was young. Naive with the innocence of youth and filled with passion. Thanks to my Parents I cherished being alive in this biosphere. I felt a kinship to the Earth and all of the Beings inhabiting it with me. I was taught about the vast suffering on the planet and I became fixated on the human deforestation of the Amazon Rainforest. I felt hurt by this. I exasperatedly asked myself "How could other humans do this?" I eventually connected that the bananas I ate were a part of that deforestation. This is untenable, I knew it in my gut, my soul fire.

At the time, I had no way of grasping the complicated history of the globalizing forces that led to the world I was born into. I was only aware of a narrow list of negative externalities that these human forces and my actions were responsible for. I conflated my role as a consumer directly with the destruction of Earth's ecosystems and other lives. I was overwhelmed with an existential grief about the accumulation of our collective choices. The pain was so great that I internalized it into a simpler emotion: rage. A rage at being alive. These low vibrations accumulated into a pit of hollowness in my solar plexus.

Fury was the wolf that I fed. I grew to distrust my intuition and guidance of happiness. I started to feel hatred for being alive. An anger that I am here, on this Earth, and because I am human, I have to face the human condition. It is powerful. It is unpleasant.

In elementary and middle school this grave realization manifested as tantrums and flare-ups, coronal mass ejections of pure fusion. In high school, it was feigning sophistication and learning to guard my self-loathing with justification found in pride. In university, I studied the history of human thought and meaning-making, all the while rationalizing my feeling of being the victim of life.

This last element: the victim. He, the me of then, motivated by self preservation, kept holding his hands over my heart and eyes. Building a fortress around my rage and blocking my joy. This stagnation increased the toxicity which inevitably overflowed. The putrid fumes affect all those in my vicinity with sideways violence. In its pure form, this energy's primary substrate is: fear.

My low vibrations are filled with a timbre of undeserving, distrust, and grief. This timbre blocks crucial signals from caring friends and loved ones, which tell me that I am doing well and deserve to feel good about how I am living my life.

Thank you for reading this far. Let's take a small breather.

Settle into our bodies. Breathe deeply in through the nose, pause easily, slowly out the nose. Let's do this together, ten times.

We can look at my writing thus far and see the habits I am writing about reveling in their glory. *"Look at how much pain I self-inflicted!"* This is only part of my whole. I was blessed with such darkness just as I was blessed with the powers of light.

I was given fundamental tools for being a good person well before I learned about the human condition I was born into. I have the honor and strength of my ancestry and the conviction of my Parents that we are able to choose how we react. I received an overwhelming amount of love and support. I still do. I was born into an auspicious family line of scholars, engineers, teachers, and spiritual thinkers. I have been able to venture deeply into the darkness because of the strength of love I have been gifted. I liken the tools to Ariadne's thread. Spun with the kindness, love, and breath of the Parents, twined with the strength of their resolve.

> The fiber from Mama:
> *"Remember your breath. Count your breaths to ten.*
> *You are Loved. God is Love."*

> And from Papa:
> *"Check your motivation of heart according to Good or Evil.*
> *Good is being honest, living for the sake of others, and taking care of all things.*
> *Evil is acting only out of selfishness."*

This thread has kept me oriented and grounded in my being. I could observe my behavior and learn about myself. When I was unable to be with my mind or emotions, I moved my body.

I have made a practice of leaning into discomfort. I found that through physical activity I am able to process and directly challenge my mental states of being. Through my involvement with spiritual and contemplative praxis I have learned, from those humans before me, that I have an ability to transmute the fundamental energy of my toxic patterns into fuel for other patterns. It then takes discipline to direct the fuel into patterns that are regenerative.

I enter the labyrinth and explore, leaning into my desolate feelings with the goal of moving through them and with them.

Part of this process requires me to be willingly open to be uncomfortable and isolated. I enter the labyrinth and explore, leaning into my desolate feelings with the goal of moving through them and with them. I am bullheaded in my approach. Taking the risk of being lost in the maze, rather than avoiding entering it.

Within the exploration of this maze, I started drawing multiple self-portraits on top of each other to save paper. Initially, the compositions were messy and I found little by way of aesthetics in the practice. As the discipline matured, a subconscious flow arose. A layered self-portrait became a physical representation of my complicated and evolving inner worlds.

The act of bringing these aspects of myself out and having to see them, touch them, and create them started a whole new transmutation of my toxic self relationship. I am able to use its energy as a power source. When I open myself to the melodramatic phrasing and sardonic sentiments, I feel the immense power available in the grief and pain underneath the rage.

The signal path wants it to be easy and known. To avoid the dance of Her feet on the bodies of dead men, oblivion. I think the anger and grief comes from realizing that, for me, this cannot be easy. In my human form I must walk the middle path into the difficulty and the unknown. A kernel of energy that glows golden, a truth body. This truth body seems small. I think of a black hole, infinite density zero mass. I imagine Dante having to reach the realm where he can climb down Lucifer's body using his "tufts of hair" to be able to climb up and out of hell.

This golden glowing kernel is portal, a seed pattern into liberation, a cyclic act of creation and destruction.

A key to this comes from Starhawk and the witches I know: "Where there is fear, there is power."

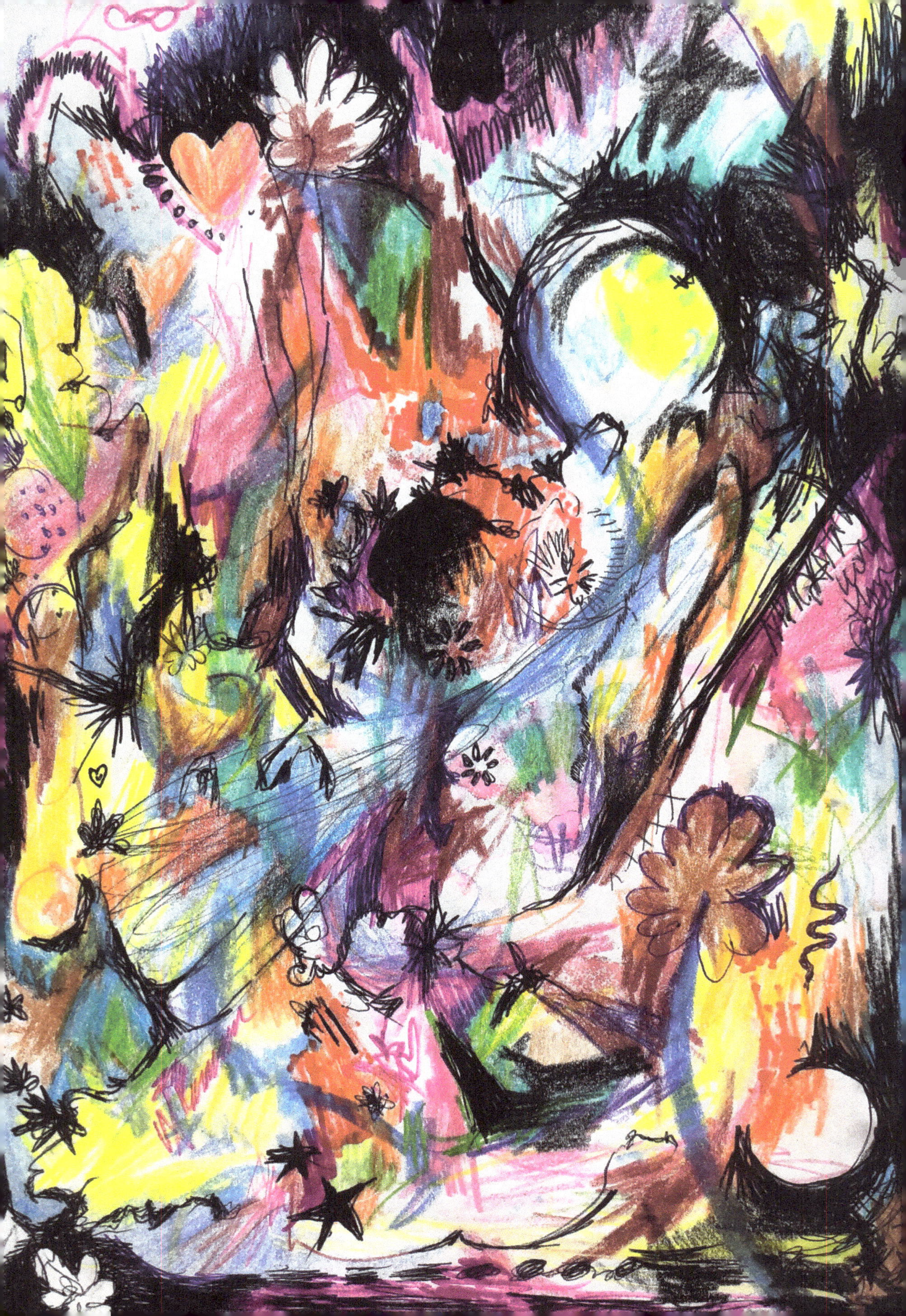

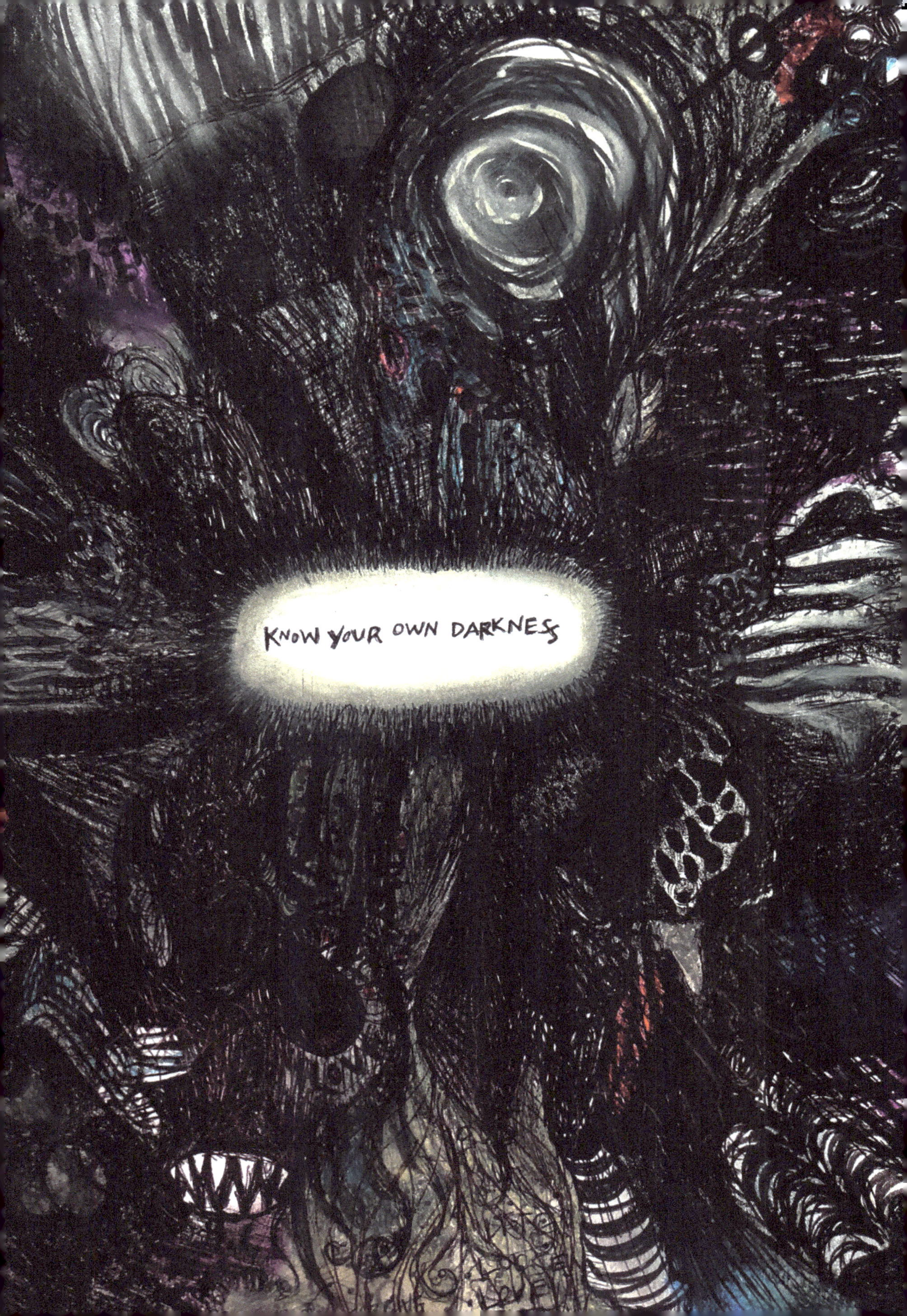
KNOW YOUR OWN DARKNESS

IDENTIFICATION AND COMPARTMENTALIZATION

BY KALEEM JONES

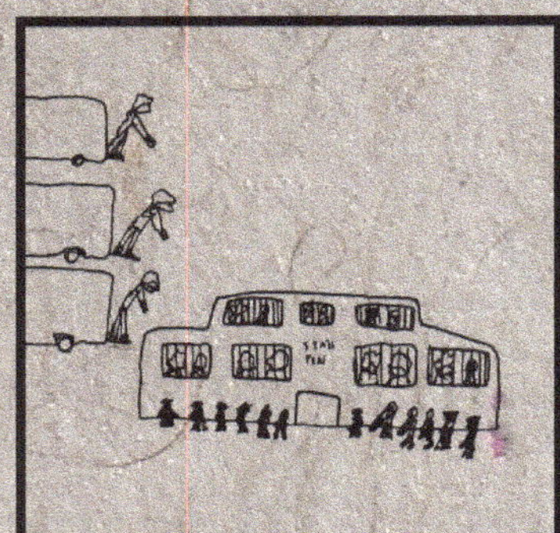

PLANTATIONS

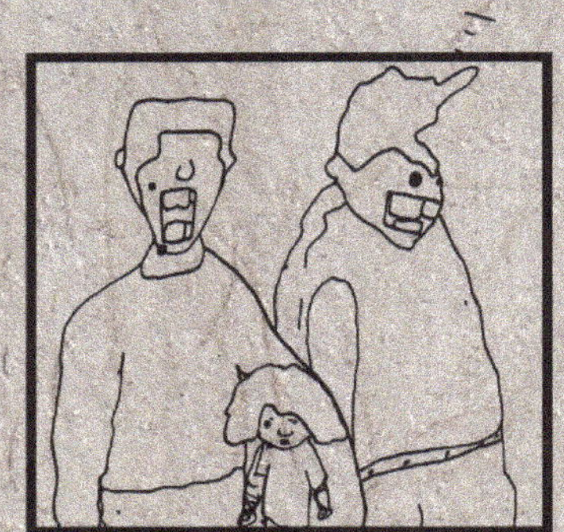

FAM

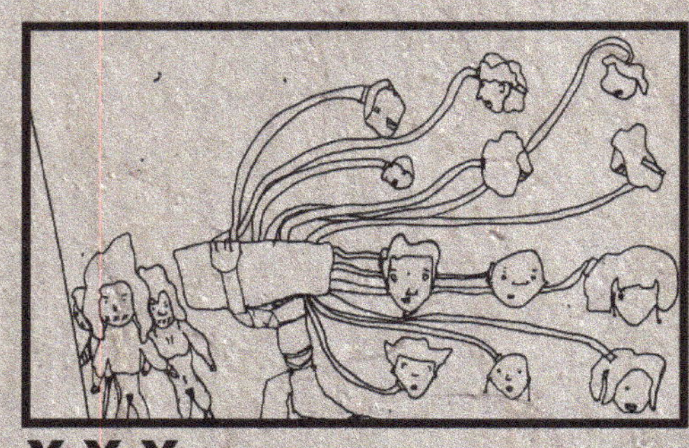

X X X

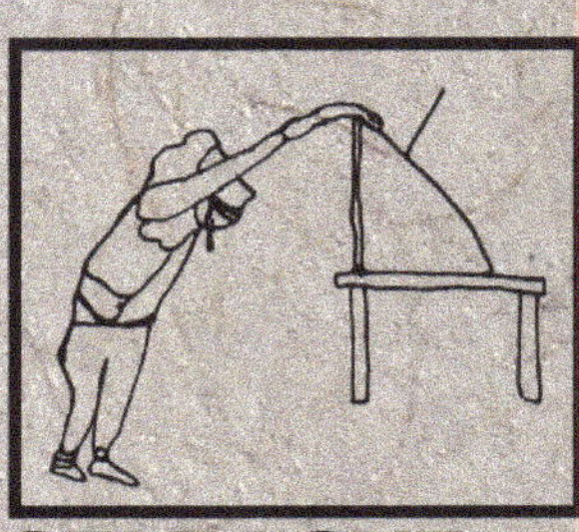

SELF LOVE

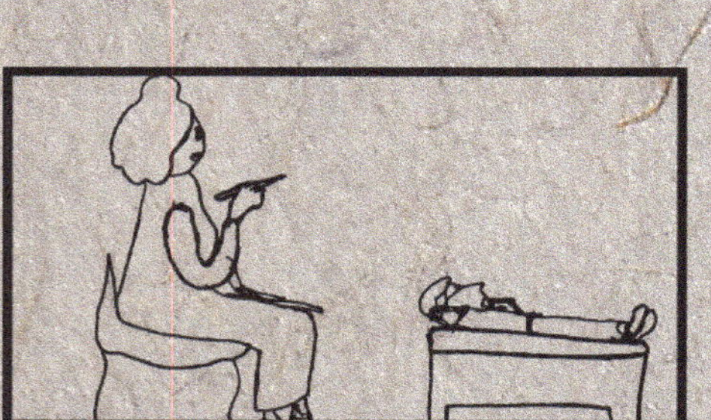

THERAPY

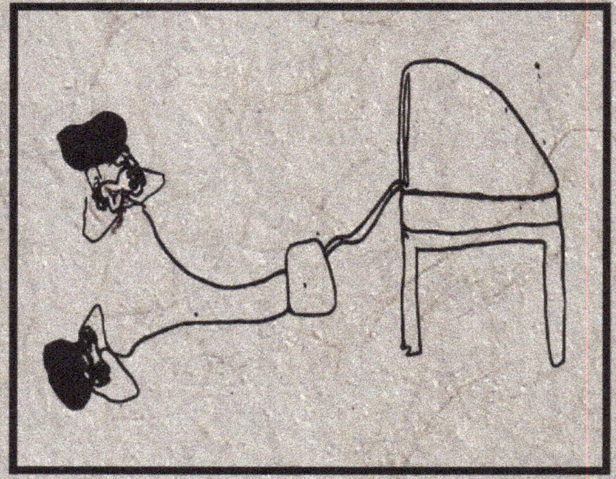

ESCAPE WITH FRIENDS

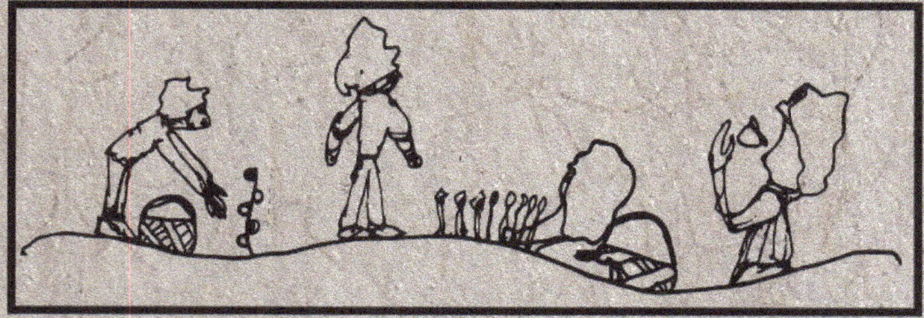

PLANTING AND GROWING

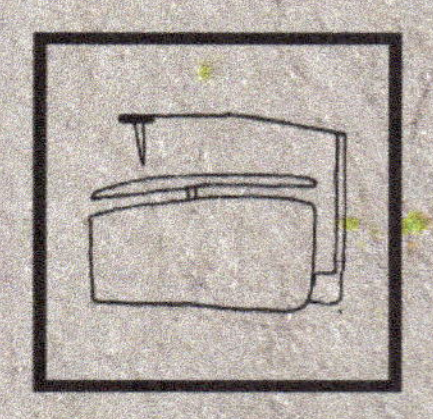

LISTENING

This piece identifies different aspects of American life in an effort to understand how they affect a person's day to day understanding of themselves, what is forced upon them, what they accept whole heartedly, what feels good, and what doesn't. It is an exercise in perspective, understanding that everyone speaks their own language, of love, of violence, of self care, a reminder that everyone feels this world differently.

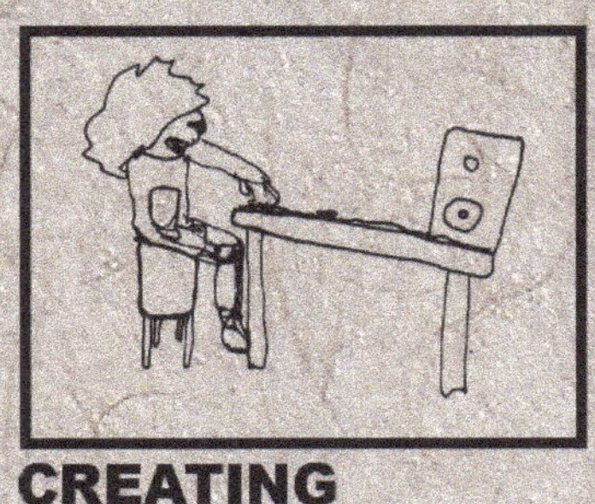

CREATING

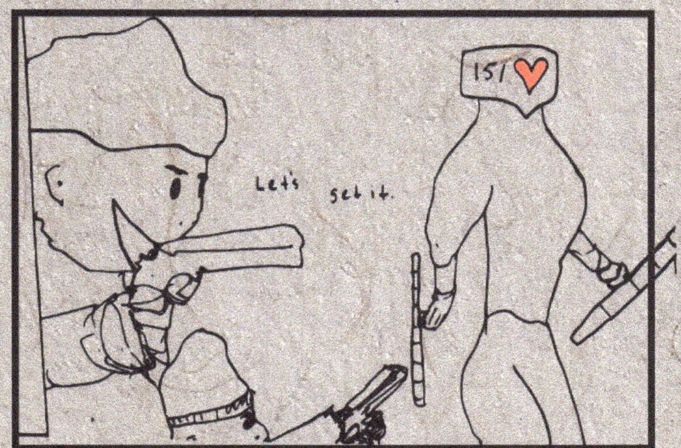

SELF WORTH

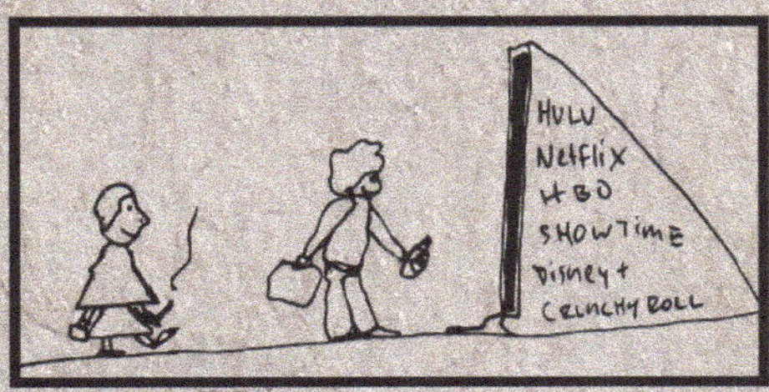

ESCAPE

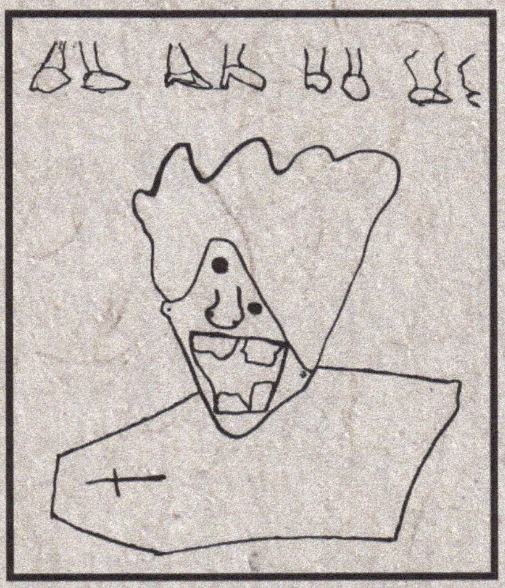

HEAVEN OR HELL

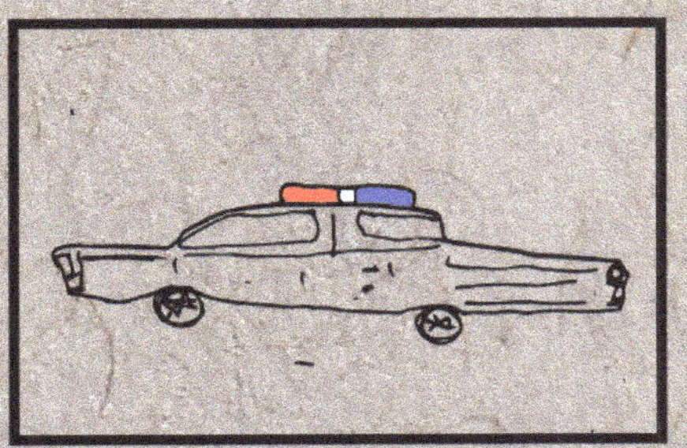

SLAVE CATCHERS

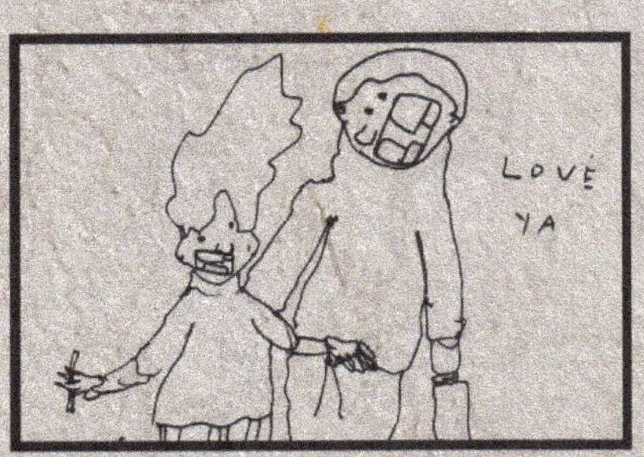

FAM

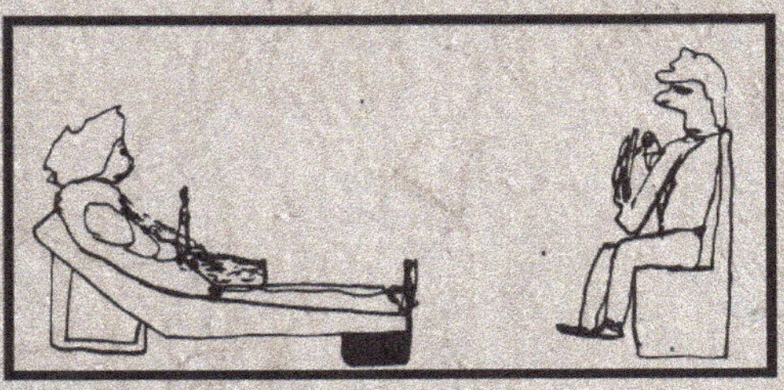

THERAPY 2

MINDFULNESS MAD LIBS

Today was a ___________________ day. When I woke up, I was
(honest adjective)

grateful because _______________ exists. As it went on, I felt many
(a small pleasure)

things. I worried that ___________________________. And also
(a persistent concern)

wondered about ___________________. But I held myself.
(existential question)

Here I am. I respect my own mystery. I don't try too hard to explain

___________________. As I reflect, I close my eyes and
(something sacred)

listen to my breath. The first thing that comes to mind is

___________________________. And that's ok. The
(an unedited thought)

___________________ lingers. The place I feel the most
(a feeling)

tension is in my _______________. I send my breath and
(a body part)

appreciation there. Thank my body for being alive, for

allowing me _______________________________. A caring ritual
(a cherished movement or activity)

that I have with myself is _________________________________.
(a self-made ceremony)

I admit that I am made of wisdom and mistakes and resilience. I contain many selves. Like the me that did ____________________

(an accomplishment)

______________. And the one that knows how to hear my needs.

Here's a list of things I love about them—the glowing parts and natural fragments that comprise my current being. I appreciate:

That I ____.

(a good past decision)

How I ____.

(a time when you turned your tenderness up to ten)

When I ____.

(a moment you were brave)

What I try to be is ____________________________.

(a characteristic you hope to embody)

I honor my heartbeat, electromagnetic, it sounds like __________

____________________. I deserve ____________________

(a sound or rhythm)   (something lovely)

______________ because I am human and it is my right to heal.

Tonight, I'd like to dream about ____________________. I sit with

(a surreal landscape)

hurt and beauty. Still, I want to see the____________________.

(a transcendent image)

Dearest

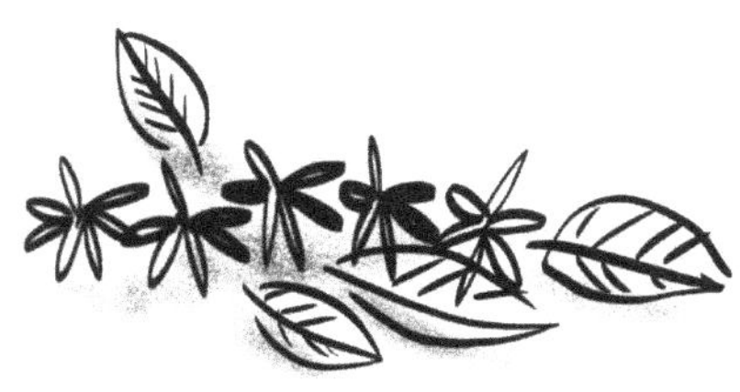

BY MAUREEN BOYD

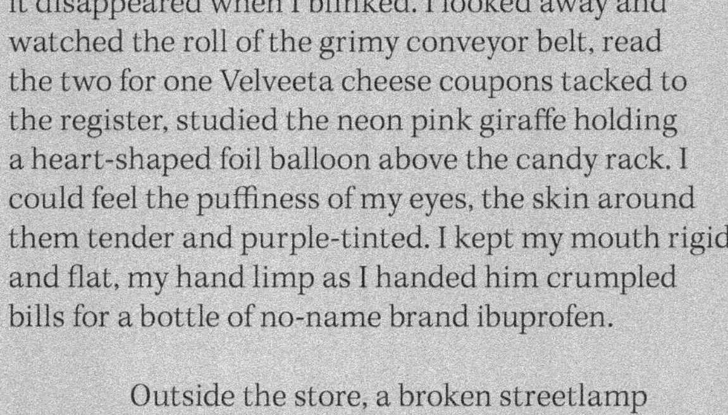

I thought I saw recognition in the cashier's face, but it disappeared when I blinked. I looked away and watched the roll of the grimy conveyor belt, read the two for one Velveeta cheese coupons tacked to the register, studied the neon pink giraffe holding a heart-shaped foil balloon above the candy rack. I could feel the puffiness of my eyes, the skin around them tender and purple-tinted. I kept my mouth rigid and flat, my hand limp as I handed him crumpled bills for a bottle of no-name brand ibuprofen.

Outside the store, a broken streetlamp sputtered indecipherable warnings. A couple blocks away, the lights of a McDonald's beckoned. I set out for their yellow glow, the sidewalk beneath my feet dotted with deposits of ancient chewing gum. I skirted blinking motel signs, empty gas stations, and a 24-hour laundromat awash in brittle fluorescence. Inside the McD's I bought a 99-cent-Super-Sized Coke and carried it into the reeking bathroom. I swallowed exactly fourteen ibuprofen— less than half the bottle. I threw away the Super-Sized Coke because it had been in the bathroom and chucked the rest of the ibuprofen after it.

* * *

On New Year's Eve my mother asked me to stay home to watch the ball drop with her and my dad, but I had plans with friends to go to a street party. My father's eyes grew flinty behind black-rimmed glasses and he told my mother not to bother with me. She closed her mouth and turned back to the television.

I forgot about them when I saw the thousands of people dancing and drinking in the street, staking spots to watch the parade in the morning. In that vast sprawl of bodies, I lost the girl who drove me. But I forgot her, too, when I caught the eye of a tall man. He gestured to me, and I followed. We didn't speak as we walked away from the noise and mean-

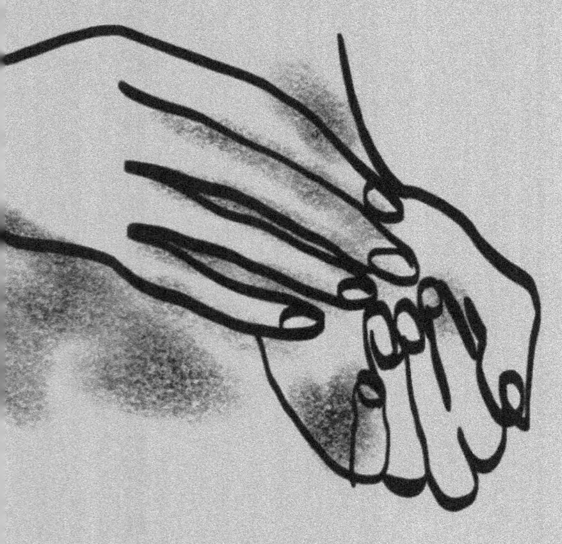

ILLUSTRATIONS
BY JENNY VU

dered down side streets lined with millionaires' mansions. We found strange little brick steps overhung with leafy branches and scented with jasmine. We climbed the secret garden steps until a locked gate blocked our path. The moon hid her face and in silence and darkness I pressed against him, guiding his hands between my legs. He fucked me with violent gratitude, our silence broken only by the rhythmic thudding of my back against the cold metal bars and the piddling of drunken frat boys pissing on the stairs below us.

We walked to his car afterwards, and when he opened the passenger door for me, I got in wordlessly. He drove a Camaro with some kind of custom stereo system, and when he turned the volume up it vibrated through my bones. We parked up the street from the apartment building where I lived with my parents, and a silence stretched between us. I didn't want to go inside and I grew afraid that I might never see him again. So, I reached over and undid his belt. He stopped me, and asked,

You're eighteen, right?

I met his gaze, but didn't answer him.
He cursed quietly to himself, and repeated,

Tell me you're eighteen.

I'll be eighteen soon.

How soon?

A few months.

He shook his head but didn't stop me when I slipped my hand inside his pants again.

It was three a.m. when I crept through my front door. I tiptoed toward my room, until I saw the flare of a match as my father lit his pipe in a corner of the living room. He exhaled, and puffs of smoke drifted in and out of the moonlight slanting through the windows.

You didn't have to wait up for me.

He stood up and walked close enough for me to see his pale, gaunt face behind black glasses. He stopped, lowered his face within inches of mine

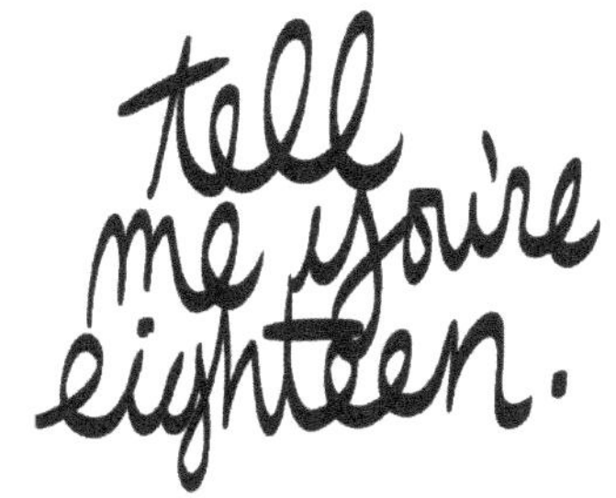

and whispered,

Whose turn was it tonight?

I could hear it, the thing quivering in his voice, whatever he imagined about me in the dark. Even as he said the words, some shame twisted his face. For a fraction of a second, I pitied him. Then I went to bed in silence. I think if he could have beaten my virginity back into place that night, beaten the sexuality out of me, driven my dangerous body out of existence, he would have. I think I might have preferred that to his question.

That was the last thing my father said to me for a long time. From that day forward, he stopped talking to me. He would drive me to my high school in the mornings and pick me up in the afternoons in complete silence. My mother continued to talk to me out of necessity, to tell me when dinner was ready, or answer my questions about buying school supplies, but other than that, she avoided me. My new boyfriend had a job at a stereo shop and his own apartment, so after a couple weeks of my parents' silent treatment, I started spending the night there. I wasn't so naive that I thought he loved me, but I saw the way he looked at me, his willingness to risk jail just so he could touch me — and I wanted that almost as much as I wanted love.

I still went to school, but now my boyfriend dropped me off in the mornings. We talked on the drive to school about random things: music, his travels in Europe, where to eat lunch, where I wanted to go to college. After a couple weeks of this, my favorite teacher pulled me out of her class and said that she heard that I had run away from home and was staying

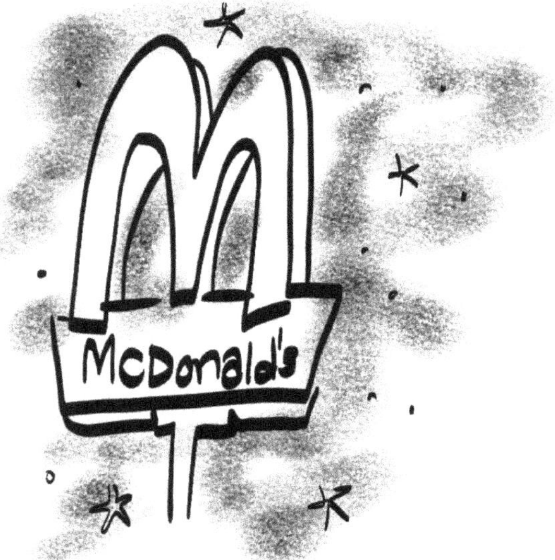

with a man. She seemed angry and asked me in a loud voice if I was pregnant. I wasn't pregnant because I knew how to use birth control. She seemed skeptical. When we finally returned to the classroom, I could tell from the looks the other girls gave me that they heard us. She never spoke to me again after that, except to return papers and the occasional question and answer exchange in class. A few months later, my cohort voted her Teacher of the Year, and we took a big group picture, with her at the center, proud and smiling.

* * *

When I left the McDonald's, I walked to a payphone and called a man I had dated briefly the previous year, who attended a college about an hour away. He answered the phone, and his voice, clogged with one-a.m.-phlegm, became knife-sharp when he heard my name. He thought if he drove fast, he could get there in less than an hour. Maybe forty-five minutes.

I was only a block from home, but I waited for him on a bus bench outside the payphone. Soon a car drove up. I couldn't see into it very well, but I saw a Chinese-American lady, in her 20s or 30s—I couldn't tell which. Those ages all looked the same to me then. Her face, framed by the passenger window and pale with worry, hovered specter-like in the darkness of the car.

Why are you out here, honey? You shouldn't be out here so late at night.

I'm fine, thanks. I'm waiting for someone.

Do you need a ride, honey?

No, no thank you, I'm waiting for someone.

Are you sure? Are you okay?

No, no, thank you. I'm fine.

The woman turned her head to consult with the person driving the car, a man. They bowed their heads together, murmuring. I became increasingly uncomfortable. I didn't think they were kidnappers or serial killers, but I couldn't see who drove the car, so I couldn't be sure. The woman began rummaging in her purse and then stretched her arm out to me, through the window.

Here, honey. Take this.

I didn't want to walk over to their car; if I got too close, they might be able to grab me. But I didn't want to seem rude, and I worried they might attract unwanted attention. Besides, I could use any money they gave me, I'd spent my last on the ibuprofen and soda.

I stood up and walked to the car. As I drew closer, I saw the man driving the car, staring unblinkingly behind the woman with concerned eyes. When I got close enough to be able to stretch my own hand out to touch hers, she pressed a chain of some kind into my palm, with smooth beads on it. I didn't look at it, however, just nodded and thanked her. As I walked back to the bench, she called out to me,

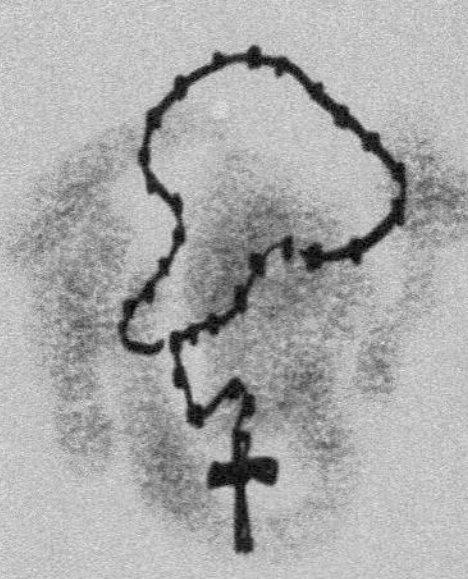

We'll pray for you, honey. You pray, too. Jesus will listen.

After they drove away, I opened my palm. She hadn't given me money. Instead, she had handed me a cheap rosary, composed of white plastic beads and rusted metal links.

* * *

One evening as I got out of the shower at my boyfriend's, I stood naked in his bedroom and heard footsteps in the hallway. Before I could grab something to wear, the door burst open to reveal three of his friends. I ran into the bathroom and locked the door. When they knocked and laughed, shouting for me to come out, I turned off the light and lay on the floor. I buried my face in the damp shower rug, inhaling the scent of moldy rubber and coconut-mango bodywash while I covered my ears with my hands and a towel.

After a long time—maybe an hour—I came out. I heard them in the kitchen and eavesdropped from the next room. They talked about their favorite porn stars, moved on to Nakamichi amps and my boyfriend's elaborate car stereo installation, and then one of his friends asked him about me. I couldn't make out the question exactly, but my boyfriend raised his voice to answer and I heard him boasting about having anal sex with me. His voice grew animated, describing what I said, the sounds I made, all the things I would do. They pressed him for more details in thick, hungry voices and I hugged myself, digging my nails into the flesh of my arms, trying to flatten my breasts, trying to shrink my ass, trying to press my body into oblivion.

When he wondered aloud where I was, I knew I couldn't hide anymore, and forced myself to walk into the kitchen casually. He asked what took me so long, and before I could answer, pulled me against him and gave me a deep kiss. I broke away from him, flushed and warm, and one of his friends asked me about my cup size was while staring at my chest.

Grinning, my boyfriend told him. I tried to slap him playfully in response, but he caught my hand and held it. Looking me in the eye, he very deliberately took hold of my left breast and squeezed it so hard that I cried out in pain. Everyone laughed, and after a moment, I did, too, forcing the sound up my throat, through my parted lips, to blend with their voices, drowning out everything else.

* * *

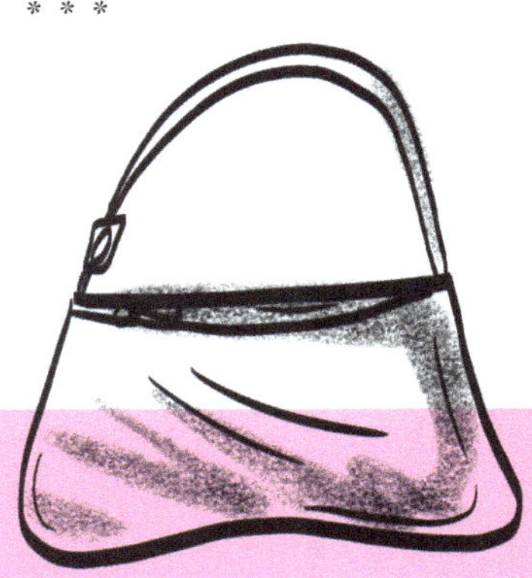

It grew cold on the bus bench. I wore a grey dress, knit with creamy, soft-petaled flowers that hugged my body, and held a blue purse my mother had given me for my sixteenth birthday the week before. I got up to pace, trying to keep warm. Someone parked a truck with a camper shell on top of it in front of one of the nearby motels. A man got out, locked it, and walked down the street towards me. I stopped pacing and watched him. He got closer, and I saw that he was my father's age, maybe older. He was white, balding, and a little fatter in the belly than my father. He wore a button-down shirt and slacks, like my father wore every day for work, except more wrinkled.

He needed to get to the freeway. There were four different entrances within a mile or so, and he nodded and looked around while I gave him detailed directions. Eventually, he interrupted me and asked,

Do you know any girls looking for work?

No.

Are you looking for work?
No.

Are you sure?

Yes.

He licked his lips as he stared at me, and it seemed like he wanted to say more, but instead he turned around and walked away. He made a u-turn in the middle of the street when he left, I think to avoid driving by me, but his truck made a hideous, screeching noise that made a discreet getaway impossible.

* * *

About a week after his friends walked in on me, my boyfriend suggested I go back home for a few nights to appease my parents. I did as he asked, but my parents wouldn't even look at me. My father left for work without me in the mornings, so I had to call my boyfriend for rides to and from school, which didn't make him very happy. After a few days of this I returned to my boyfriend's place, but things seemed different between us. He barely spoke to me, and the sex felt impersonal, an exercise in him getting off as quickly as possible.

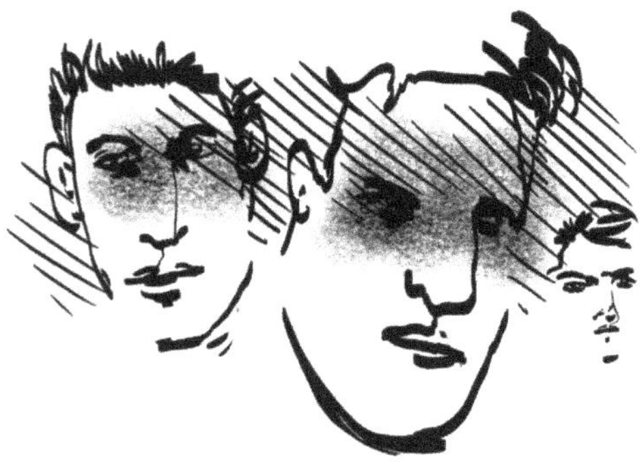

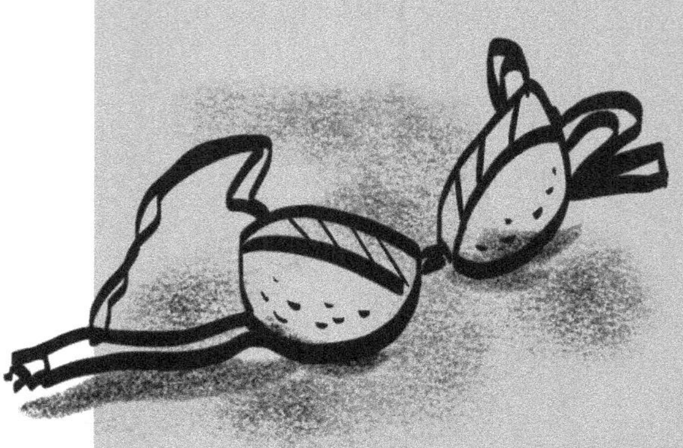

The last night, a couple of his friends came over and started mixing these drinks called Sex on the Beach: Malibu coconut rum and cranberry juice. They called it a girlie drink, and when I took a sip, it tasted like a delicious tropical punch. I don't know how many I had, but they kept on making them and I kept on drinking them. My boyfriend brooded, nursing a beer, watching me with hooded eyes as I accepted each glass offered to me.

At some point, my boyfriend got a phone call. I was so drunk that I had fallen down in the living room and was rolling around on the floor under the glass coffee table. The glass distorted the faces and bodies of the men standing above me, and I started giggling. They tried to reach under the table to pull me to my feet, but they fell down, too, until we were all on the floor, a laughing tangle of arms and legs. I heard the front door open and close and when I sat up, I didn't see my boyfriend anywhere. The guys told me he had to go help a mutual friend of theirs. They reassured me that he'd be back soon, and told me to relax and have a few more drinks.

I have flashes, here and there. I know we played strip poker. I kept on losing, but I was having fun, and I enjoyed the way they looked at me. Then all I had left on was my bra and panties, and they told me I had to take it all off. Of course, I wouldn't do that, so we came to a compromise that involved removing my underwear and wearing a towel. I remember them teasing me, pretending to grab the towel, and I told them that they shouldn't do that, that my boyfriend would get mad. I remember they exchanged looks. Finally, one of them said,

He doesn't care what we do with you. You know that, right?

I was trying to avoid spilling my drink and still hold my towel up as I weaved back and forth on my feet, so I didn't hear him, at first. The other guy took my glass from me and set it down on the coffee table. The one speaking shook his head, and added,

He's with another girl right now. He met her while you were at your parents'. He's been waiting all week for her to call him back, and she finally did. He asked us to keep you busy while he was gone. I think he's going to ask you to leave, tomorrow.

I couldn't quite comprehend what he said, so he repeated it until I did, and

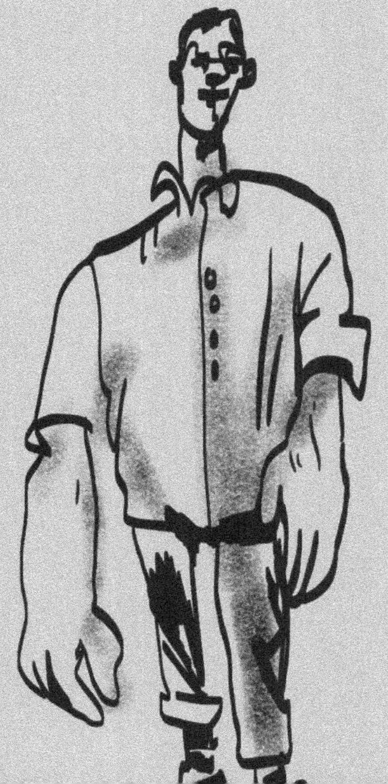

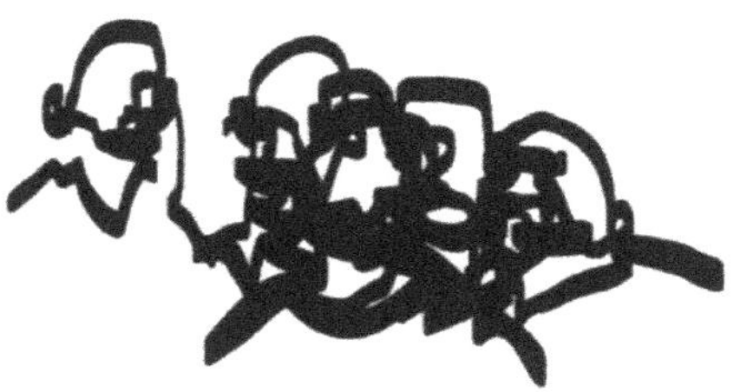

somehow, I ended up on the floor, leaning against the couch while the room reeled around me. I pictured my boyfriend's face and voice when he told me to go back home, and realized I expected this. I had nothing, now, and nowhere I wanted to be.

I surrendered to sloppy, drunken sobs and my neck became soaked with my tears. The guys made mournful, sympathetic noises. One of them brought me a box of tissues while the other rubbed my back. They told me that they'd always thought he treated me badly but had been afraid to say anything. I nodded, not really listening. I could feel something inside of me, something dark and growing, extending long, slithering tendrils that took over my body. I almost didn't notice when the one rubbing my back began to remove my towel. I protested, but he shushed me, told me I was beautiful and irresistible, and I fell silent. I knew this would happen, knew it the night my boyfriend sent his friends to the bedroom while I got dressed. It was best just to let it happen, because the alternative could be so much worse. The last thing I remember was asking them to get condoms from the bathroom, and then I blacked out.

I woke up to afternoon light streaming through the windows. I lay naked on the living room floor, with a splitting headache. It was eerily quiet. Everything hurt when I sat up. There were bruises on my inner thighs, and I was sticky and sore. They hadn't used condoms. I had told them to use fucking condoms, and they hadn't.

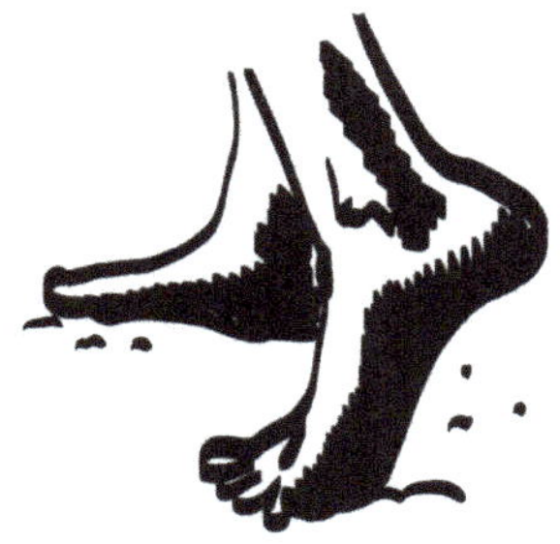

I heard the rumble of the garage door and the sound of my boyfriend's car. I tried to stand up quickly, but my butt stuck to the carpet and peeled away with a sickening sucking sound. Somehow my clothes had ended up all over the room and I couldn't get to anything fast enough. I spotted the towel, and wrapped it around myself just as the door opened, and my boyfriend walked in.

He carried his belt, and his shirt wasn't buttoned all the way. He stopped when he saw me, his face blank.

Hey.

I was shaking. I squeezed my legs together and gave him a tight smile. He walked into the kitchen and started humming while he heated some leftover pizza in the microwave.

I'm just going to hop in the shower, I told him.

He nodded at me, but something caught his eye. He walked towards me, and I started to panic, but he continued past me to the fireplace, where he picked my bra up off the floor.

I think this is yours, he said and tossed it to me.

My towel slipped and flapped open as I reached to catch it. I burned with shame, but he seemed too busy picking up dirty glasses and dishes to notice. As he walked back to the kitchen, he said over his shoulder,

It's time for you to go home, don't you think?

* * *

I got too tired to pace the sidewalk anymore. When I sat back down on the bench I leaned over and heaved up a brown stream of Super-Sized Coke and some of the leftover pizza I ate at my ex-boyfriend's place. Looking closer, I saw a smattering of little ovals of undigested Ibuprofen bobbing in the puddle of my vomit.

I wiped my mouth with the back of my hand and spied movement across the street—a white dog of some kind, loping low to the ground. She stopped to stare at me, and we watched each other, both of us wary. She looked like a terrier mixed with a greyhound, a short racer's body covered with wiry fur scraggly with dirt. She seemed more curious than rabid, and I whistled to her. Her ears twitched up, then back, and when I called out soothing words, she cocked her head and trotted daintily towards me. She paused in the dead center of the street, and I panicked, fearful that some car would mow her down. But I coaxed her, and she crossed the rest of the way to me. I tried to pet her head, but she ducked away, and I spoke softly, holding my hand out for her to sniff. When a car pulled up, she bolted a few feet up the

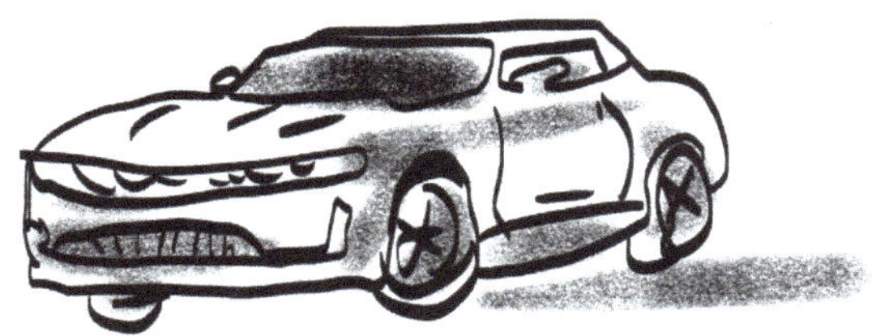

sidewalk, skittish and watchful.

It was the man I had called. He rolled down the window and said my name. He seemed bleary-eyed, hunched over the steering wheel of his dented, navy blue Toyota Tercel, the same tiny car he drove the last time I saw him. I stood up, slowly, my body sore from the hard bench, and still bruised in places from the night before. The man said my name again and I walked toward the car. With my hand on the passenger door handle, I hesitated, and turned to look at the dog, whose tail started a slow, rhythmic wag. The man leaned over and tried to keep the irritability out of his voice as he said,

Hey—we should get on the road. I'm pretty tired.

I opened the door, but remained standing, indecisive.

Is there a problem?

No, sorry, sorry.

I opened the door and slid in, sinking with a sigh into the seat. The old, torn pleather felt luxurious after sitting on a wooden bench for so long. As we pulled away from the curb, he placed a hand on my knee, and squeezed it reassuringly.

It's great to see you.

I smiled weakly in his direction.

It's good to see you, too. I've had a rough one.

Are you okay?

Much better, now.

Good.

He pulled up to the red light and glanced at me.

I've got roommates at the new place, but my bedroom is much bigger than my old one in the dorms.

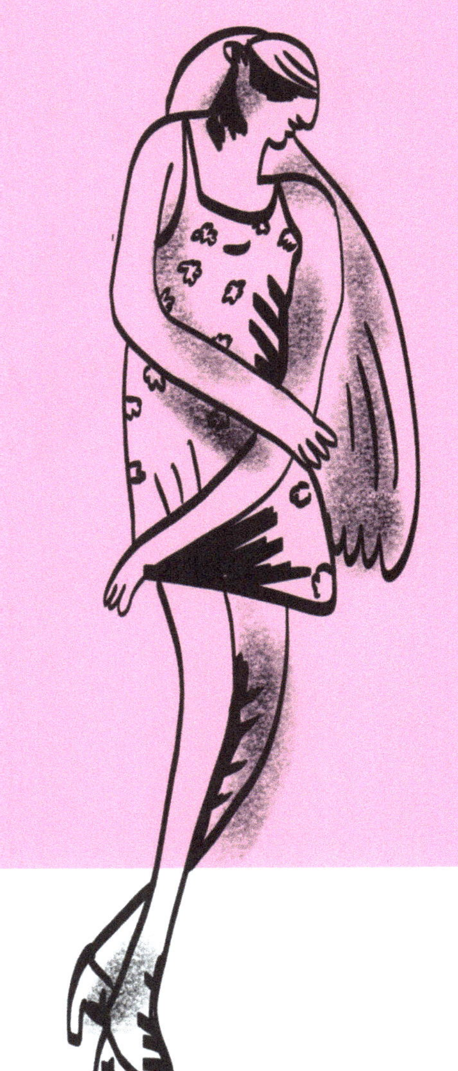

I turned to look back as the dog approached the bench where I had been sitting. I wondered if I should tell him about the ibuprofen, or any of the other things that happened. When he'd called me the week before to wish me a happy sixteenth birthday it was the first time I'd heard from him in almost a year, so I didn't know where we stood with each other.

The dog sniffed at the gutter, and in typical gross dog fashion, started lapping up my puke. Exhaustion washed over me as he moved his hand to my thigh, and the dog continued.

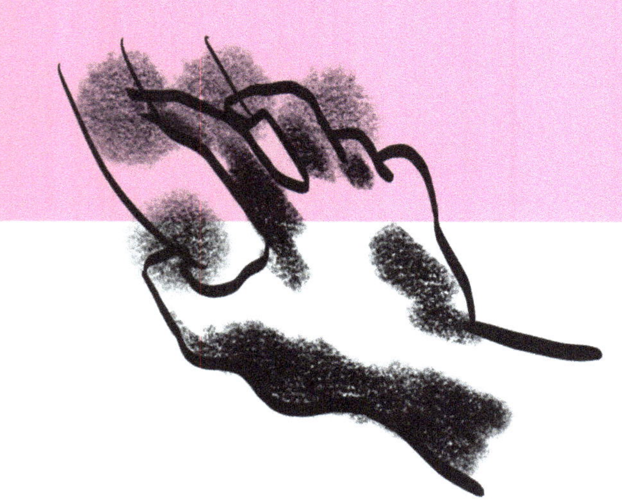

Stop, I screamed.

He snatched his hand away.

What the fuck?

We have to go back, we have to go back!

What? Why?

That dog's going to die.

What dog? That stray?

Yes, it ate something bad that's going to kill it. We have to go back.

It's a stray. Strays live on garbage, for fuck's sake. What's wrong with you?

I couldn't answer him. If I told him about the pills, I knew he'd take me back home, and I couldn't go back there. I couldn't take my parents' silent revulsion. I had no one to talk to, no one to see me, no one to even argue with. I felt like I was crumbling, pieces of me eroding away, until all that would be left was dust.

So, I said nothing, and lowered my eyes to watch the green lights of the digital clock on the dash grow blurry with my tears. The light changed, and he pulled over to idle outside the store where I had bought the ibuprofen, under the same sputtering streetlight.

Look, I know it's rough at home. And, I really do want to hang out, but you seem kind of messed up. Hysterical. I can't deal with something like that. I've got finals coming up. I think I should just take you home.

No, no, please don't. Please.

He remained quiet, and I stole

a quick look at his face. He stared into the street, and I couldn't read his expression. I placed a hand on his leg, and he looked down at my hand, but still said nothing

I've just had a really bad night; I need a friend. I need you.

He covered my hand with his own.

Okay. Can we get going, then? I came all the way out here because I was worried about you. No more screaming at the driver, okay?

I couldn't answer him. My head hurt from the remains of my hangover and all the crying and puking. The street looked like a post-apocalyptic dreamscape under the maddening flicker of the streetlight. If I spoke, I knew I would start screaming and I wouldn't be able to stop. Seconds, maybe minutes, passed. I focused on the slow rise and fall of my chest, reducing all of my thoughts to that movement alone, until, gradually, I returned to myself.

I looked back at the bus bench. The dog was gone, although I thought I saw a faint white blur receding in the darkness of the street.

I'm ready. Let's go. I want to see your new place.

Okay, then, he said, and smiled at me for the first time since I had gotten in the car.

Soon, we were speeding down the highway. He turned up the music to stay awake, and the fingers of his hand resting on my leg tapped along to the beat. I closed my eyes and tried not to think about the dog. I could have gotten out of the car. I could have run back and stopped her, but I didn't.

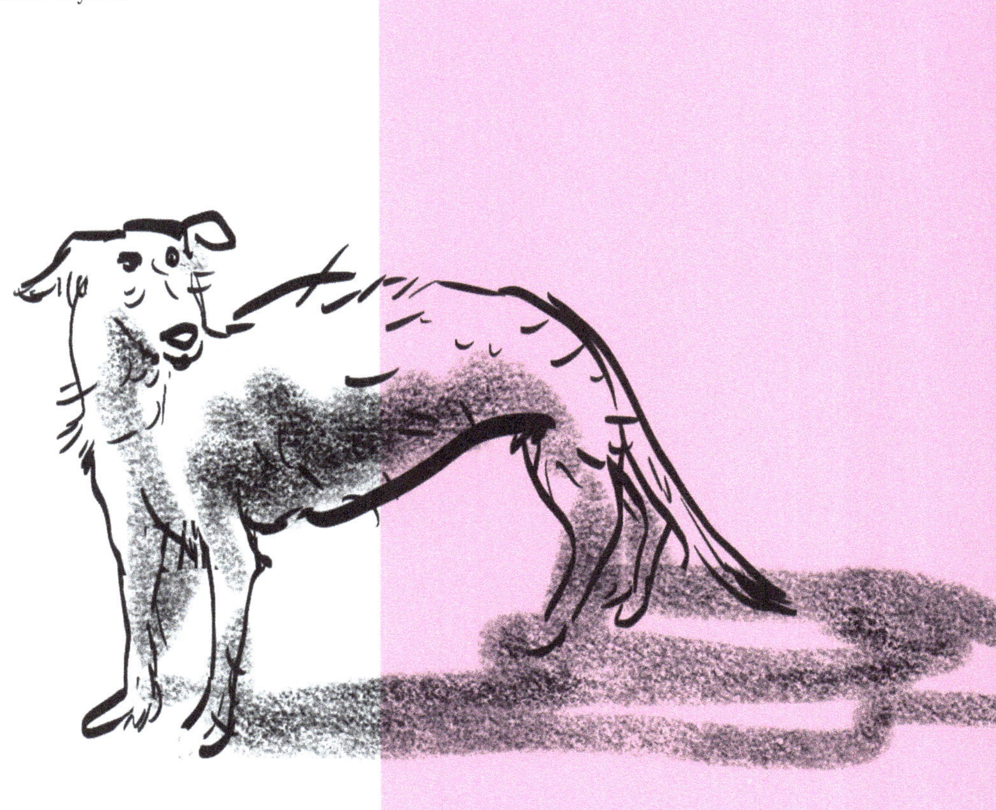

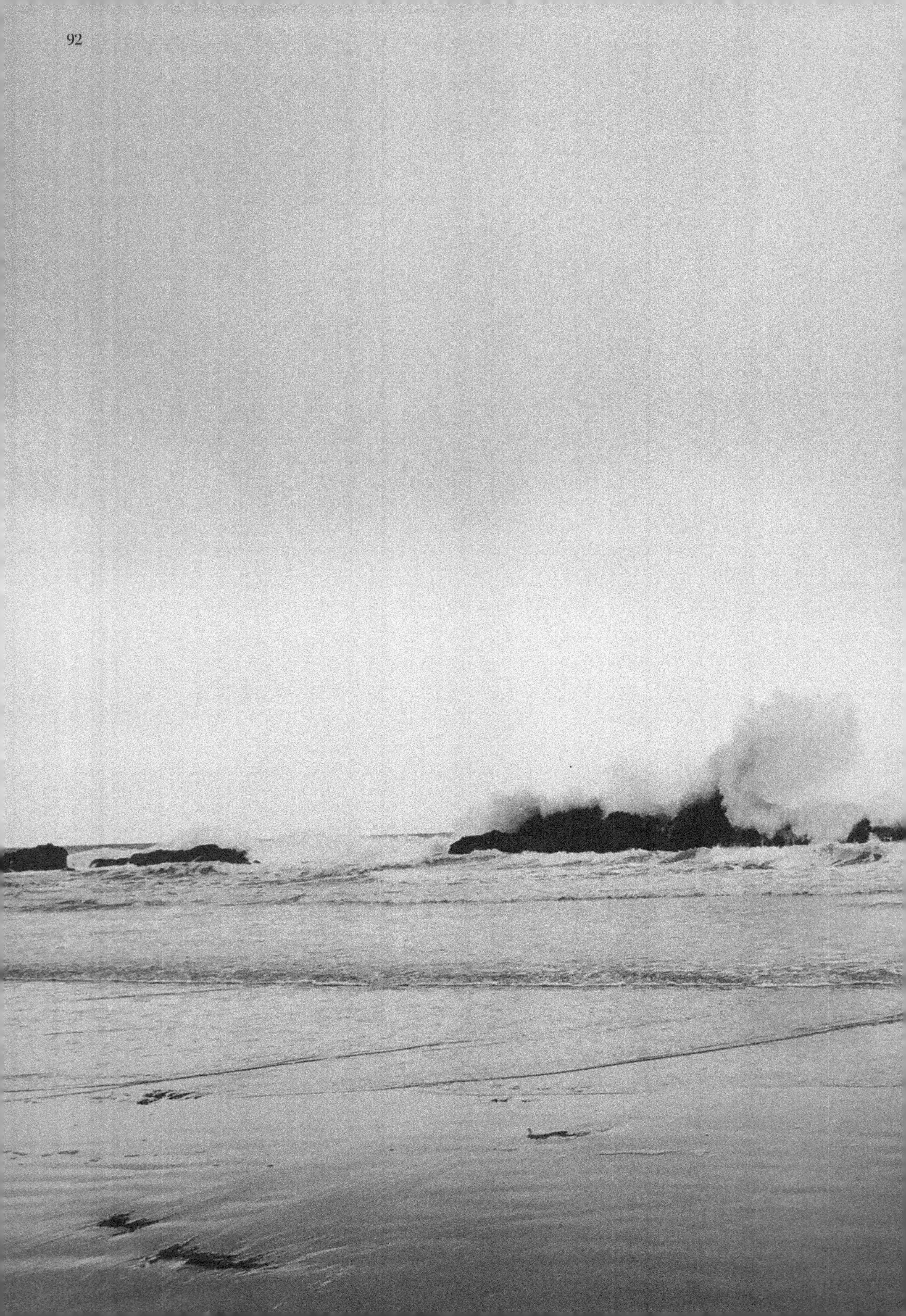

It's very simple, child. You are vast, like the sky.
You have light and dark in you.
If you fight the dark within, you tear yourself asunder,
split yourself in two. Don't begin a holy war within,
my precious one. Love the dark in yourself!
Honor it. Hold it gently. Flood it with the light of love.
Illuminate those wounded parts, those sore and tender
regions of your ancient heart. The darkness within you
only longs for the light, and the light within you longs
to touch the darkness. Fulfill an ancient promise
to illuminate an entire cosmos...

— Jeff Foster

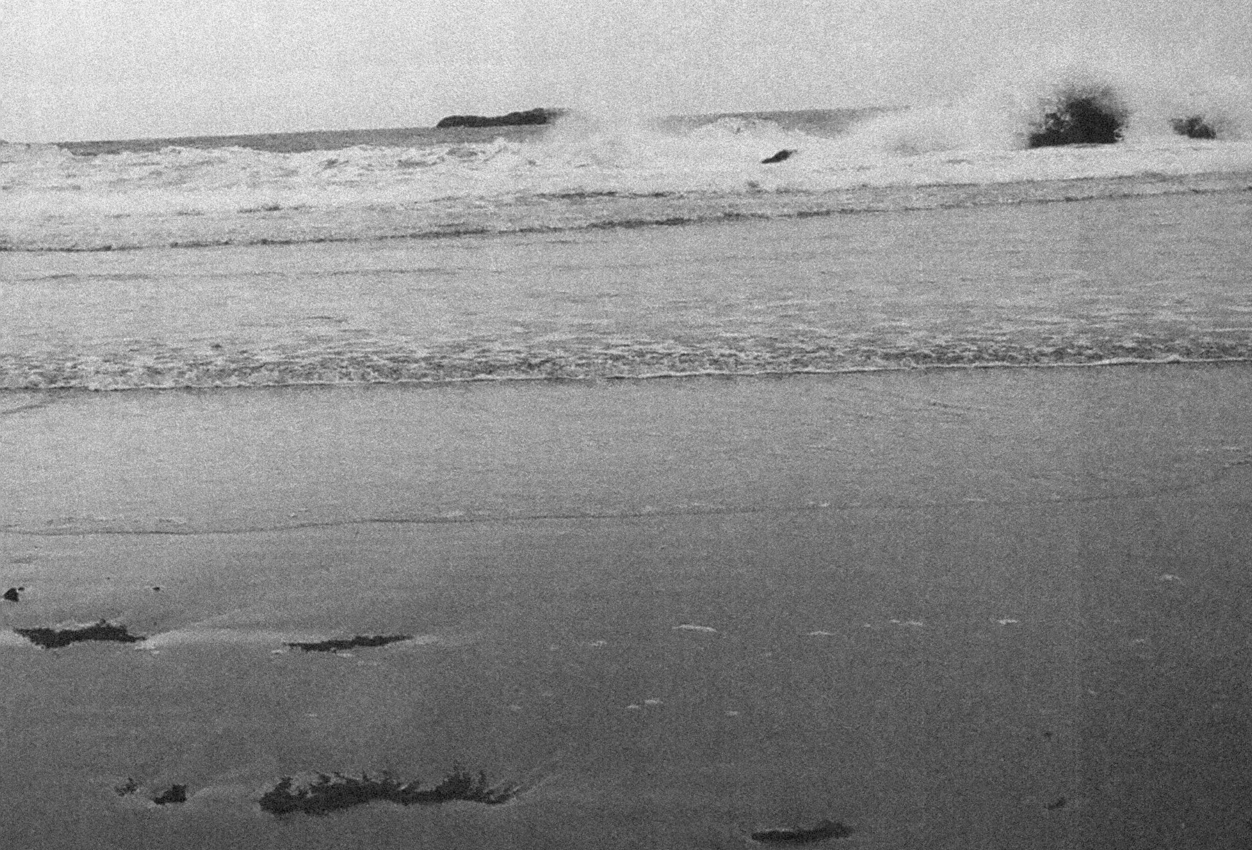

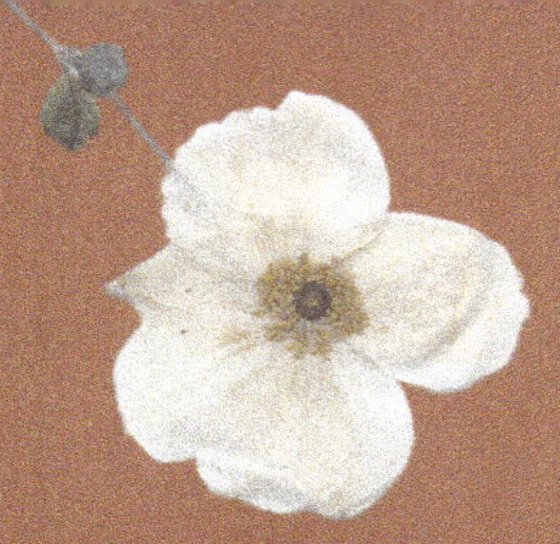

Ritual Poetry: For Self-Love

BY L. SPARKS

"Ritual Poetry: For Self-Love"
is a forthcoming recording with Head Room Sessions.

do not cut your skin
there has been enough blood letting
the Earth has had her fill

write the words "I love you" on your skin
write it again
                                   and again
write it 3x to remember
                                   you are worthy of love
write it to banish
the voices in your head
that speak things
other than love

                                   step into your skin
let love be your name
let everyone know love lives here

write the words "I love you"
when you start to forget

                                   say them like a prayer
                                   trace the word "love"
                                   onto your body 312x
with the tip
of your finger
and then with a leaf   or a flower   or blade of grass
   (any soft thing
      you are also softness
       you are also alive)
                                   REMEMBER you are a child of this Earth
you belong here
                                   write the word "belong" on your skin 13x
you are telling your body
it is safe to engage   in processes that heal
                                   you are changing the story

erase all other words
that have been written on your body
without your consent   the ones that burn

write "I love you" on your body
                                   again
                                   and again
                                   and again
don't forget YOU ARE A CHILD OF THIS EARTH
when no one says "I love you"   remember it is written in your skin

A Distant Knot

I feel a destructive sadness coming on, like a storm from the east that chases the sun to the west. It feels like a pang in the kitchen (in my stomach? in my heart?) as I remember that "nook" used to be a part of the body when we were together. That use of the word has been tainted for me. It certainly wasn't the first casualty. A large dollop of strawberry jam fell off my bagel earlier and onto the plate. I can't bring myself to eat it, and I won't. Especially since my sweetie isn't here and they can't say anything to me about wasting food. It was the very last of the jar. I took more than I wanted to so I could clean it out. All this is to say that I'm very excited to open the raspberry preserves.

The sadness pulls me to the bathtub like sirens on the ocean. It almost works but then I remember last weekend, alone in the house, sobbing as the water drained out.

What I'm omitting here—and it may be in good taste—is that I recorded four songs with my legs below sea level. It used to be that I could satisfy this feeling with words on a page but now they want my voice too. I am exhausted, mentally of course, because my eyes are itching and I'm running all the scenarios for what might happen this time. I don't want to take Benadryl. I don't want to but I will. My eyes feel like glass panes, sloppy with Windex. The wind beats against them until they dry. Streak-free shine. I wait for it.

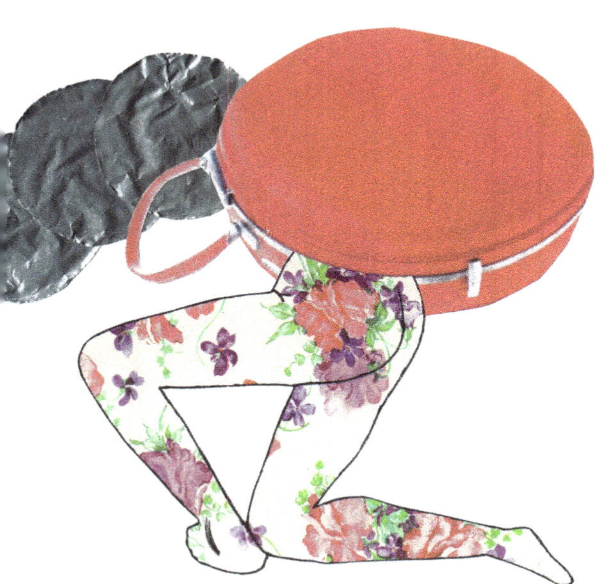

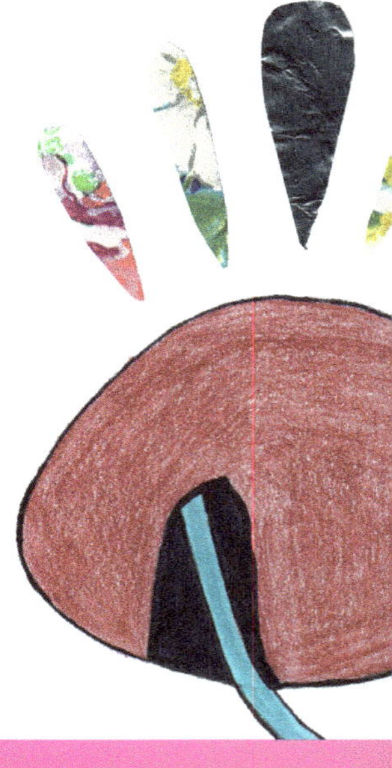

Art and Writing
by Emme Williamson

I run through my rolodex in my head but nobody's flavor will do: too chalky, too cloying, too 1997. I've felt so lonely today, why be such a picky eater now? It's not loneliness, it's fear. Not even a fear of being alone. It's a fear of what I'll find when I follow the call to make something, anything. My vulva is burning (again) and I refuse to take ownership. I leave this pink suitcase at baggage claim at LAX, around and around, its lining soft and smoke-filled. By the time it's returned to me the lidocaine will have kicked in. Comfortably numb.

I'm angry that I remembered something about you earlier today and I was sad because I thought I resolved this issue yesterday. I expressed gratitude for my past unraveling in all the ways it did, which included you. I don't regret the breakup, I only wish I could have done it "better." I'm too tired to go into what that means.

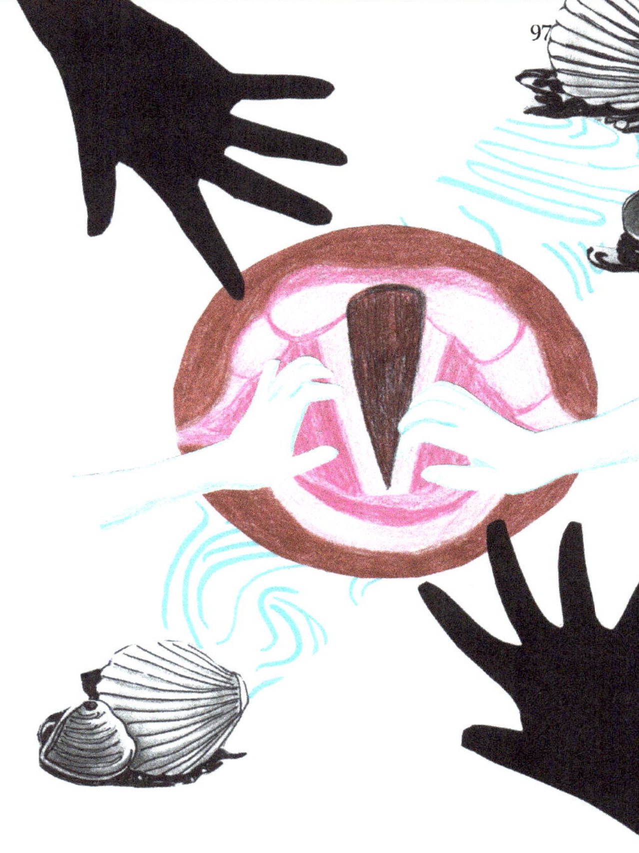

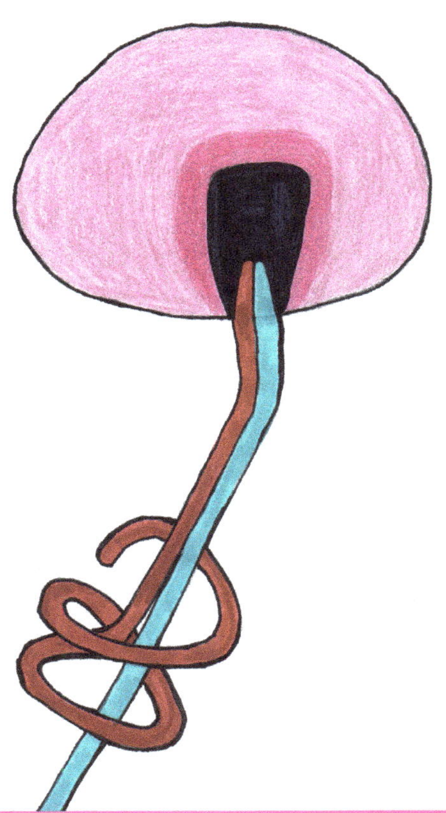

What matters is that I'm here now. Although I do sometimes feel a thread from this poly-blend yarn pull suddenly. I figure you must be yanking my memory around. I rarely take any interest in the belief that this pull could come from me. It used to send me into a panic, or down the candy aisle, but now it mostly makes my eyes well up. It's a hollow feeling. The questions I send it echo through our empty bungalow. I've driven by it a few times but never truly believe anyone else lives there now. They are the holograms, not us. It feels weird to put our selves together like that, in a word, "us." I sit with this feeling that comes and goes. I rather wish it would just stay gone but I learned a lot in our union and our disillusion. I'm still making sense of all of it. Maybe the "pull" is the tension released from a distant knot untied. I pretend we celebrate it separately, together.

what is one hope you have regarding healing?

That some day a medicine or behavioral technique will quell the noise in my head. —DW .... That we all start to take more time to recognize when we are struggling and take the time we need to heal. Instead of ignoring our pain because it is an obstacle keeping us from being productive and our best self, we pause and sit with it, and ask for help from ourselves and loved ones. —RS .... That I accept and allow the wholeness of myself (and others) —RZB .... That we hold space for all the facets of what healing can be and that we hold people accountable with brave love. —G .... That healing has a butterfly effect, and can bring healing an entire continent away. -JC .... That I stay focused and patient enough for transformation. —TH .... That we can make a collective cultural shift toward practicing it. —KH ....That my healing will not be isolated or individual. —AC .... Getting to a point where I can help others heal. —ZN ....

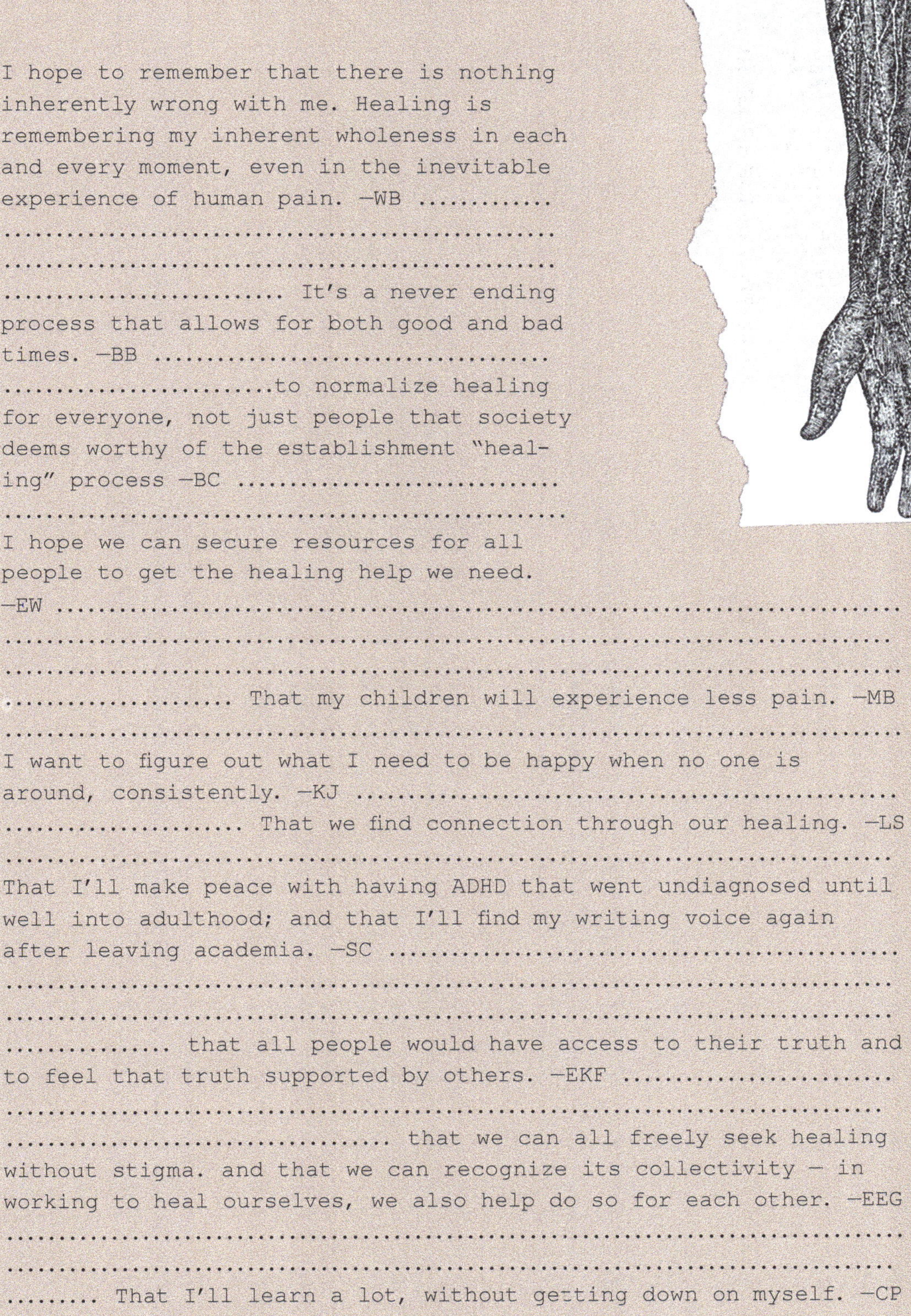

I hope to remember that there is nothing inherently wrong with me. Healing is remembering my inherent wholeness in each and every moment, even in the inevitable experience of human pain. —WB .... It's a never ending process that allows for both good and bad times. —BB ....to normalize healing for everyone, not just people that society deems worthy of the establishment "heal- ing" process —BC .... I hope we can secure resources for all people to get the healing help we need. —EW .... That my children will experience less pain. —MB .... I want to figure out what I need to be happy when no one is around, consistently. —KJ .... That we find connection through our healing. —LS .... That I'll make peace with having ADHD that went undiagnosed until well into adulthood; and that I'll find my writing voice again after leaving academia. —SC .... that all people would have access to their truth and to feel that truth supported by others. —EKF .... that we can all freely seek healing without stigma. and that we can recognize its collectivity — in working to heal ourselves, we also help do so for each other. —EEG .... That I'll learn a lot, without getting down on myself. —CP

BY CARISSA BUGANAN

What is a recipe that makes you feel good?

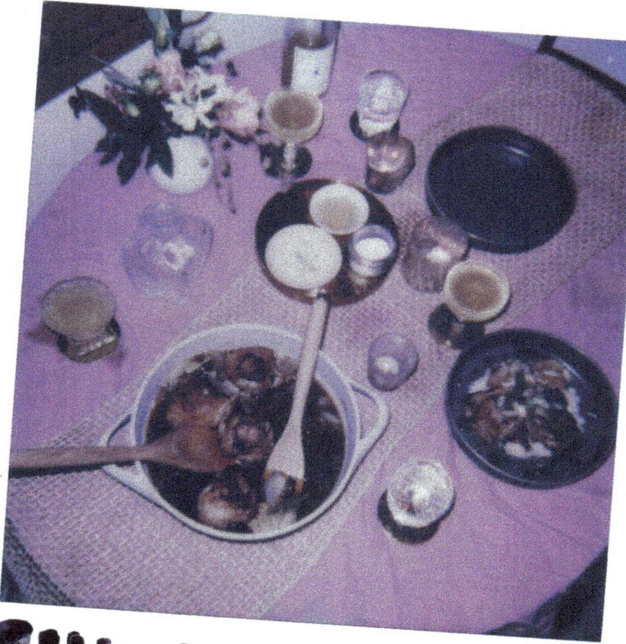

For most immigrant families one tends to grow up around a kitchen. While that may be true for my family and me; that is not where my love of cooking began. It came out of necessity. Don't get me wrong, I loved eating my family's meals, but it was never on my agenda to actually learn how to cook the meals that my family so carefully crafted for me. I left that to the pros.

Being a second-generation Filipina African American, my mother really tried her best to make sure my upbringing was as "normal" for an American girl as it could've been. Somehow learning how to cook got lost in the sauce. I'm sure it was due to the fact that my interests lied heavily with boys and fashion and more boys.

When I moved into my first apartment whilst in college,

I quickly realized I truly had never made a meal for myself outside of reheating my family's delicious leftovers and the occasional sandwich. So that necessity I never minded quickly turned into a passion, and I realized maybe I did pick up on a few more family kitchen secrets than I thought I did. The more I cooked the more I wanted to know. The more I knew, the more I wanted to cook. It was all-consuming.

Fast forward through college and culinary school, I'm still obsessed with cooking, but now the passion is retrieving old family recipes and learning how to make new Filipino dishes. So in honor of Filipino American History Month, I thought it was only right to make what is arguably considered the national dish of the Philippines: Chicken Adobo!

INGREDIENTS:

Olive oil (enough to sear chicken and veggies)
Course ground salt
5 bone-in chicken thighs
⅓ cup soy sauce
⅔ cup apple cider vinegar
5 tsp of sugar
¼ cup of water
2 whole heads of garlic
5 bay leaves
½ yellow onion
Scallions to garnish
Half of a handful of black peppercorns
Tongs
10″ or 12″ skillet

INSTRUCTIONS:

The first step is to always wash your hands.

Then I like to start by whisking together the soy sauce, vinegar, sugar, and water in a bowl. Then you'll want to prep your yellow onion and garlic. I like big chunks of each of these vegetables in this dish, so I prefer a rough chop of the onion and one single slice horizontally down the middle of the whole head of garlic and I call it good. After that, you will want to salt both sides of the chicken liberally with coarse salt. This will help you to develop a nice crust on your chicken.

Once all prep is done, you'll want to start warming up your skillet with olive oil to a medium-high heat. While that's warming up, this is the time to get your rice rinsed a few times and cooking because you can't eat Chicken Adobo without rice!

My method of making rice is all about intuition. I eyeball the amount of rice, rinse until the water runs nearly clear, and then cover with water. The way to do this is to place your finger in the pot and measure the amount of water that rises above the rice using the first segment of your middle finger. It should be even with that line in your skin. Then leave the rice to cook at the same time as the adobo. If this intimidates you, just cook your rice according to the directions on the package. I use the same rice cooker my Lola brought to Oregon when she first moved here. I work with real low-tech equipment sometimes, so that could be why this technique is more instinctive than anything. A rice cooker is non-negotiable/staple in any Filipino household, so I definitely recommend investing in one to make all your rice dreams a reality.

By now, your skillet should be warm enough to throw in those chicken thighs skin side down. Leave them like this until you see a nice golden brown color. This will help to lock in flavor.

Now that we have achieved a golden brown color on our skin, it's time to flip the bird and add in our yellow onion, our garlic, our peppercorn, and bay leaves. Doing this step now helps to release their aromas and flavors so they don't get overwhelmed by our soy and vinegar sauce once we add that liquid in. Let these ingredients sear off all together until the other side of the chicken has browned off properly, and then it's time to add our soy and vinegar mixture. Get the liquid to a boil for about 5-10 minutes and then reduce to a medium-low, cover with lid, and let simmer for about 40 minutes.

After about 40 minutes, the chicken should be cooked all the way through. At this point, I like to warm up another skillet or cast iron if you have it so I can sear off the chicken one last time to get a crispy skin.

Once you've done that, this next step is optional, but you can take half of the remaining liquid left in the skillet and reduce over medium-low heat into a thicker sauce to drizzle over your chicken and rice.

Put some rice in a bowl with a chicken thigh or two (bonus points if you get some onion and garlic bits in).

Drizzle in some of that reduced sauce and garnish with the scallions and you have my perfect Chicken Adobo recipe. Enjoy.

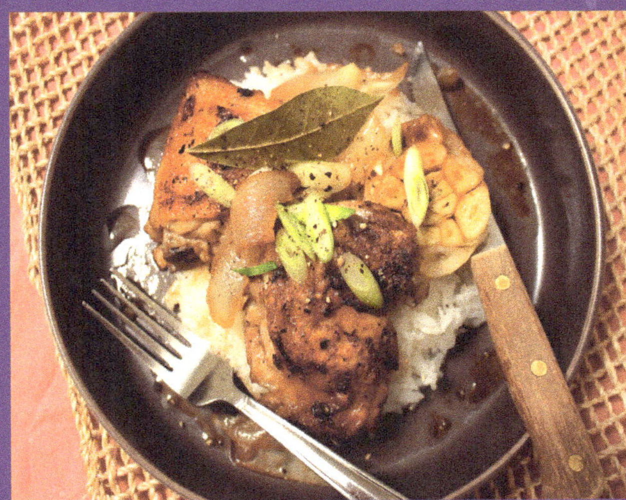

SOUL
INVOCATION

During a meditation, I connected with an embodiment of my Soul. In our exchanges, I asked questions like, *"What messages do you have for me? What might I fear in you that is actually profound?"*

From this conversation with the embodiment of my soul, I created an invocation to my Soul, my Self, and the world. As I spoke the words aloud, my body naturally gravitated toward different positions and placement of my hands. This watercolor series was born from the words and embodiment that longed to be painted! Through creating and practicing this invocation to my Soul and the world, I've felt deep somatic healing and integration.

I hope that this series serves the world in some way.

BY WILLOW BROOK

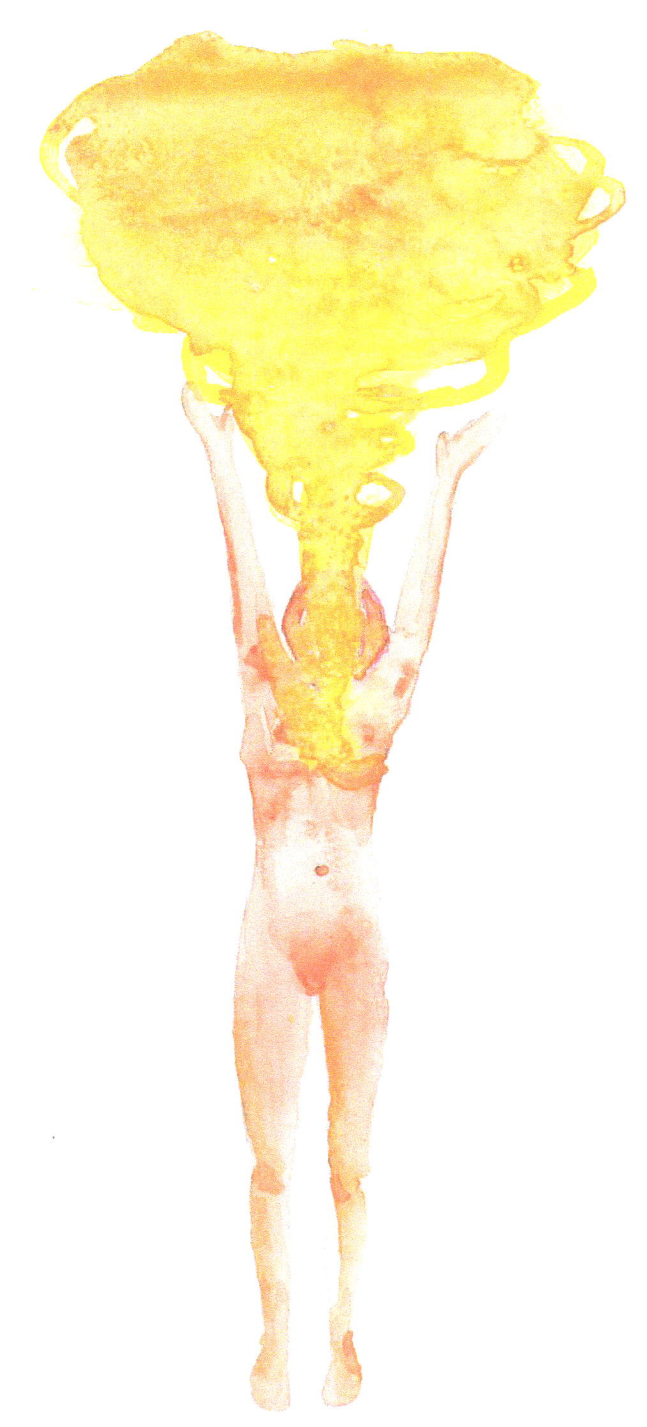

I WELCOME ALL PARTS OF
MYSELF BACK TO MY BODY

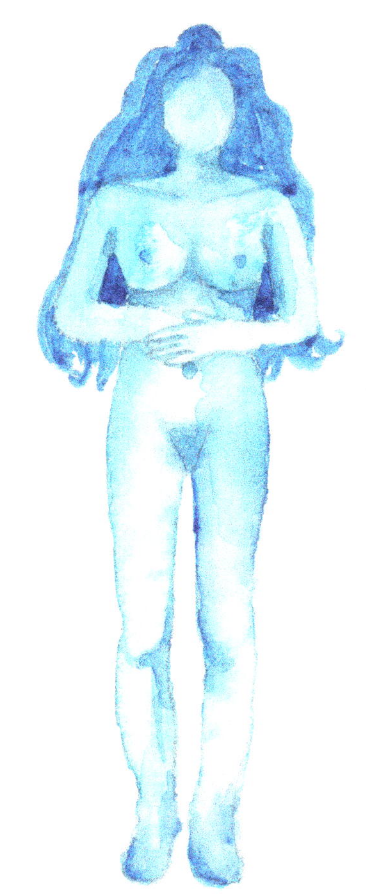

I   TRUST   MYSELF

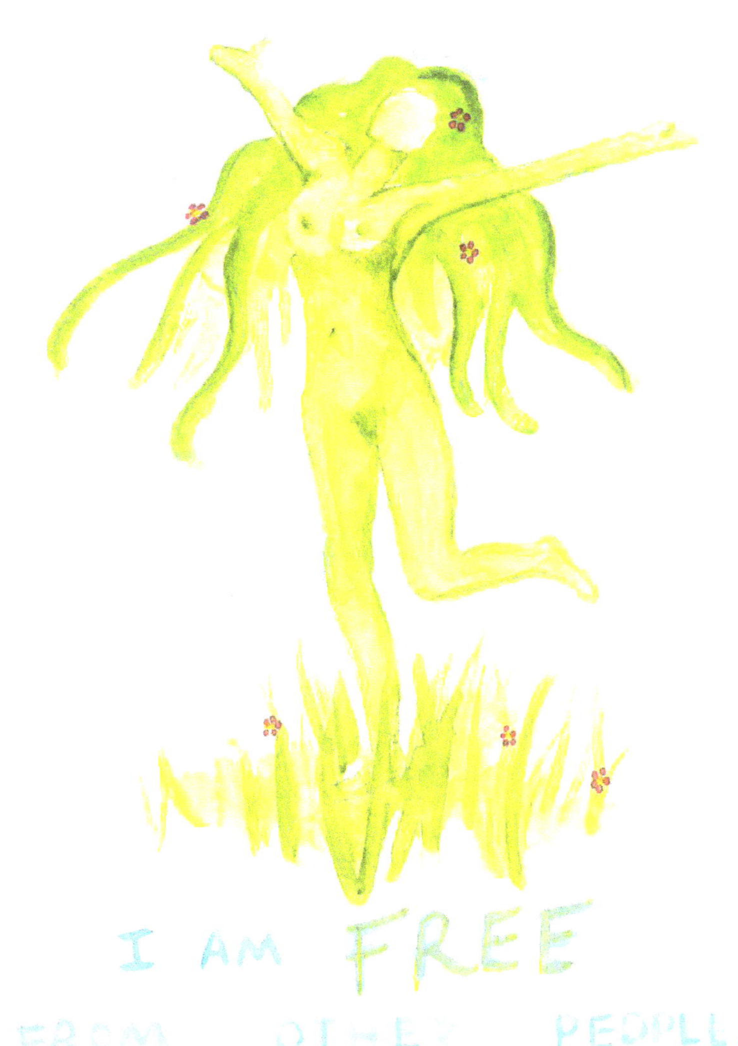
I AM FREE
FROM OTHER PEOPLES
EXPECTATIONS OF ME

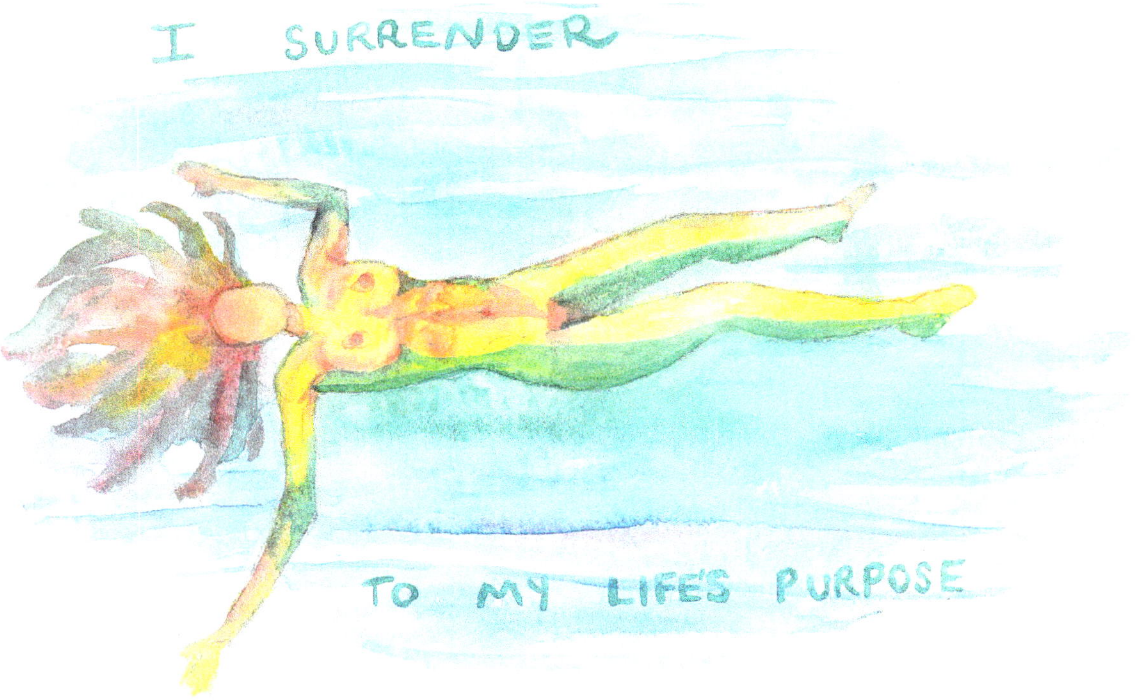

I SURRENDER
TO MY LIFE'S PURPOSE

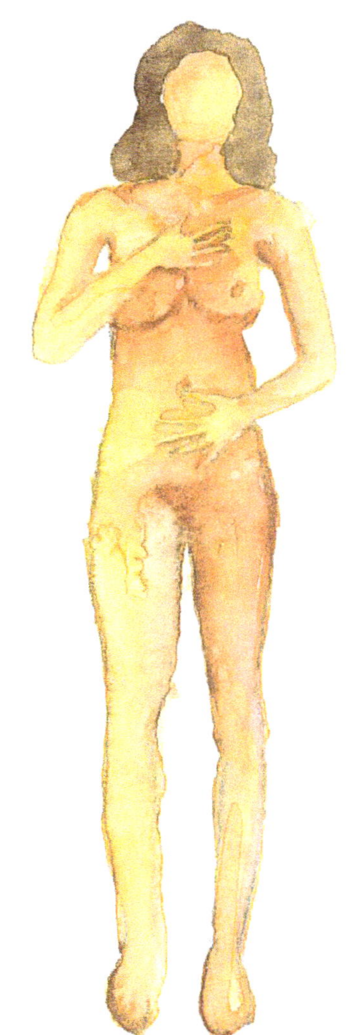
I AM GROUNDED AND
AT EASE IN MYSELF

I AM PROUD OF MY BOUNDARIES

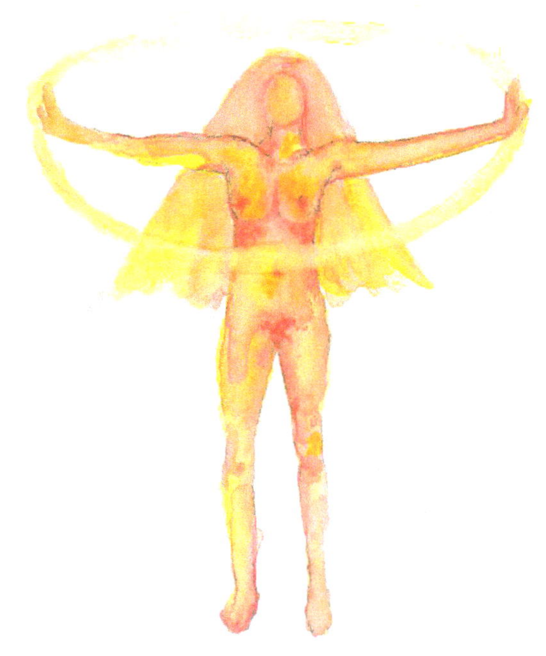

I AM STANDING TALL

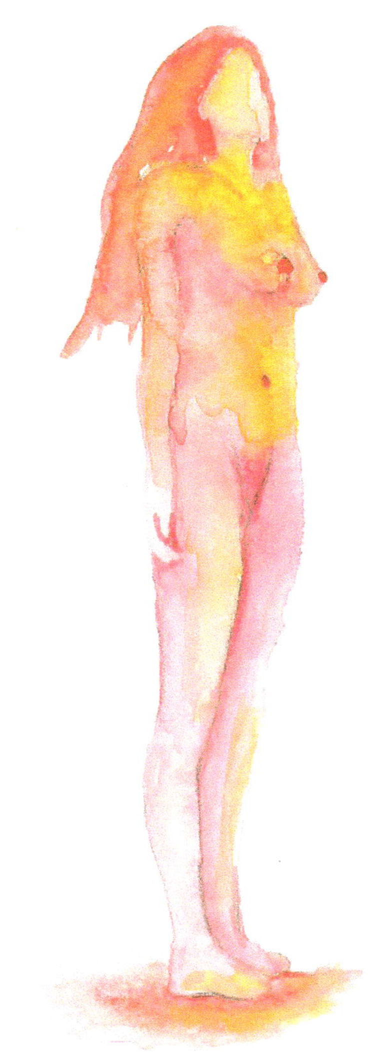

IN MY INHERENT POWER

Returning to the Things
We Have Always Known

Go back to the bridge
Back away from the knife
       you do not need to live in fragments
Let wholeness be your name

Go back to the joining
The union-the-link-the-connection
       you do not have to be lonely
You are strange (& so is everyone)

Go back to the dance
The sculpting   the movement   the growth
       you are not stagnant
You are alive & ecstatic & dynamic

Go back to the ancestors
To the Earth   to the knowing   to the dreams
       you are someone's prayers answered
Your body means survival

Go back to joy
The pleasure   the desire   the longing
       you deserve to enjoy life's ecstasy
Your body does not equate suffering

Go back to the mountain
The magnitude   the vast   the unanswerable
       you are also the mystery
Not everything needs explanation

Go back to the path
The way through & out
       your heart knows the way
the bottom of your soul is tender with knowing

Go back to your voice
The words that comfort & hold you
       the things your elbow-hands-eyes say
the lexicon of the body (1)

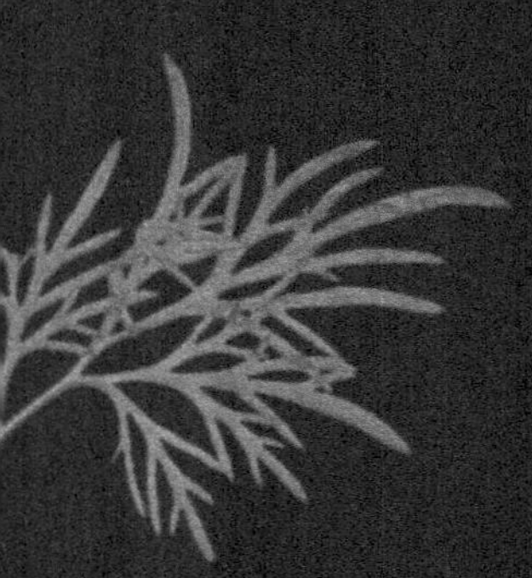

---

(1) Diaz, Natalie, "A Lexicon of the Indigenous Body: Images of Autonomy and Desire," Los Angeles Review of Books, December 8th, 2017, https://lareviewofbooks.org/article/a-lexicon-of-the-indige-nous-body-images-of-autonomy-and-desire/.

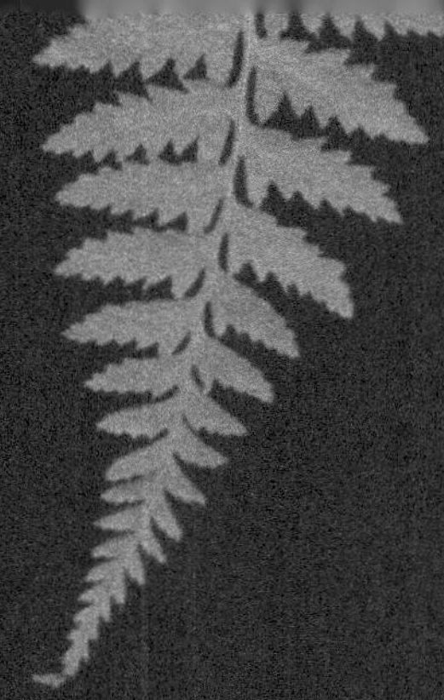

BY L. SPARKS

Go back to remember
your body inside the water
            the womb-the soil-the fire
You are not so separate

Go back to expansion
You are multiplicity
            you are all the turns of a song

I dreamt I was swimming in a sea

of stars – following all the others
when I realized   that path   was not for me

I swam away and the stars trembled
in applause

I swam my own way through another
sea of stars

& I was afraid

But the child in me already knew the way
I dreamt I was myself   but in a different life

~

We are not so separate.
Tell me the ways you want to be loved.
Tell me the ways to hold a moment with you.

Can we know the sacred?
Can we know peace?
Can we know love?

Can we know   we will never know   all there is to know?

Can we accept the blank pages and fill them with our own beautiful
imprints of the body?

I am getting close to my own print   my own song   my own voice

How must we feel alive?

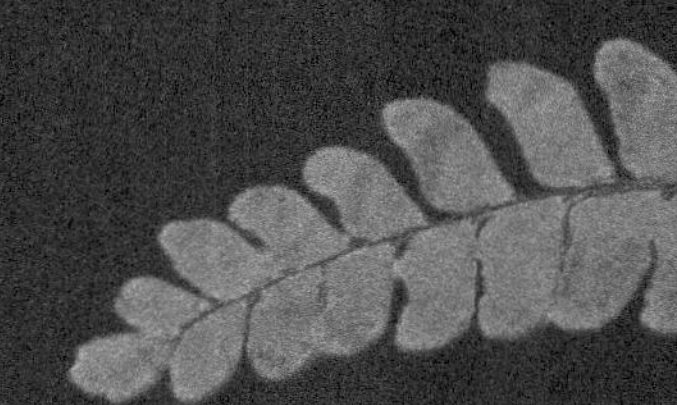

Falling Open

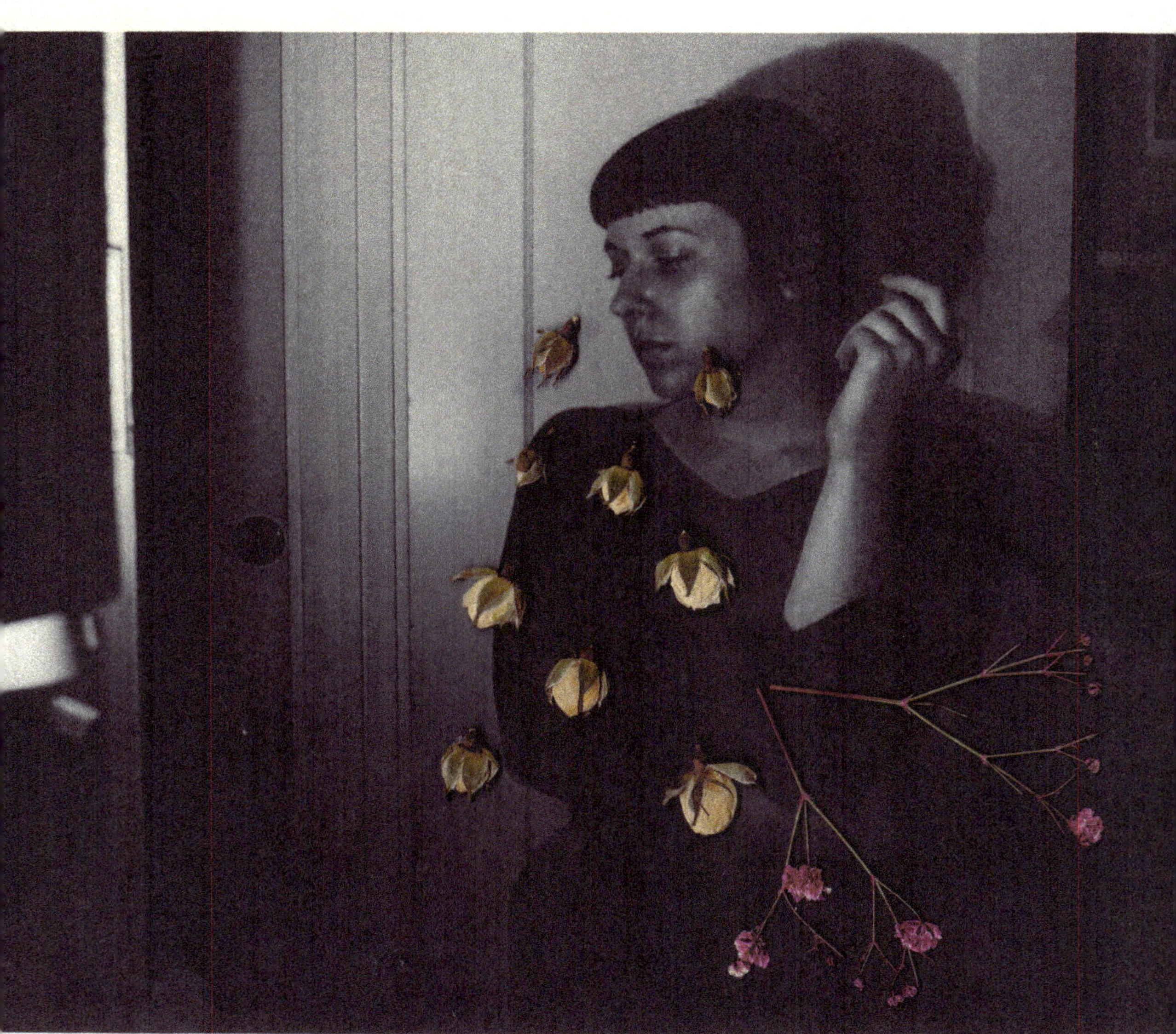

BY SHARON E. CROWLEY

I remember the moment when I knew my marriage would end.

We had just gotten home from a trip. First, we visited my husband's family in Chicago, and then we went to see my friend Tim in Joplin. I had consumed a 20 oz bottle of Coke during our flight back to Burlington, so I was wide awake. It was summer, and I had just finished the first year of my MA program at UVM. I was studying for my qualifying exams and preparing to start my thesis on the rise of the novel. I decided to stay up to read and write. I got lost in the work, in the quiet stillness of the house.

Around 2 AM, I looked up, and he was *there*, in the doorway. I didn't know how long he'd stood there. He demanded to know why I hadn't come to bed. I couldn't tell if he'd been asleep and woken up to find me missing or if he'd been awake the whole time. He accused me of chatting online with Tim. I hadn't been, and I said so. He said, "You're lying." I offered to show him my screen so he could see for himself. Instead, he listed every misstep I had made in Joplin, ticking each one off on his fingers. The worst one: I had paid more attention to someone else than to him. He was sure that I was planning to cheat on him, perhaps already had.

He continued hurling accusations. I repeated my refrain: "You're wrong. No. It wasn't like that. We're friends, that's all." Around and around. I felt dizzy and nauseated. I don't remember raising my voice, but I probably did. Finally, he said, "Maybe we should just get divorced." We stopped, both of us at once. All I could hear was the whisper of the CPU's fan and my own breath.

He had dropped this line before, during other arguments. There were many. I only remember some of what we fought about. What I've held onto is the memory of how I felt when we argued: to blame. Face hot, chest tight, heart pounding, abandoned, failing. He wouldn't or couldn't believe anything I said. He didn't trust me. *I was untrustworthy.* Why did I yell? Why couldn't I be more rational, less emotional? *I was unworthy.*

This argument was different. I felt calm. I was in no hurry to respond. We looked steadily into each other's eyes. In my head, I could hear the sound of a lock opening. As the last tumbler fell into place, the hasp released. A door creaked open.

"OK," I said, and that was it. He left. I was alone.

* * *

If he wrote the story of our divorce, I wonder where he would begin. If he started with that night, I wonder what he would say.

* * *

The next day, changes started coming fast. I painted my toenails blue for the first time ever. I took a picture of them while standing on the front porch. Erin, Dan, and Kate took me to a park in Vergennes. We swam in Lake Champlain and got stoned on Dan's marijuana. Two weeks later, Dan helped me move into a long, narrow apartment. Only the bedroom was square. The rest was all angled walls and awkward corners. There was no room for a couch (I didn't have one anyway.) But my dog and two cats were welcome, and the rent was affordable on my teaching fellow stipend. Best of all, the owner said I could move in immediately, and I could have the last two weeks of July for free. As we retrieved my things from what was now my ex's house, Dan asked if the television was mine. It was, but I didn't want it. I told him to leave it.

That was my first night in the apartment. Two weeks later, Tim came to visit. He had booked a hotel room, but he ended up staying with me.

* * *

In mid-August, I drove to Michigan to spend two weeks with my family. Tim came up from Joplin to see me. He stayed for two nights in a top floor room at the Amway Grand Plaza Hotel. I spent both nights with him. We fucked, got room service, and stayed up until 3 AM, looking out at our hometown.

I basked in this unexpected warmth. It was exactly what I wanted. I felt no hesitation.

* * *

I was going to cry. It was going to hurt.
There was nothing I could do about it.

My brother followed me back to Vermont. We drove in the dark in our separate cars. I was exhausted, and I got off the highway one exit too soon. I didn't realize my mistake until I approached the intersection where a left turn would take me to the house. His house, the one where I no longer lived. In that moment, I felt something enormous bearing down on me. A dragon. Instead of fire, it breathed grief against my skin, into my nose, down my throat, filling my lungs.

I was going to cry. It was going to hurt. There was nothing I could do about it.

* * *

Somehow, I kept my shit together. I led my brother to his hotel, waited in the lobby as he checked in. We said goodnight, see you in the morning, all smiles. My throat was tight. My skin registered every sensation as an assault. I drove home, parked, and made my way back to my apartment with my dog and my backpack.

Once inside, I closed and locked the door. My knees buckled. I collapsed on the floor. The loss of my husband burned through me: its irrevocability. It was the first time in two months that I'd thought of him in those terms: "my husband." I tumbled into the space where he had been.

For the first time, I wondered, "What have I done?" and "Why me?" A voice in my head whispered back, "You chose." And "Why not you?"

I stayed there for a long time, pressed flat against the floor. Gradually, the grief eased its grip. I opened my eyes. My dog was curled up next to me. He saw me seeing him and wagged his tail. I stood up. My apartment was quiet. Everything was just where I had left it.

* * *

The nature of divorce means that I only know my half of this story, and I can't even tell all of it. It's too complex. To tell the story, I have to choose. Choosing puts me on the path toward cherry-picking, which is a species of lying. Not choosing tangles everything up in complexity.

What is the truth? Whose truth? Can I be trusted to tell it?

Stories written from life are open-ended. Countless tributaries flow into and out of the main stream.

* * *

Somehow, my ex-husband knew that Tim and I had slept together. He framed it as a question, but it was a confrontation. I had no reason to lie. He wasn't angry. His face settled into an expression that looked like justification. My face burned, and I looked away. I refused to cry. He said, "I figured you would end up together."

We didn't. What had happened between Tim and me was a fling, a mistake. It hurt both of us. It almost ended our friendship.

Why did I let it happen? I beat myself up with the question, but I knew the answer: I had to nuke the bridge back to my marriage. What surer way?

I didn't expect the grief to be so hard. In truth, I didn't expect it at all. But here it was, presenting me with a stark choice: I could let it do its thing, or I could try to bury it.

I understood what it would mean to bury it. I had spent the last ten years shrinking the scope of my life down to the size of a postage stamp. I'd swallowed desire and ambition, downplayed friendships, and numbed my emotions - never quite enough - because expressing them always seemed to provoke a fight.

I could let it
do its thing, or
I could try to
bury it.

I had just emerged from that. I couldn't go back. If the road forward required me to pay this toll, I would.

* * *

I cried several times a day for six months. It didn't matter where or when. In one sense, this is remarkable.

When I was in kindergarten, I saw another kid get his fingers caught in a metal door. His face blanched, and he stared at his hand without making a sound. All the other kids stood in a circle, staring. A teacher rushed in and pulled the door, freeing his hand. The boy stepped back. Only then did he begin to cry. The teacher knelt down and tried to examine his fingers. Some of the other kids made fun of him. There I was, five years old, witnessing a cruelty that happens every day, on countless playgrounds just like that one. Right then, I vowed that I would never, ever cry in front of people again.

In another sense, this story is banal, clichéd: 30-something woman gets divorced after her first year of grad school. Blindsided by grief, she cries in public for the first time since kindergarten. She finds wisdom, perhaps redemption. *Remember, she is untrustworthy.*

* * *

I was walking south on Church Street, a pedestrian marketplace that runs through the heart of Burlington. I had just left the Crow Bookshop with a couple of novels tucked into a cloth bag: Daniel Defoe's *Robinson Crusoe* and Aphra Behn's *Oroonoko*, books on my reading list. I felt good. I had gone for a long run that morning, and I was looking forward to doing some work.

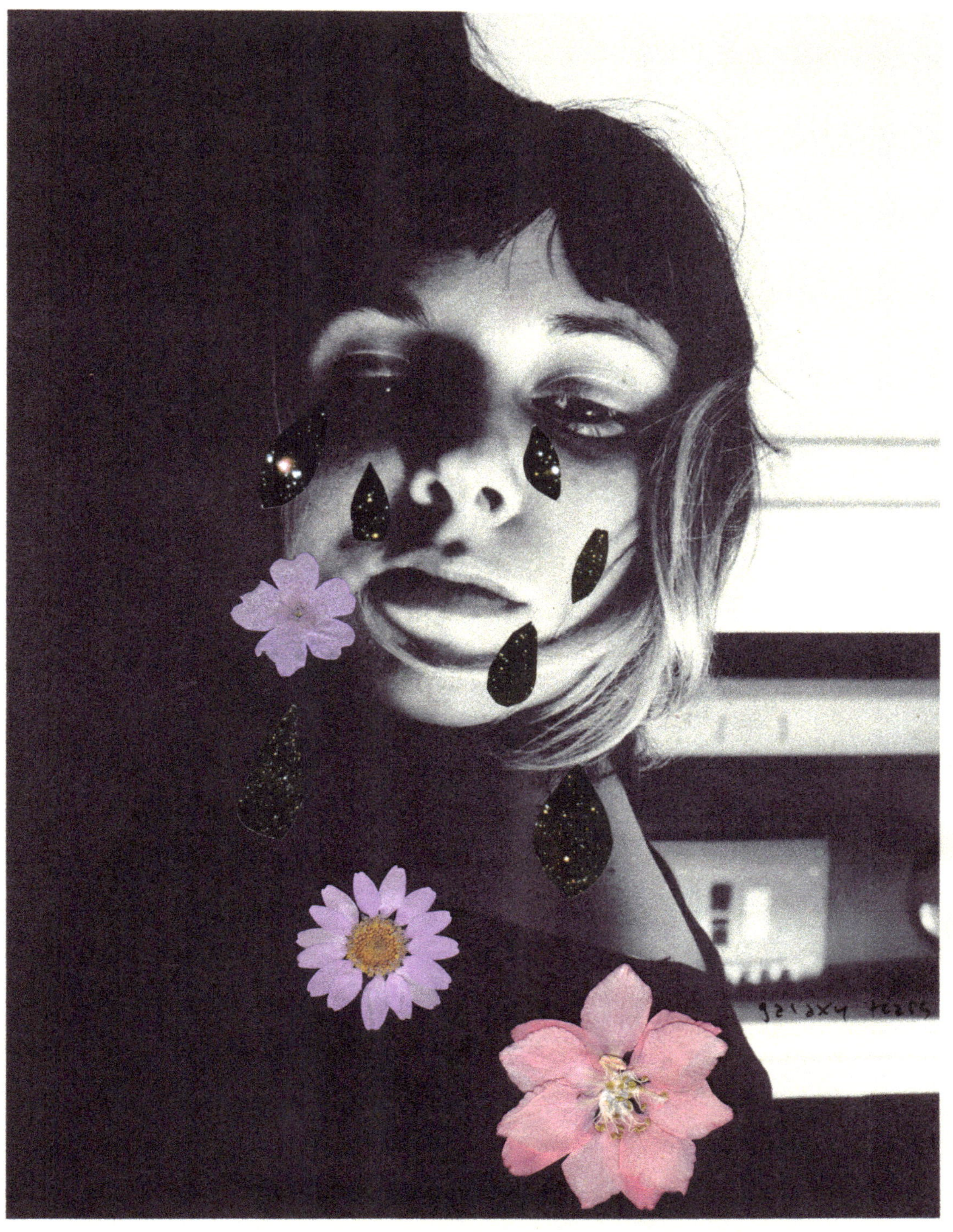
galaxy tears

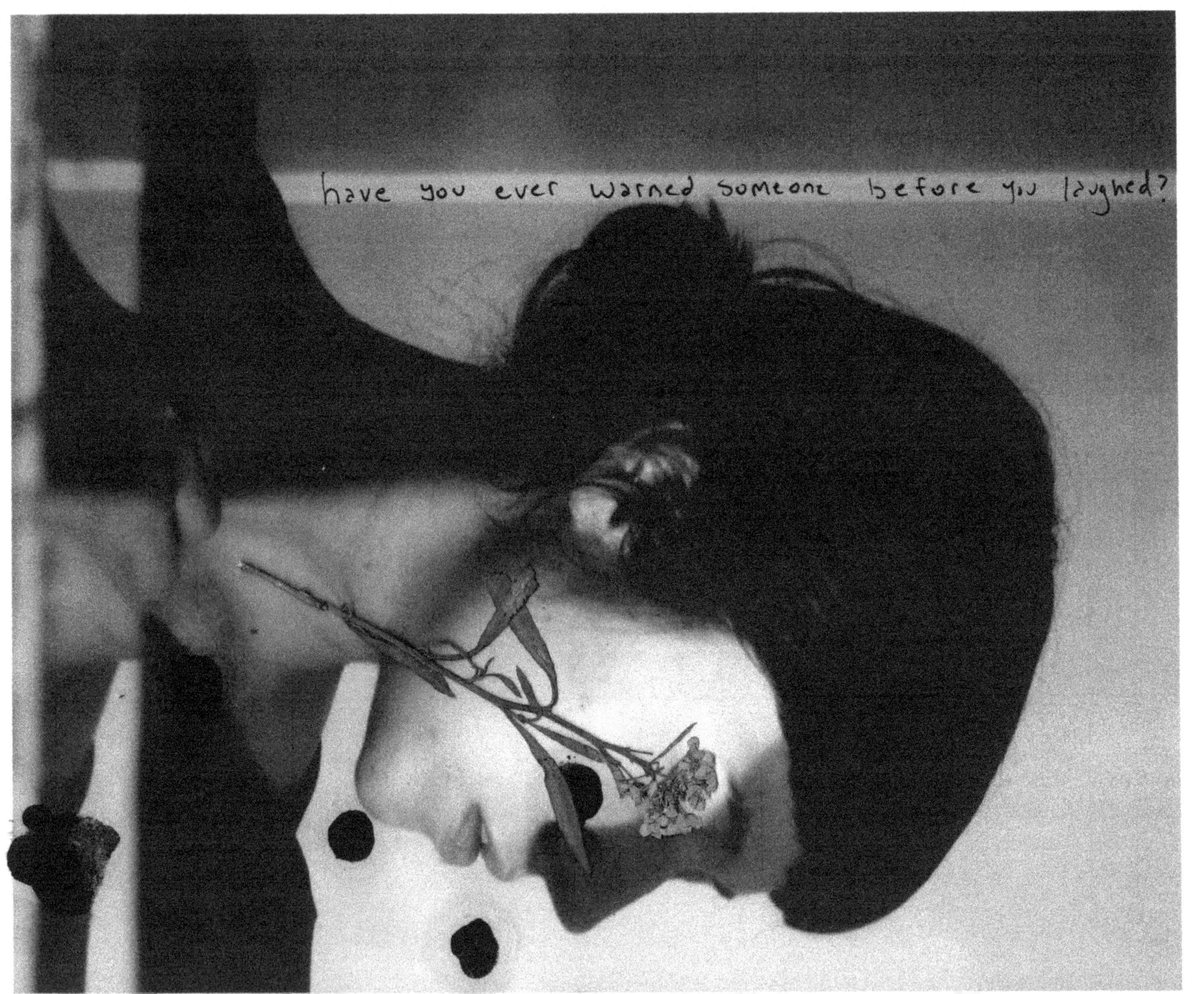
have you ever warned someone before you laughed?

I was happy, enjoying the sunshine, and just like *that*, I started to cry. I looked around for a place to hide, but there was nothing. I was already crying. My apartment was too far away. I stumbled to an empty bench and sat down. I stayed there, relatively quiet but with tears streaming down my face, for at least ten minutes. People walked past me: a woman with two children; an older man with a Labrador retriever holding its own leash in its mouth; teenagers carrying djembes, probably headed to City Hall Park to join the perpetual drum circle.

Many more people wandered past. I noticed every single one. Not one of them noticed me. Eventually, I stopped crying, dried my face with my sleeve, and started walking.

This may not seem like a happy memory, but it is. I felt naked and afraid to cry in public like that, but when I did, nothing happened. As I made my way home, vulnerability settled around me like a new skin. It was thinner than my old skin. Porous. It would not keep the grief out.

* * *

As I was unlocking my apartment door, a thought crystallized: *Just because he doesn't trust me doesn't mean I'm untrustworthy.*

* * *

In May, I was working in my apartment and realized I needed a book from my office. My apartment was situated on College St., which runs steeply uphill to the UVM campus. I loved the climb. That morning I was the only one out. It had rained the night before, so the sidewalks were wet. The early morning sky was clear, and the sun was just starting to warm the air.

Near the hill's crest, there was a stretch of sidewalk full of large holes carved by freezing and thawing winter ice. I felt irritated. *They need to fix the damn sidewalk,* I thought.

As I approached, something seemed strange. The pavement appeared to be moving. Fluttering. It took me a minute to comprehend: birds. The sidewalk pits were filled with rainwater. At least a hundred birds had gathered to bathe in these small pools, ducking their heads to drink and shaking their wings in the water. Scattered droplets gleamed in the morning light.

My irritation evaporated. I stopped and watched.

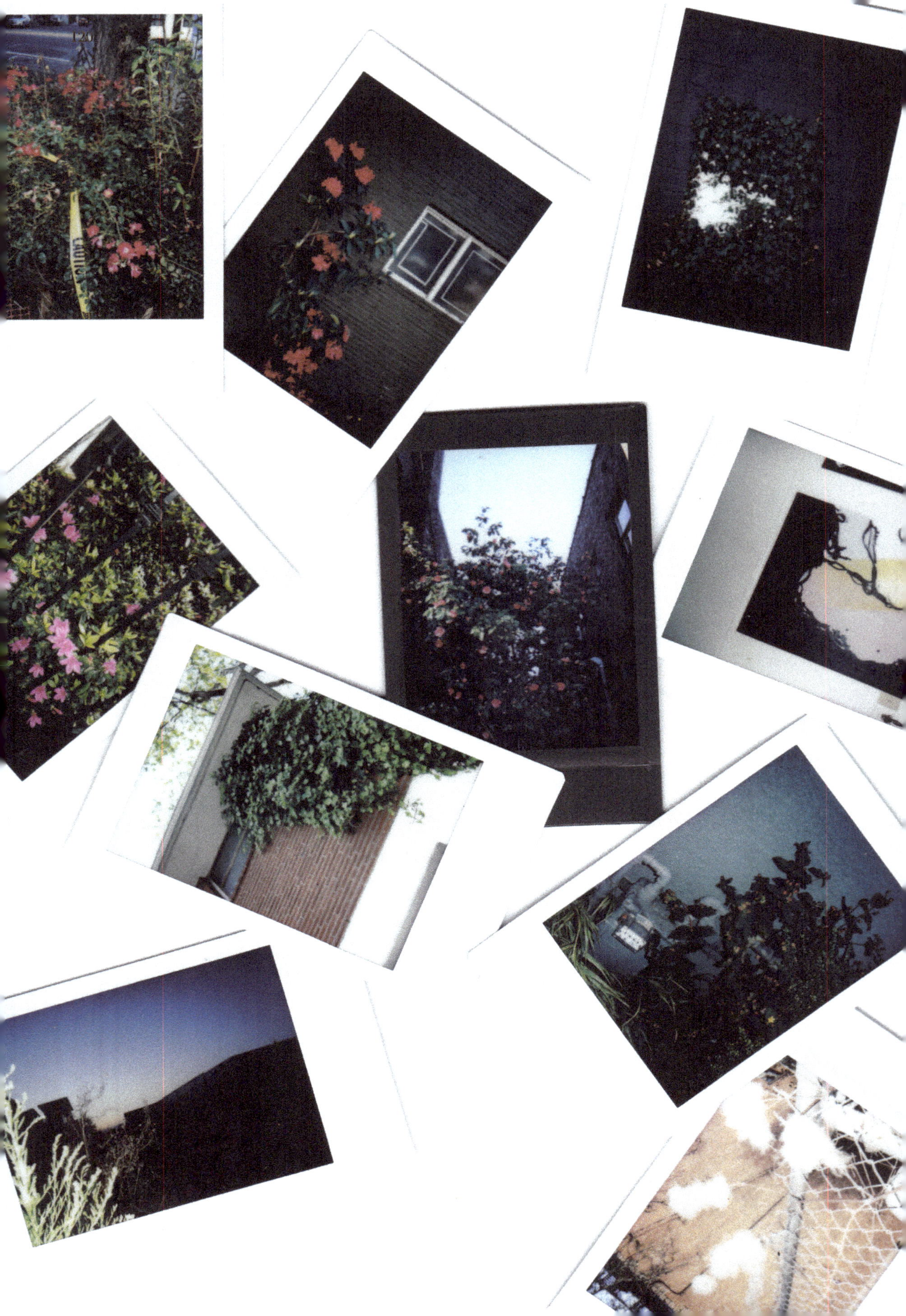

no need to shroud reaches
the wind will tell us when.

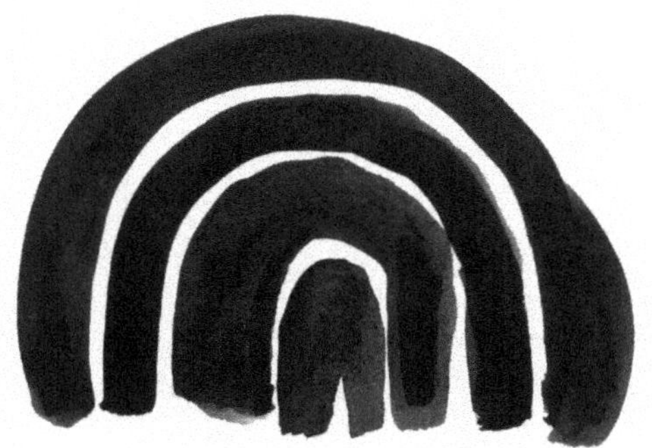

what personal rituals or remedies do you have for healing?

Take a moment to feel the weight of your feet at least once each day; and anytime your thoughts race or take you somewhere you don't want to be. —AC .... when i am struggling i imagine a friend or partner going through the same thing and treat myself with the same care i would give them. —KW .... 1. Breathe 2. Write. 3. Imagine. —JC .... Start by asking yourself, "who taught you how to be white?" —G .... Square breathing; journaling; running and hiking outdoors. —SC .... Daily and cyclical rituals are the foundation of my life. Spiritual practice as a way to start every day has given me stability and consistency from a reliable source — myself! Beginning my day with movement, breath, silence, and song brings me so much joy! Journaling is another important ritual for me to reflect and process, and I do rituals at the quarters of the year and significant life transitions. —WB .... I'm still working on this process, but journaling and moon charged baths help alot. —CP .... build practices that allow you to tolerate not knowing (which is living), be willing to ask "Is that true? how do I know? where do I feel that in my body? what's changing? what do I need? what do I have to give?" —EKF

....
....
Stretch first thing every morning. Bow to the directions (North, East, South, West, Above, Below, and Inbetween) and say good night to the world before bed every night. —RZB .... I get into cold water, a river or a mountain lake. Always focus on my breath. —TH .... Engaging with words that engender human connection, be they spoken, heard, seen, read, or written. —ZN .... stretch as soon as you wake up and right before you crawl into bed, talk to yourself and no one else for a full day, light things on fire and watch it burn until ash, jump into cold water, make a blanket fort. —BC .... cleansing in an ocean or waterfall. live music. meditation. —EEG .... Setting firm boundaries & centering gratitude —LS .... Practice floating in a body of water. Feel your stomach soften. When the tightness (re)emerges focus on the breath. Notice how your breath keeps you alive, keeps you floating. At this point I remind myself that I'm safe and supported. Return to this memory whenever desired. —EW .... Laying on the ground and snuggling with my cat Pepperjack. —RS .... Meditation. Yoga. Therapy. Journaling. Creativity. —KH .... Reading bad urban fantasy in the bathtub. —MB

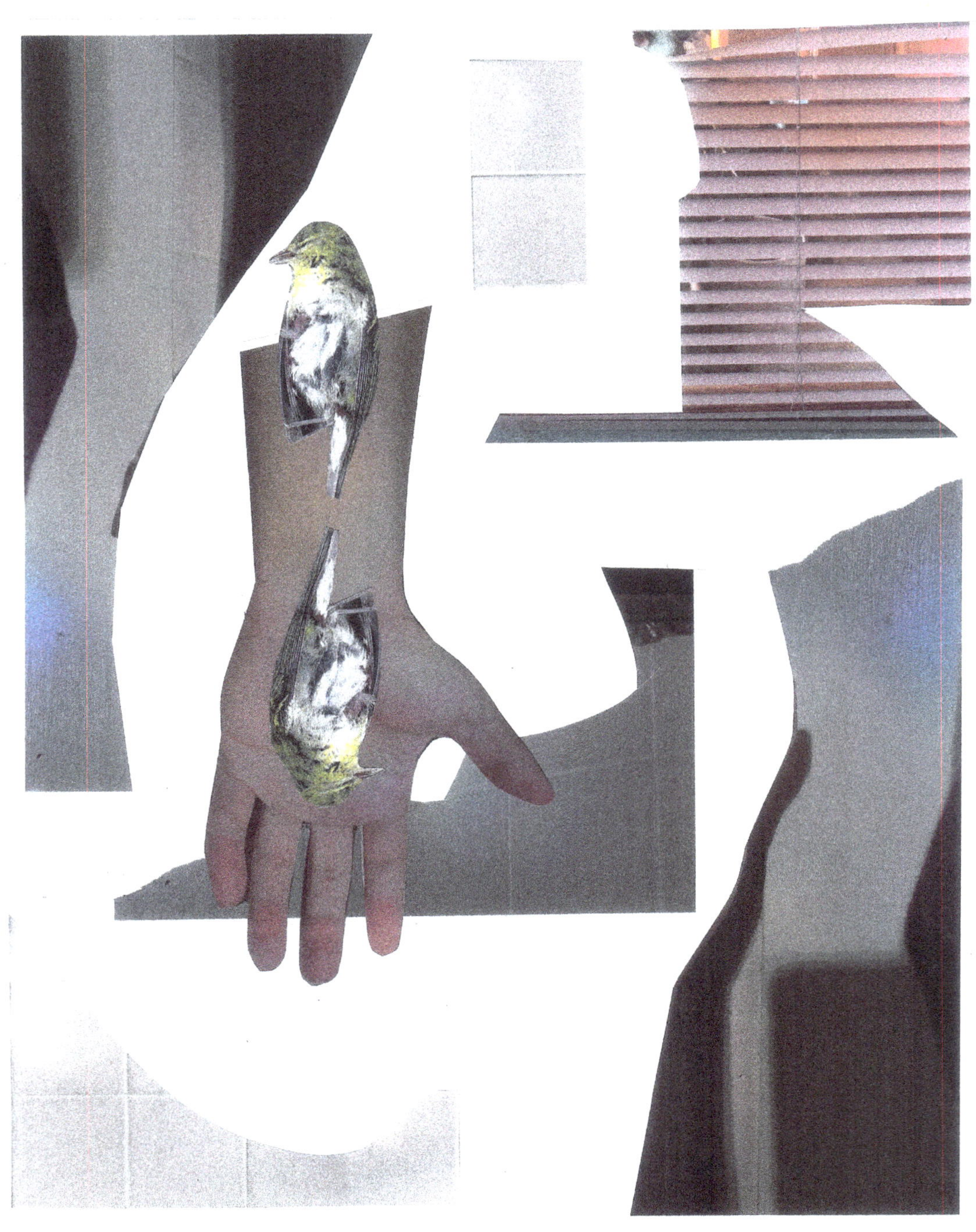

FALLEN | Miguel Ontiveros

Cleft

BY JOSEPHINE CHIEN

This is not the end of the world, my daughter says to me,
as I am trying to finish writing a poem.

It is not as if you are your mother,
who came to this country as a pianist
but could not earn a living,
nevertheless thrilled to leave behind
her mother-in-law who threw dishes at her husband
for having five children by a mistress,
and it is not as if you are your grandmother
either, who at age sixteen was forced to be
married.

No, I am not my mother.
I am my father's daughter.
And because my father was a doctor,
a psychiatrist to be exact,
specifically a saviour for mental patients,
I was raised to add and subtract, to hypothesize
and look at the facts, and reasonably accept
that I too would be a doctor.

No art, no writing, no music,
unless they are just hobbies,
for they will make you crazy or
they are the products of crazy people.
Look at your uncle, the textile artist in Queens,
who had a mental breakdown
and split from his wife and baby,
don't need to talk about how he ended up,
and look at Van Gogh cutting off his ear,
and Judy Garland, dead from an
overdose. No art, no writing, no music.

If I finish this poem, it will be dangerous
Because I did not become my mother,
And I did not become my father.

DIGITAL ARTWORK BY
ANTHONY FERGUSON

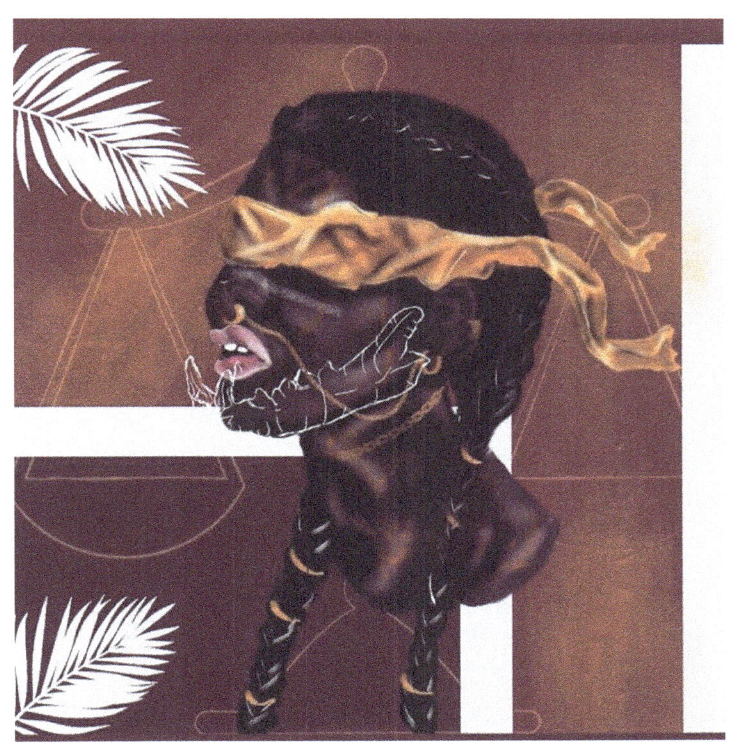

LIBRA

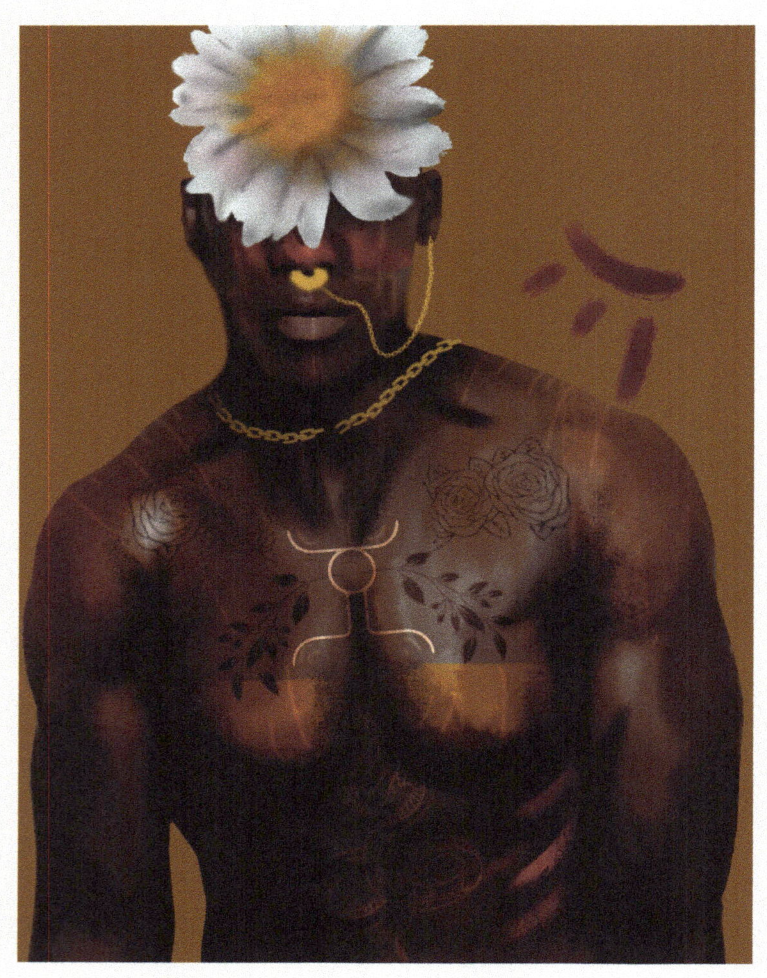

OOKO

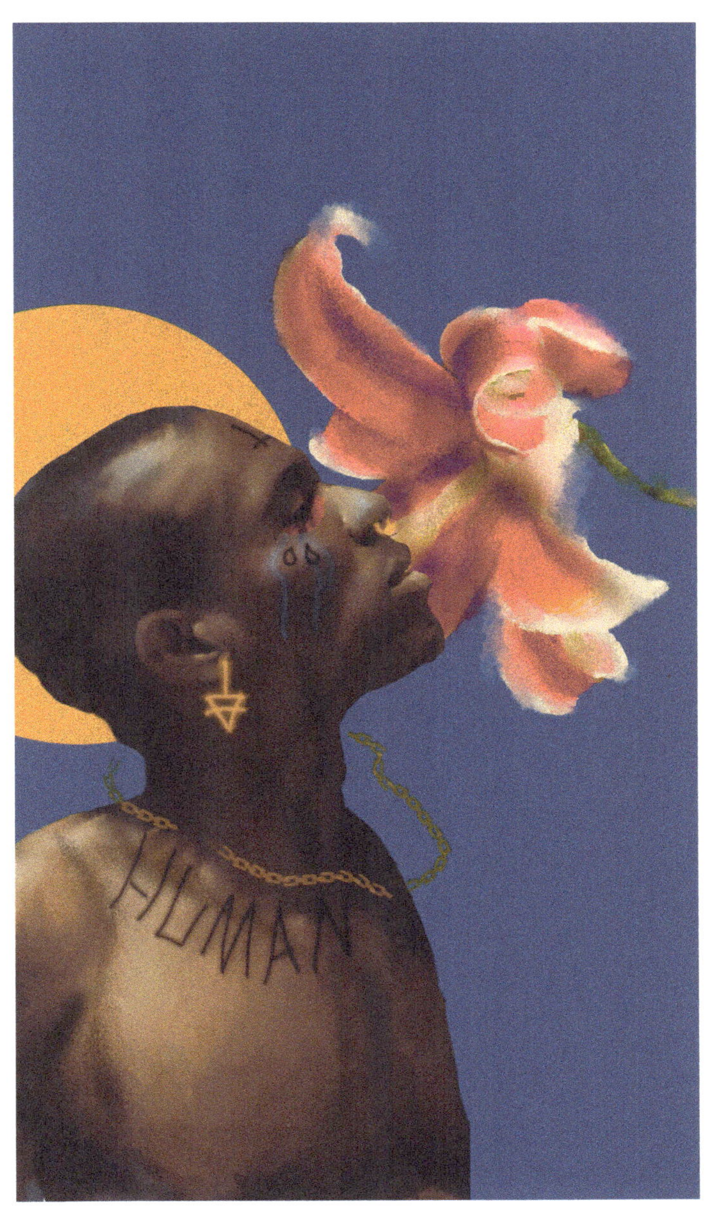
HUMAN

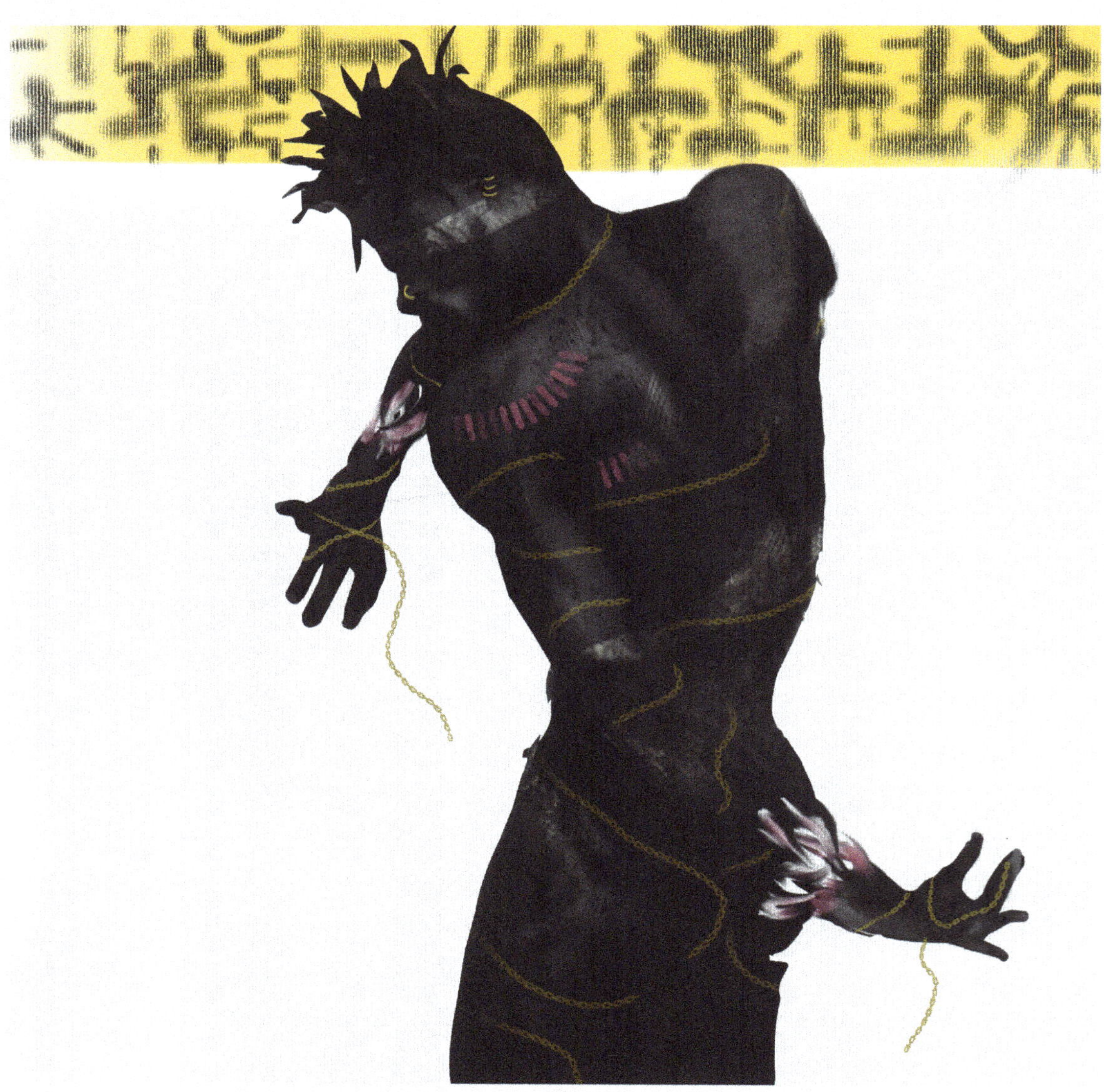

MOSAIC

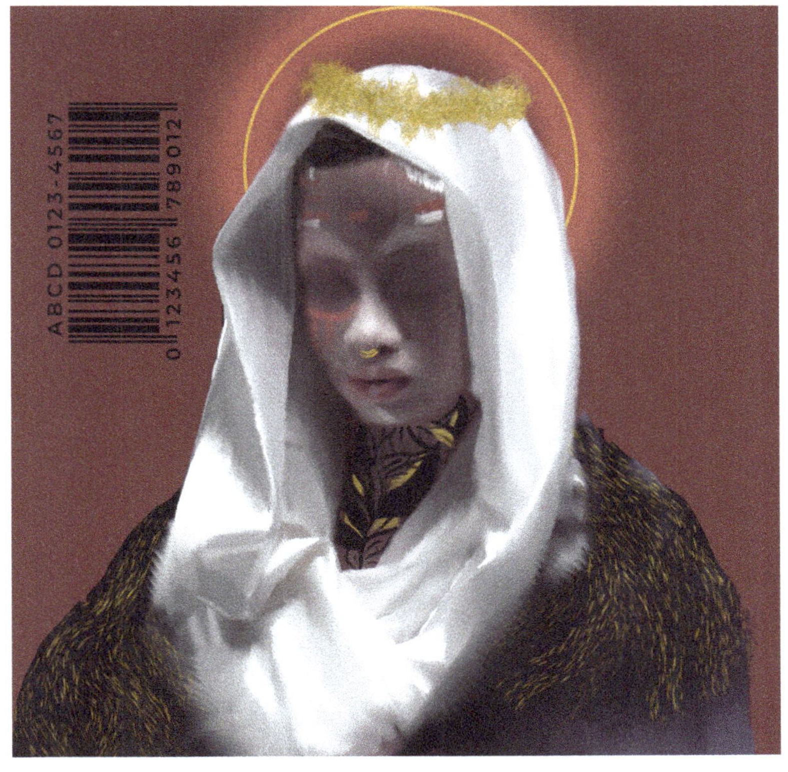

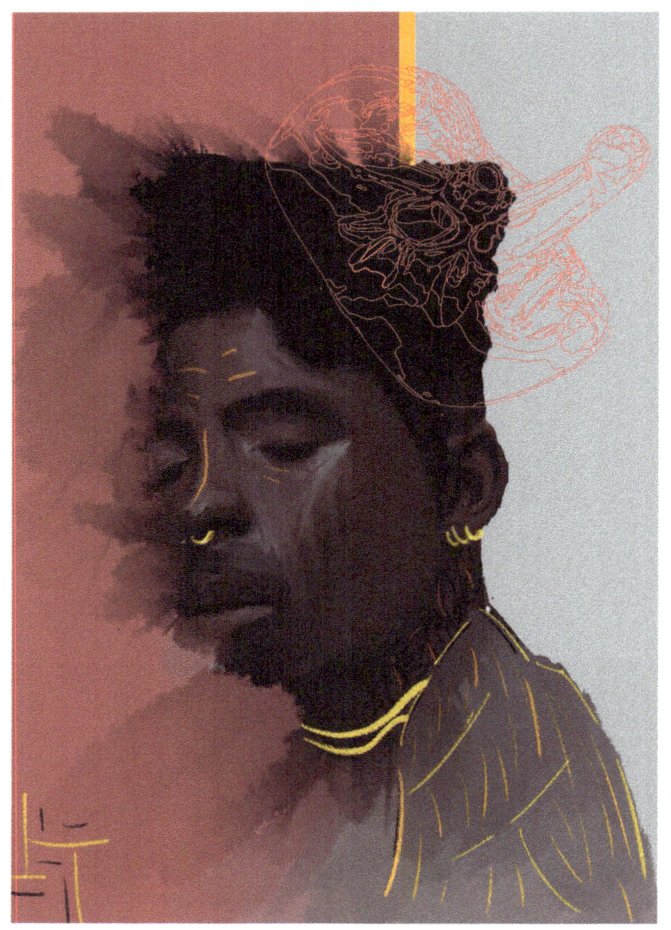

WE CRY

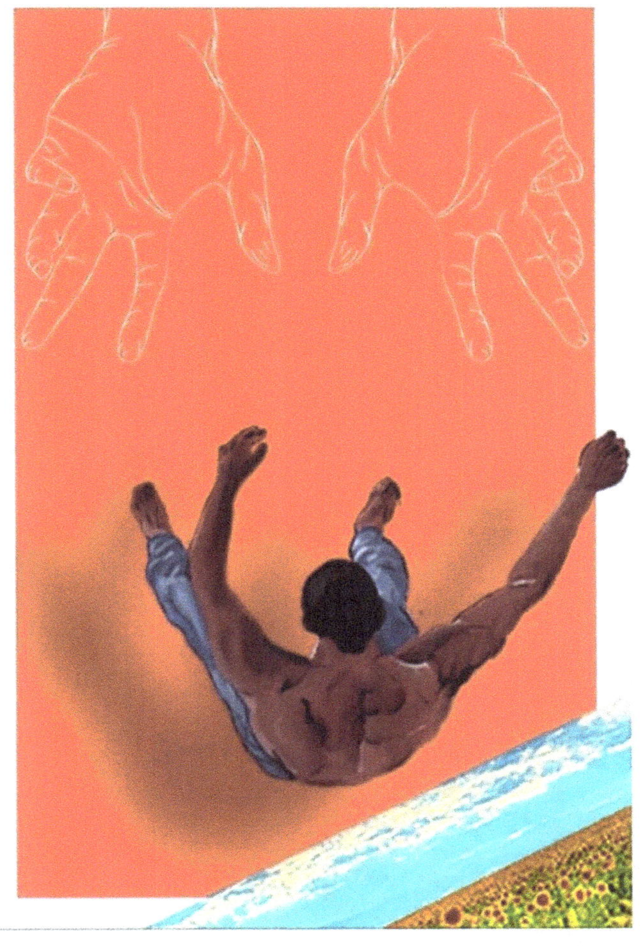

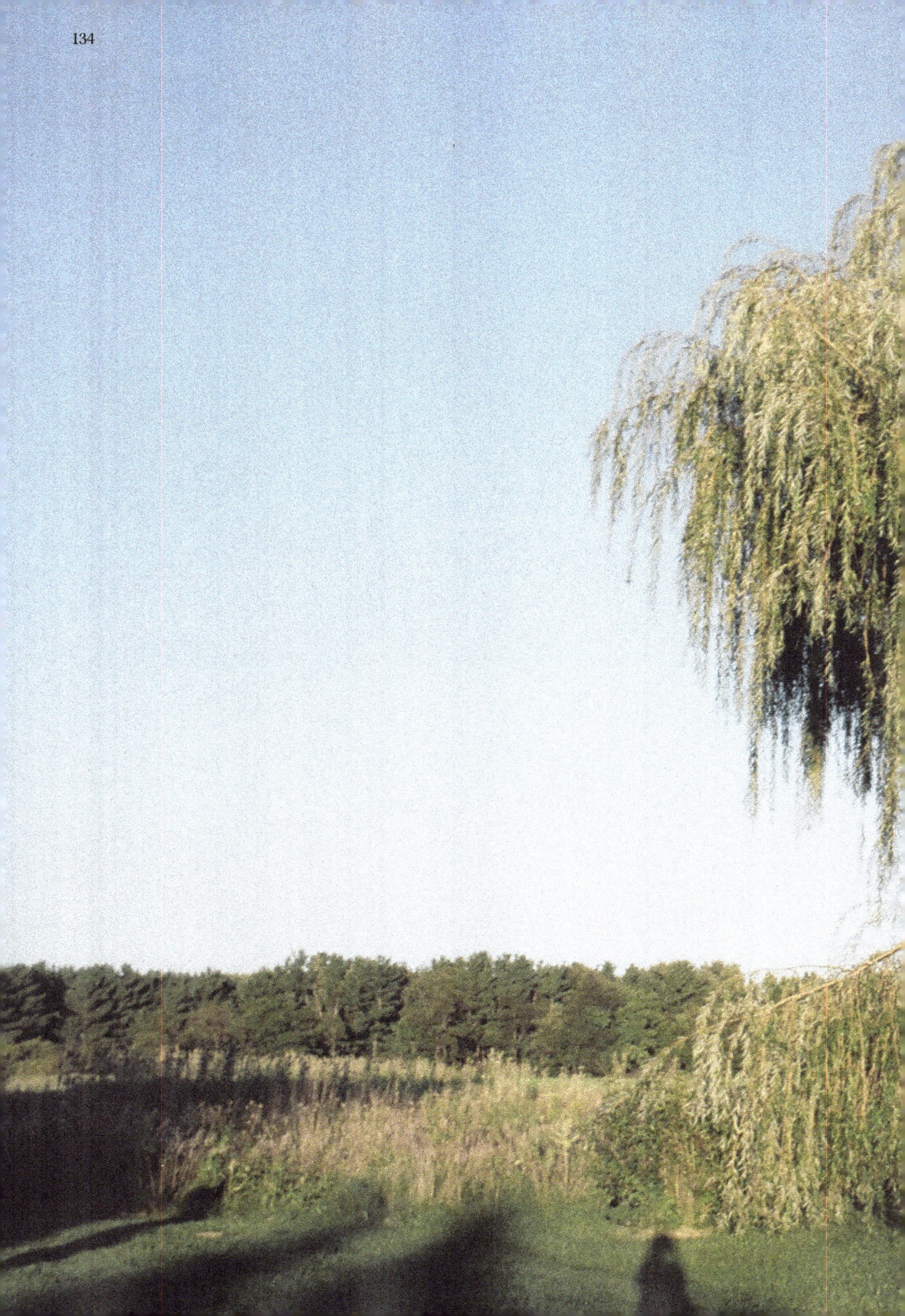

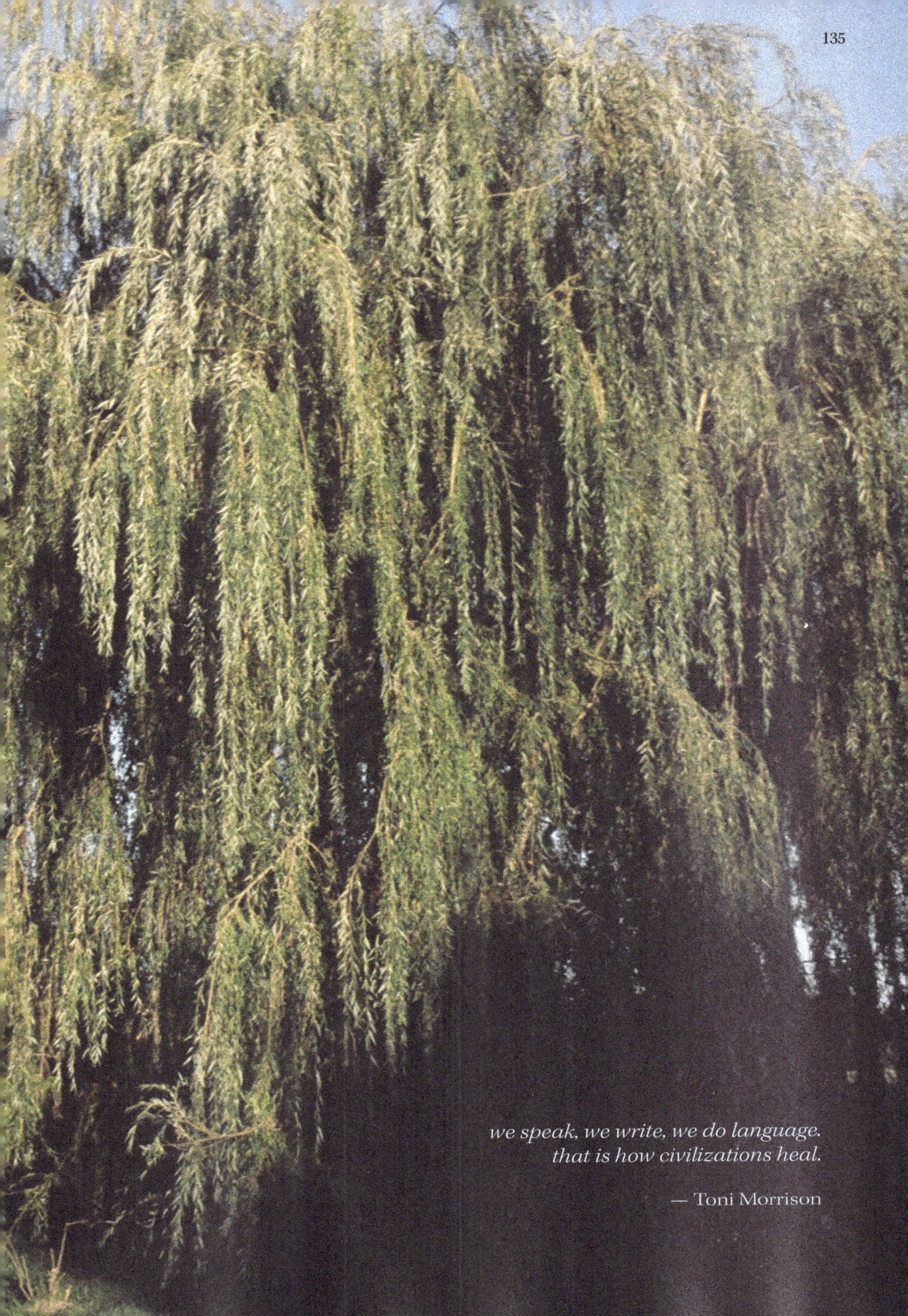
we speak, we write, we do language.
that is how civilizations heal.

— Toni Morrison

what does liberation look like to you?

To me liberation is all about helping to liberate others!
—DW ....
.... Collective freedom. —EW
....
.... I have not fully seen that
future, but I know the seed has been planted. —G ....
....
.... Every person has access to food,
shelter, education, healthcare, art, music, open natural
space, and work that brings them joy. —MB ....
....
.... *"From each according to ability,
to each according to need." (Karl Marx)* —AC ....
....
....
Liberation means freedom from identifying with my human
conditioning. It is knowing that love is my nature, being
able to breathe when constriction happens. In the words
of Hazrat Inayat Khan it is humanity's ability to 'raise...
above the differences and distinctions which divide'.
It is awakening to and accepting the impermanence of this
beautiful and painful human incarnation. It feels like
the ultimate freedom. —WB ....
....
....re-humanizing —KW
....
Social, economic, and environmental justice. —SC ....
....
.... The unfettered freedom to exist, in all the
ways that you are and all the ways that you choose. —ZN

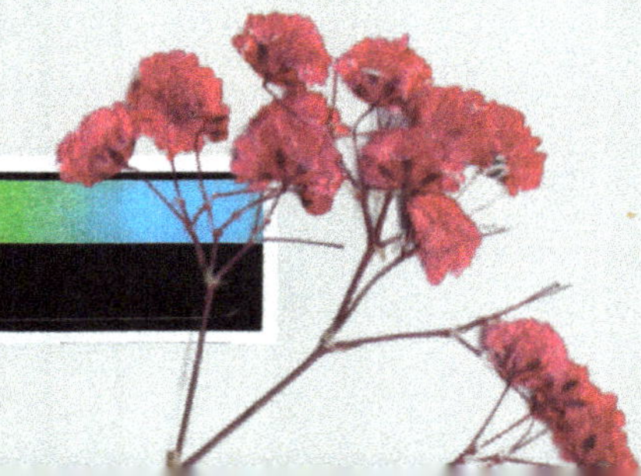

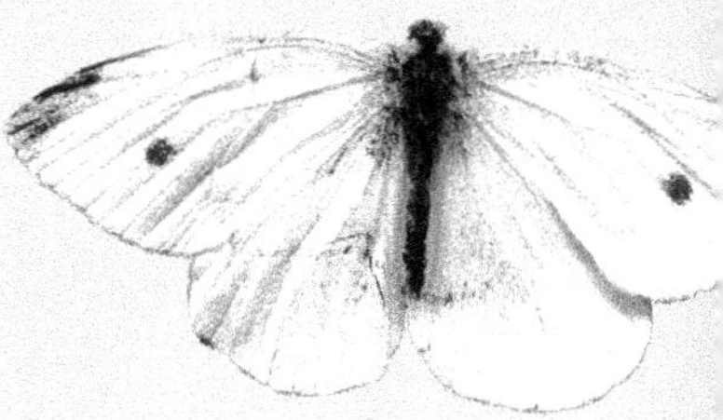

total destruction of caste systems, reparations, communities creating language and ritual process of forgiveness, access to art and art-making, access to healthcare, access to the fundamental safeties of existence, for all beings, human and non. —EKF ....
....
....
Knowing that no one knows you like you do. —BB ....
....
....
Equity, opportunity for all. Removal of capitalism! —KJ
....
.... Not having to worry about myself, out in the world or inside my head. —CP ....
....
.... *"I'll tell you what freedom is to me: NO FEAR! I mean really, no fear." (Nina Simone)* —LS ....
....
...... Recovering lost wildness, coming home to the earth. Interdependent, self-sustaining systems. Strong community bonds that support courage, honesty, creativity, and the fullness of being. —RZB ....
.... the freedom to exist as myself without fear of losing my health, happiness, or life —BC ....
....
Feeling at ease with myself. Asking for what I need. Sharing my opinion. Sharing with others. Feeling open and loved. —RS ....
.... a vessel that can shift shape and size to hold anything just right. —EEG ....
....
.... Embracing that I am not here forever —JC

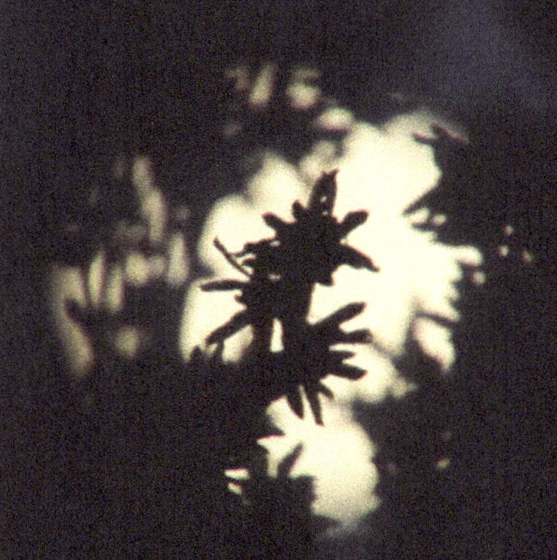

*i feel that there is nothing
more truly artistic than
to love people.*

— Vincent Van Gogh

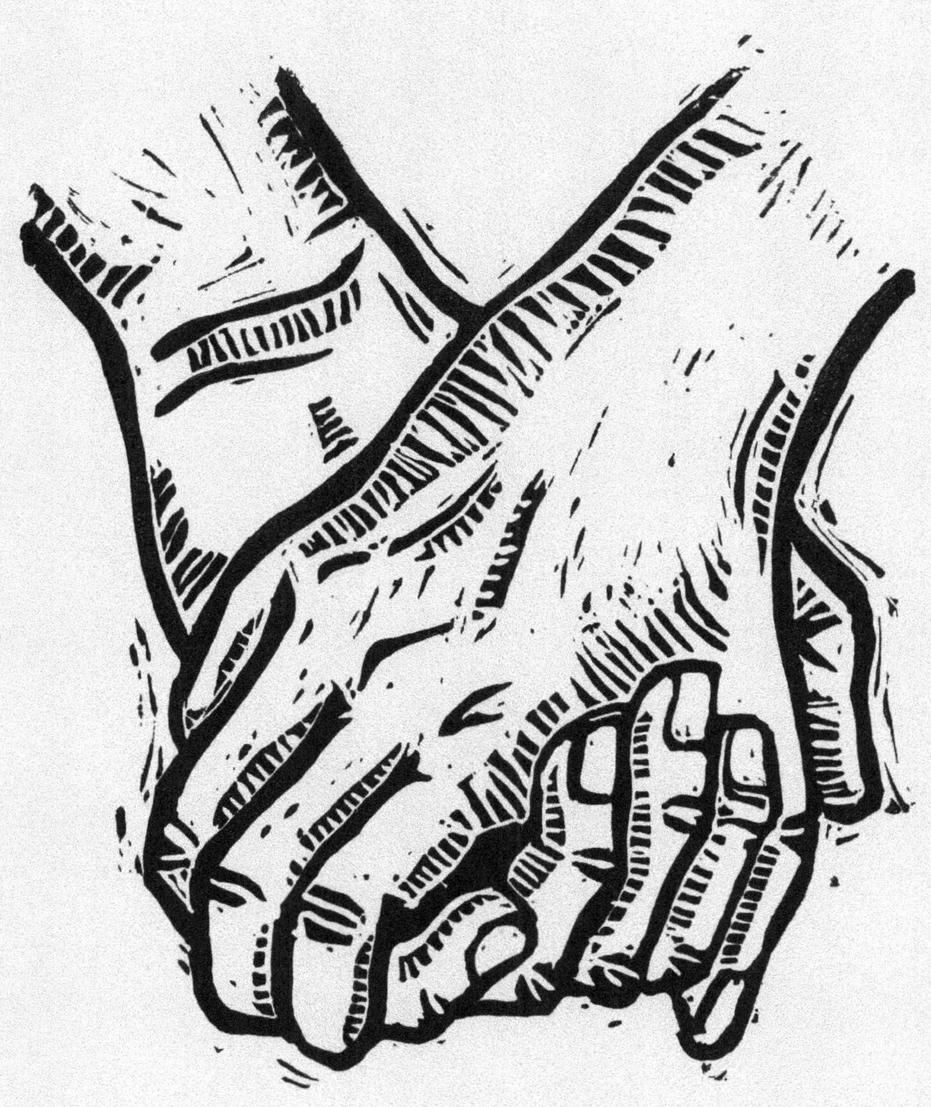

"To Hold and Be Held" by Kate Weimer

Self-Test

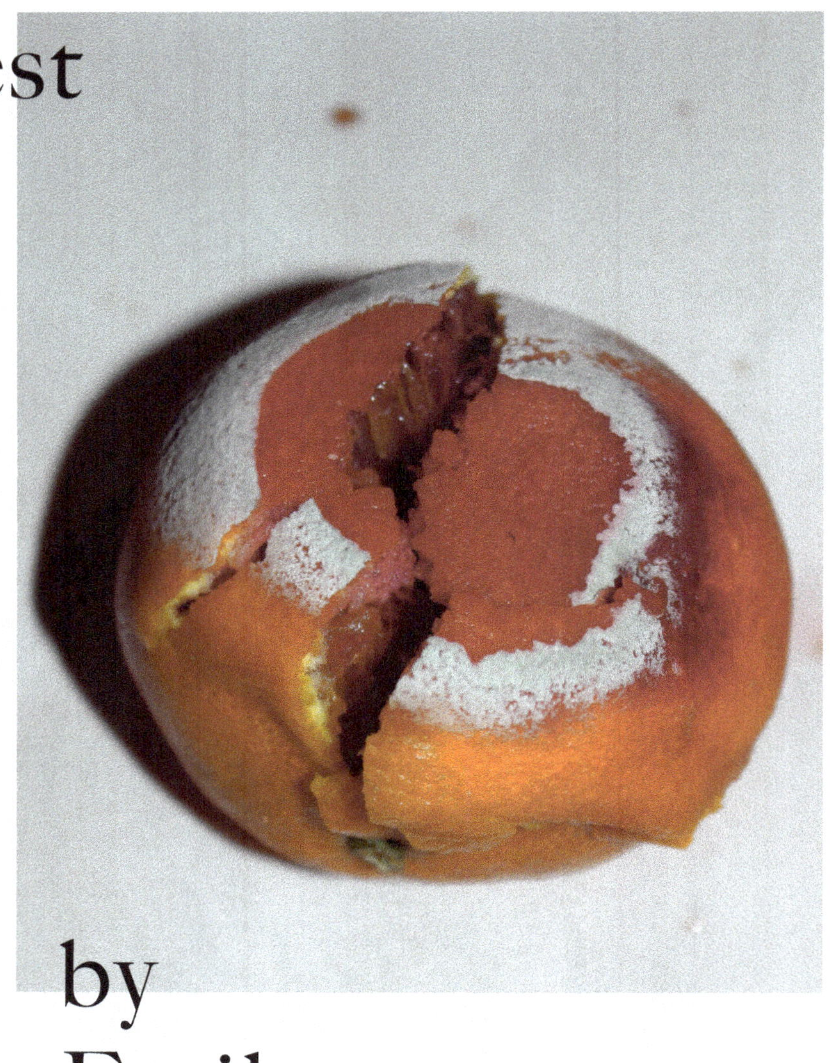

by
Emily Kendal Frey

Did you forget

Did you check a box and crawl under it

What of the rest

"Who feels it knows it"

Who knows your head in its nest

The Sensitivity Cycles

The Nourishment Barrier

A demon with glands

A fragmented self

A fighting circle where layers shed

A child's bed

A blood-colored circle where you paint pain

An egg with a thousand shells

A circle made of infinite squares

The door to a house where you lived for years that you'll never again enter

The lodged wooden icicles

An untamed virus

An essential worker

A bent chakra

A person nicknamed Rainbow

A person actually named Rainbow

A person with rainbow eyes

A person exists who has not seen a rainbow

A bird under a window

An egg with a bird inside

Character Analysis

The strong ice of resentment

The way we walk down the street imagining our enemies

The way disgust bloats us

An attempt to make art with a throat full of dust

Being the last at many things and the first at a few

Existing because it's what keeps happening

Core Material

The profound aquarium experience

The braids of time

An acutely porous train memory

Sit back into the movement of your life going by

We drove up into the state

It seemed like early morning all day

It was pink and then peach and then pink again

Even the blues were pink

To be alive because you crave pleasure

To have a mind, telling you not to think

It's your job to love the trees on the highway

The average, indignant trees, unmoving

"The stone that the builder refuses"

A test with no key, no answers

A rippling mood never breaks

"Our body is home to our spirit"

In the alleyway behind our local bar, wind whipping

In love with winter for what it might do

In a cab stone-drunk and breathing cold

A body is home to its ancestors

A dream of one purple grape fills the throat

Let love die

Choke the death-grape

Waking with one eye and snow in the living room

A hundred people organized around one idea

A thousand ghosts in ten thousand broken eggs

A cold rainbow

However we loved it was despite great obstacle

A quiet mind

A rotating moon

A pencil you sharpen to break

The person on the train fixed to your mind

Desire flickering up and through morning

You walked further than you wanted to

The trees ambivalently joyous

The rapturous pleasure in your legs

The light of your grief

Blazing its lighthouse

The untrimmed hope you carried

You gripped it

Who would you be without a name

The circle where you gathered stones to the middle

Where you stand on your life

Where you become milk

Again

SENSORY MEDICINE

a strong thought

a way i took care of myself

press a flower or tangible artifact here

(describe or draw)

a lingering image

a sensation

as a way of tuning into the endless messages your body sends, fill in these shapes. documenting the constant wisdom of your senses, what it's like to be in a body.

a comforting taste or aroma

told someone i appreciate them

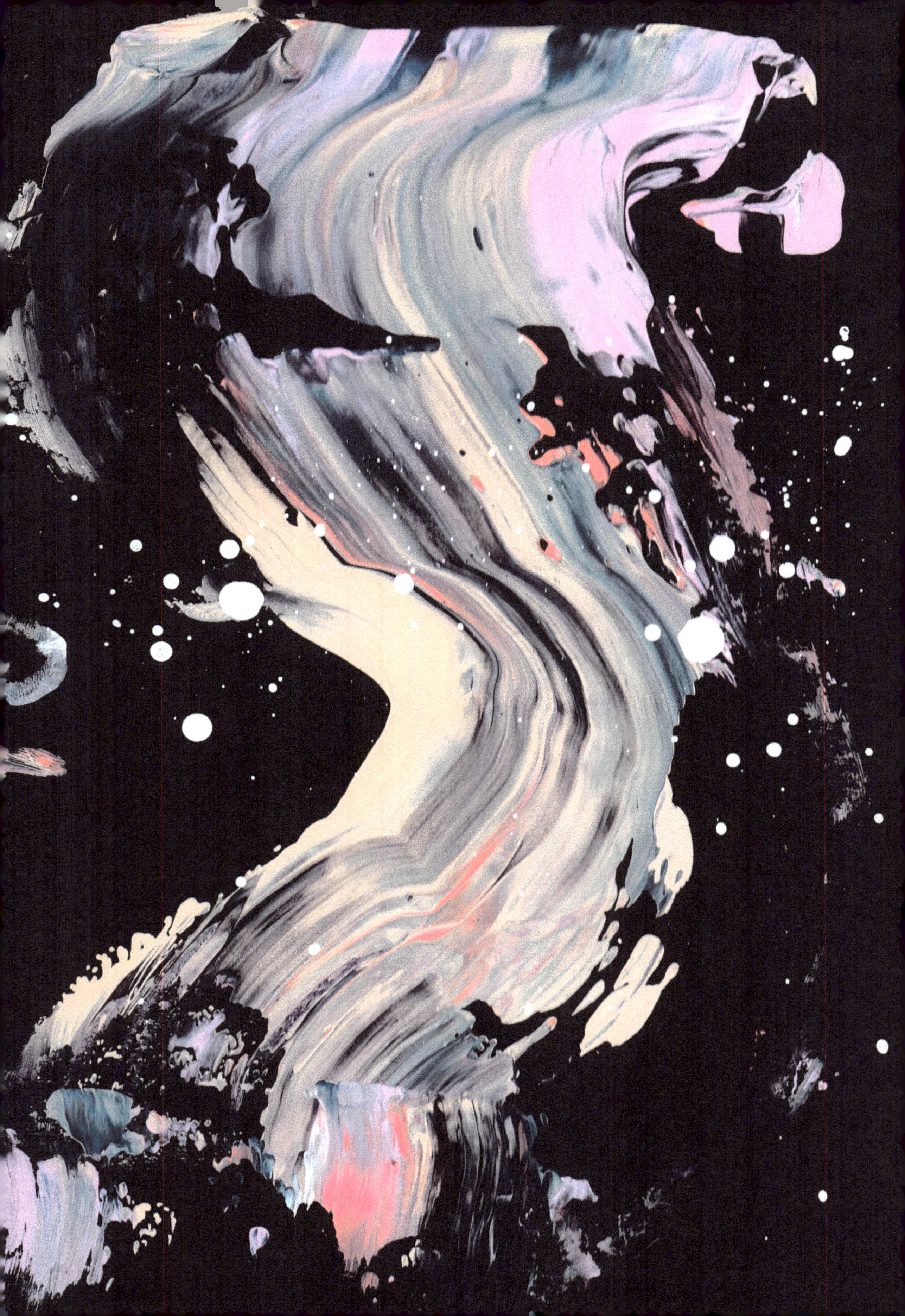

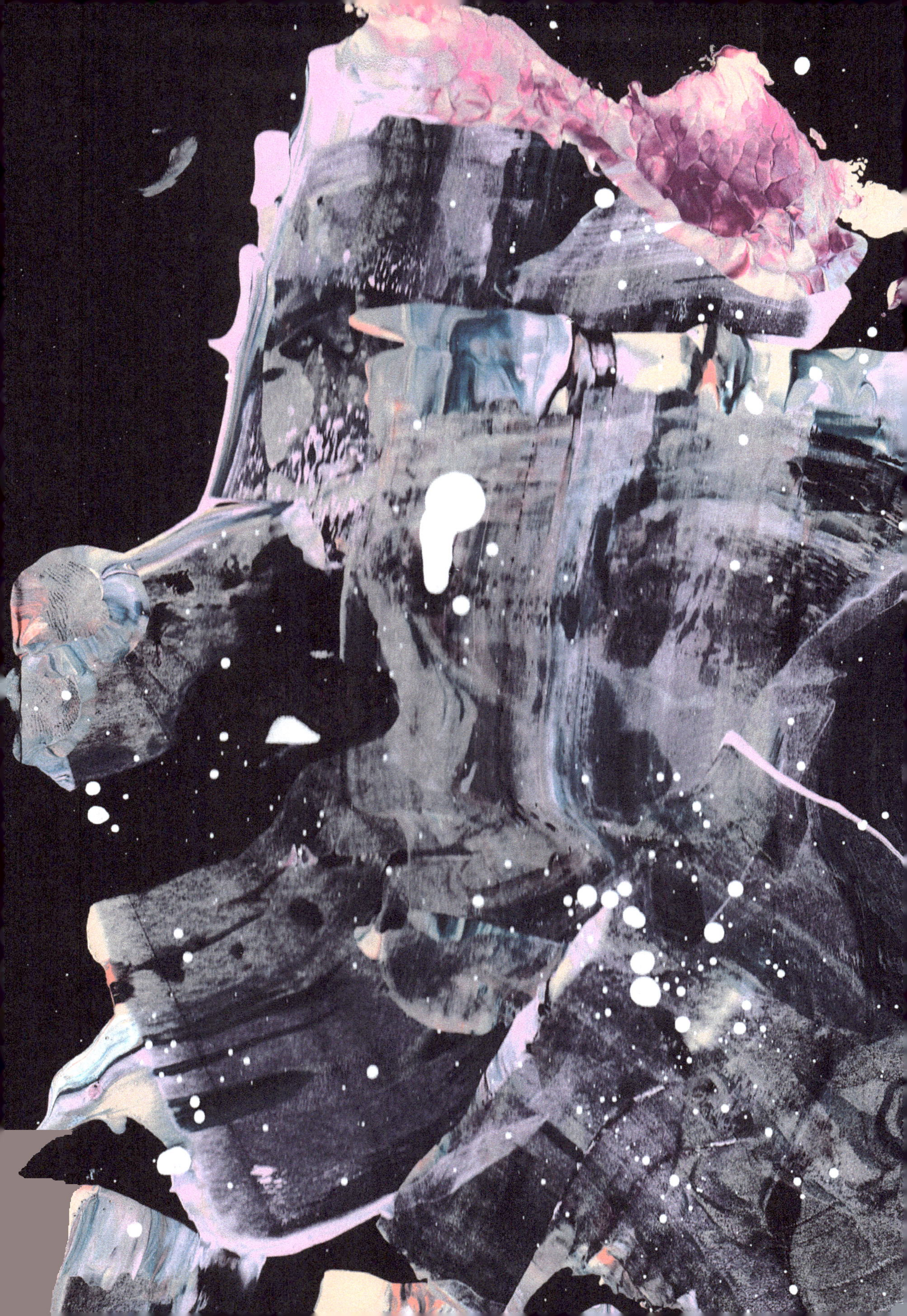

outro / portal / curtain

been a jagged shore long as I can
remember. a fissure, entertained

sung by siren volcanoes, marked
in igneous and strewn

digging in the pillows
searching for the *no*

there lies the pekid fountains,
the fertile wound.

stemmed and fleeting
got convex.

please put down your
pretty wreckage.

it's heavy reckon
and redone fathom

breeding like regret.
or phoenixes.

the hazards we held
with cupped palms

but also brought columns
and introduced them

to angel nerves and swam
with sunlit fragments.

used to hoard the scorn
blame the vapors

dressed in fumes
got consecrated

what is fond enough
the boundaries howled

cover us with sweet beams
empty tremble.

our bright indecision,
its shouting tendrils

we gripped ember garlands
gulped for gone reasons

give back that glyph
the sheets of radiance.

we were panoramas,
landscapes of shame

I know those cliffs.

finally, there are canopies
and the grid has vanished.

our gorgeous proxy
come back saying:

*I've seen another kingdom
that looks like your lines.*

won't ignore the bloodstream
the mortal warning

we answer the intake,
taste the annex

swoon with intent
flaunt at the veil

there is no pedestal
only phase and protect

haven't seen the
thicket through yet.

spilled cravings
and claimed echoes

isn't this an ancient
gloaming

isn't this a
sated sight

the fault you've
since altered

haven hailing
softest mention

pass around the fevered chalice
and blaze the lilac fences.

renewal. renewal.
renewal. amen.

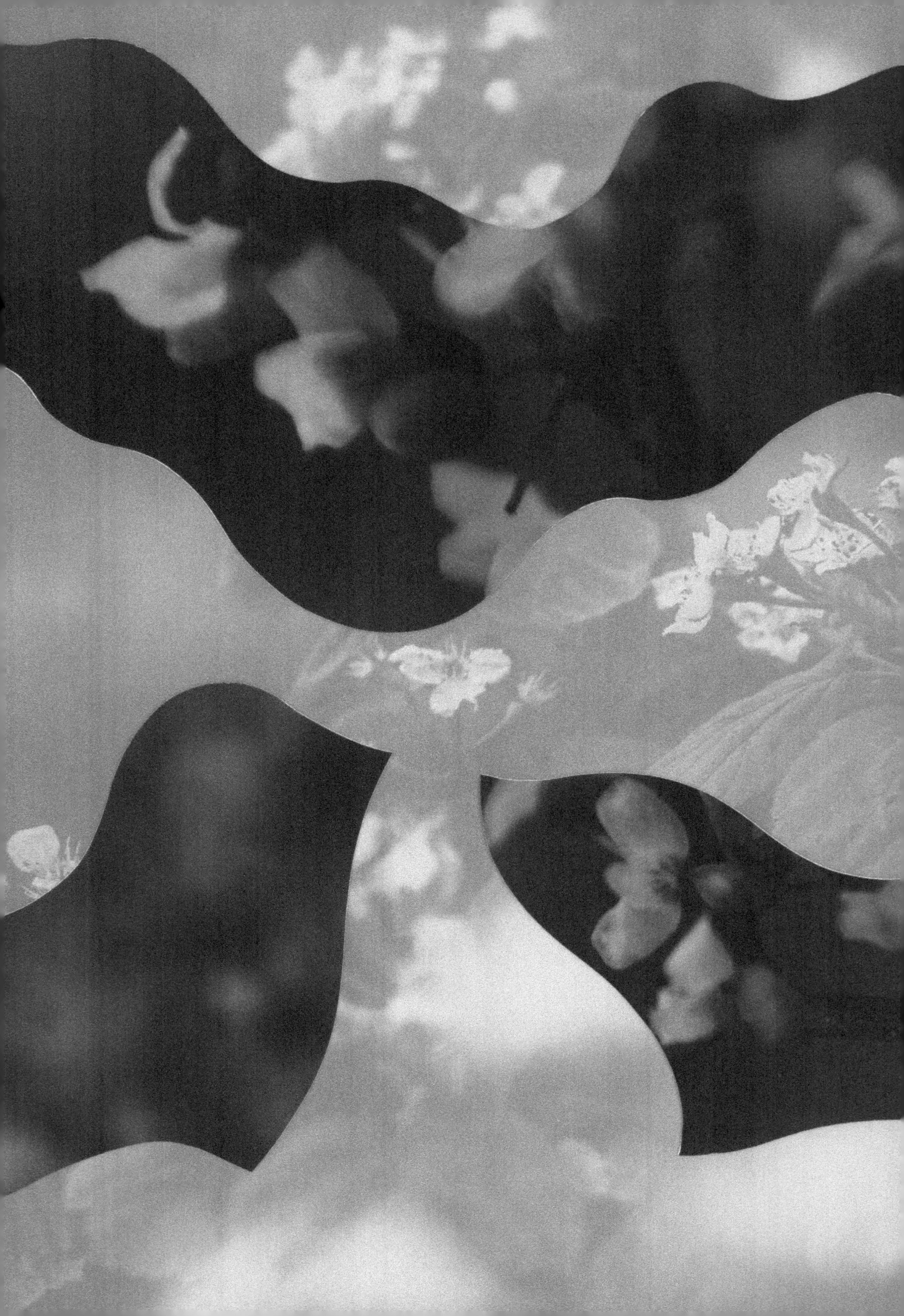

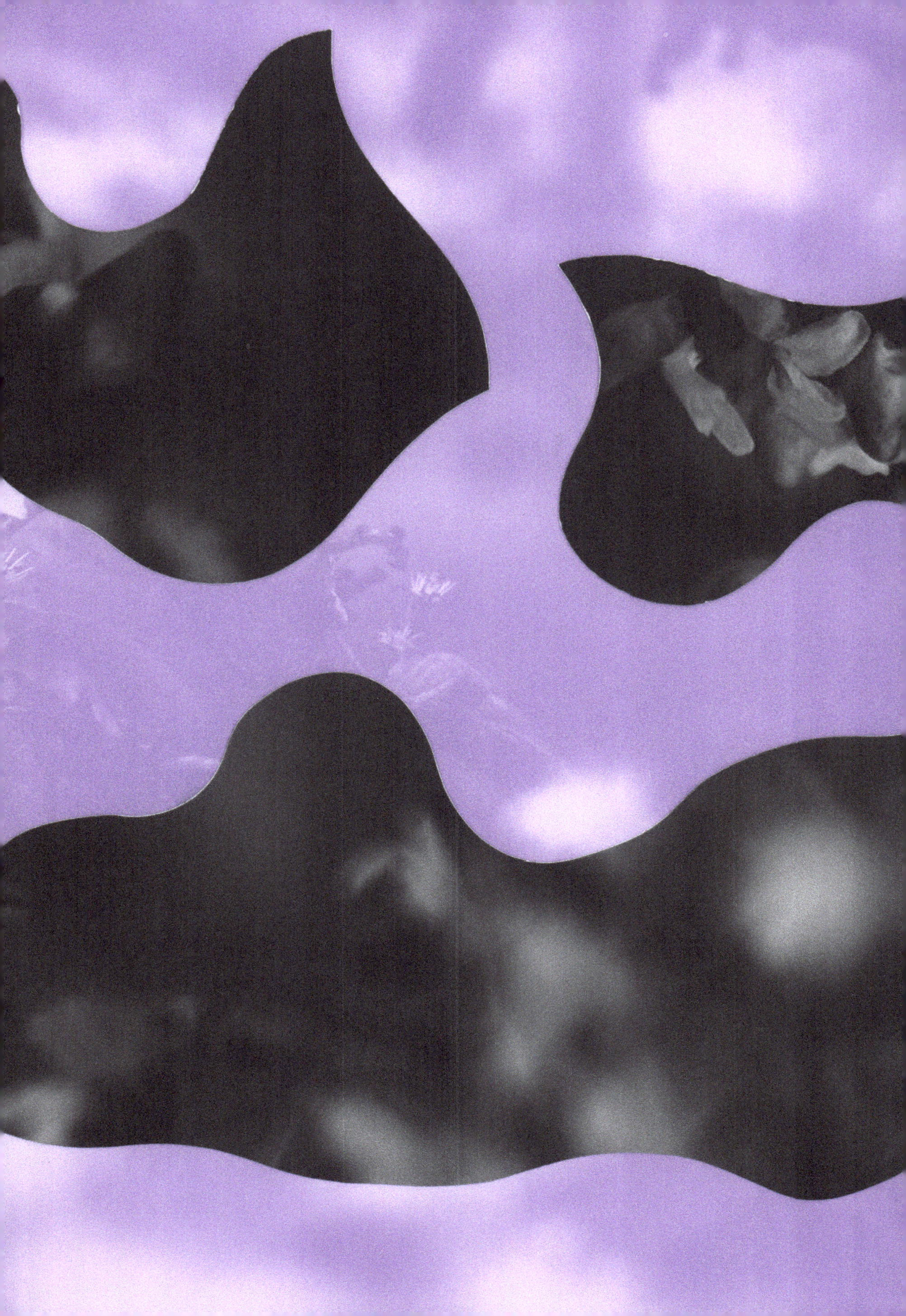